The View From the Back of the Bus

John 'Deebo' Wesley

The View From the Back of the Bus

CONTENTS

Upon my uncircumcised lips thou has laid a reply. Thou has upheld my soul, strengthening my loins and restoring my power; my foot has stood in the realm of ungodliness. I have been a snare to those who rebel, but healing to those of them who repent,
prudence to the simple, and steadfastness to the fearful of heart. To traitors Thou has made of me a mockery and scorn, but a counsel of truth and understanding to the upright of way. I have been iniquity for the wicked, ill-repute on the lips of the fierce, the scoffers have gnashed their teeth. I have been a byword to traitors,
the assembly of the wicked has raged against me; they have roared like turbulent seas and their towering waves have spat out mud and slime.
But to the elect of righteousness Thou hast made me a banner, and a discerning interpreter of wonderful mysteries, to try those who practice truth and to test those who love correction. To the interpreters of error I have been an opponent, but a man of peace to all those who see true things. To all those who seek smooth things I have been a spirit of zeal; like the sound of the roaring of many waters so have the deceivers thundered against me; all their thoughts were devilish scheming. They have cast towards the Pit the life of the man whose mouth Thou has confirmed, and into whose heart Thou has put teaching and understanding, that he might open a fountain of knowledge to all men of insight. They have exchanged them for lips of uncircumcision, and for the foreign tongue of a people without understanding, that they might come to ruin in their straying. The Complete Dead Sea Scrolls in English (Thanksgiving Hymns (IQH, IQ36, 4Q427-32) Part II Hymn 6 Penguin Classics

John 10:1 *G Verily, verily, I say unto you, He that entereth not by the door into the sheepfold, but climbeth up some other way, the same is a thief and a robber.*

John 10:2 *But he that entereth in by the door is the shepherd of the sheep.*

John 10:3 *To him the porter openeth; and the sheep hear his voice: and he calleth his own sheep by name, and leadeth them out.*

John 10:4 *And when he putteth forth his own sheep, he goeth before them, and the sheep follow him: for they know his voice.*

John 10:5 *And a stranger will they not follow, but will flee from him: for they know not the voice of strangers.*

John 10:6 *This parable spake Jesus unto them: but they understood not what things they were which he spake unto them.*

Chapter I - Introit

Chapter I - Introit
Occasionally, I get startled by a level of incompetence, bordering on what would happen (is happening) when criminally insane people are at the helms of major institutions in American life. As much as I love hyperbole, I only resort to it when there is a fire, and one must hose something down. The gates of hell may not prevail upon the church, but the fires of hell will sure enough singe, roast and set parts of it on fire and this is what we find in major Christian denominations and Black Christianity splitting over sexuality and other fundamental issues.

As a former Methodist by upbringing and a United Methodist by Seminary training, I follow current UMC events at a curious distance. I am like a lone wolf, ostracized from the pack, just hanging around the margins. Just today at General Conference 4-24-24, and it is only Day 2 mind you, I saw what can only be described as a 'doo-doo storm'. Imagine well paid Bishops and Representatives, sitting around the dying Body of Christ, casting lots on his earthy possessions, his cloak, tunic, and outer garments. They are casting lots in 'Holy Conferencing', 'Holy discernment', and under the auspices of the Holy Spirit, for the broken body of the Church. A Church Body, splitting the property of God (the Churches up) part by part, retaining pieces for themselves because of course that is only fair, and they must be 'fair' in dividing the broken Body of Christ! Oh, for shame. Fairness is a worldly legal, public relations and humanistic concept, forever talked about and fought over, but rarely established in fact or principle. The only 'principle' in these deliberations is that each side wants to retain for itself as much real estate, and as much theological and administrative power as possible. Today I'd like to exegete the whole UM News Digest Web version. Do not worry. You will not have to read the whole thing. Neither did I. I tried, but I could not. We will just analyze, emphasis on the word 'anal' the proceedings as described by the Official UM News and Communications Service itself. Consistent with my Seminary training, which was subsidized by the United Methodist Church Education Funds, the reader and I will exegete The United Methodist Communications blasts regarding Day 2 of the delayed and long-awaited General Conference. This was the Conference after the 2018 General Conference that was supposed to fix everything but didn't, and also after the 2022 Conference scheduled to fix the mutinous disaster created by not fixing anything at the 2018 General Conference and making it precipitously worse.

1. Bishop Holston: Become 'who God needs us to be'

No wonder Americans of all races are abandoning Christianity and the Denominational church with that kind of non-sense. How does one become Bishop with a $250,000 per year salary and not know 'who God needs us to be' or thinks that 'who God needs us to be is somehow debatable'. We know what God 'needs us to be', it is outlined very clearly in the Bible, and furthermore because everyone in the Bible is either a man or a woman, one might presume God needs us to be 'men and women' of God. But that answer is too obvious for Bishop Holston, and he wants the United Methodist Church to 'be' what God needs it to 'be' in a transformative sense, without having the foggiest notion either of what God needs it to 'be', or how to get there from here...other than the fact on the first of the month the process of the church 'being' what it needs to be is him getting his check direct deposited in his account.

We might exegete Bishop's statement further and wonder if God has needs? To argue an omnipotent and omniscient God has 'needs' is quite a leap. And if He had needs, would he tell us? Is this not rather presumptuous of man to suggest God needs him, without daring to make the dialectical leap. What if Man needs God and God's rules, far more than God needs us! We need God way more than God needs us, to go poking our noses around in scripture changing things that don't make sense (to man). Indeed, such a God as needs man? Sheer Blasphemy and by a well-paid Bishiop no less! Since the dawn of creation God has been in the business of compelling man, beasts, animals, flora, fauna, animate and inanimate materials, but now God needs man? God needs man to tell him what a man and a woman are (or aren't)? God needing us to inform him of such matters is akin to Bishop Holstein asking his Hispanic maid and landscaper who barely knows English, to articulate for him the complexities of the Trinity in English. That is the kind of God postmodern Christianity serves, a pathetic, weak (g)od that doesn't know his butt hole from his mouth (if said god doesn't recognize the difference between a vagina and a penis in biological and reproductive terms). This is the God the current United Methodist Church is pushing on traditional Methodism and the American public.

As I stated earlier, no wonder people are leaving in droves. You come to God for answers. So you ask this United Methodist God for answers and this God doesn't even know what a man and a woman are, even though both males and females are scattered throughout mammals, reptiles, fish, trees, and plants! What an ignorant God...or is he just playing stupid and impotent for the sake of stupid human beings who will not cease from digging the holes that trap them further and further until they cave in and they suffocate under the weight of their hideous piles of theological excavated dirt. If Bishop Holstein would have asked his Hispanic landscaper and maid how to build tunnels, it wouldn't have been politically correct, but it would be more logical than asking him to explain the theological nuances of the Trinity, or human beings sitting around speculating how to legislate a mammalian sexuality that was here hundreds of thousands of years before humans even thought there was a question. That's why all they can come up with is hocus-pocus mumbo-jumbo LGBTQIA+ sexual algebra. As I said, no wonder people are leaving the church in droves. As welcoming as the new UMC is, even the people it claims to be so welcoming to, aren't joining in droves because of the new openness and acceptance.

The UMC, once God's church, will now happily and joyfully admit it doesn't know what a man and a woman are, and will expeditiously cede the matter to secular authorities, and human will, wit and fancy. Inclinations of all sorts and types are justified, by presuming that they all come from God. This is even though no alcoholic or drug addict is presumed by the Church to have been designed by God with, that is to say born with, a love for alcohol and drugs and the church and society must simply let him do it. What kind of church is that? Even though this church doesn't know what a man and woman are (absent sexual algebra), I noticed that they (United Methodist Church Communications) have a presence on Facebook, X (Twitter), YouTube, and two other social media symbols I have no idea what they represent. Brothers and sisters this is worse than New Testament ideas about what it meant to be worldly and materialistic, concupiscent, and to serve mammon. If you claim you don't submit to mammon, but then serve the world mammon created in defiance of God, you're still serving mammon. Can you use mammon (to evangelism and reach the masses with nonsense theology and a weak ignorant god), without serving mammon. Let us ask Jesus who when confronted by the Pharisees for casting out demons in the name of Beelzebub, said a house divided cannot stand.

Matthew 12:21-26 21 And in his name shall the Gentiles trust. 22 Then was brought unto him one possessed with a devil, blind, and dumb: and he healed him, insomuch that the blind and dumb both spake and saw. 23 And all the people were amazed, and said, Is not this the son of David? 24 But when the Pharisees heard it, they said, This fellow doth not cast out devils, but by Beelzebub the prince of the devils. 25 And Jesus knew their thoughts, and said unto them, Every kingdom divided against itself is brought to desolation; and every city or house divided against itself shall not stand: 26 And if Satan cast out Satan, he is divided against himself; how shall then his kingdom stand?

How can one cast out demons in the name of one? Jesus was casting out demons and reaching people by the power God, the current UMC has a multi-million dollar per year communications department devoted to casting out mammon by means of mammon. What else would a church in such dire straits as 50 years of membership decline do? What else can they do but view their problems as 'communications technology' issues, as opposed to analyzing the precise value of what they are communicating (a Jesus that apart from being God manifest in the flesh, doesn't know what a man and a woman are and must be corrected)? It is easy to throw money and computers at problems rather than attacking problems with prayer, God, the Word, the Holy Spirit, and/or Jesus. What else can they do but prefer to be hip and relevant, rather than right or on the traditional 'Way' of their elders in the Wesleyan faith on some 'ride or die' stuff? Standing up for the tradition of our Wesleyan elders and upholding biblical standards in basic matters would take courage. Courage is something this current crop doesn't have. They pretend like they have courage, the courage to do hard things, and take hard stands, but their courage stops at who signs their checks. The Wesleyan Conservative side is struggling itself, and furthermore due to its rightward position in the cultural landscape doesn't feel it owes the Black Church, Black Methodism, anything other than lip service, which of course is all Black Methodism can repay them with. Striking out independently is impossible for our Ebony bishops (and many Black UMC pastors) because none of them rose to their present height by their preaching, evangelism, or talent, and thus were they to do anything independently, they know it would sink faster than the proverbial millstone tied around deceivers' necks for deceiving a child of God.

Matthew 18:6 But whoso shall offend one of these little ones which believe in me, it were better for him that a millstone were hanged about his neck, and that he were drowned in the depth of the sea.

Organizing Black United Methodists conservative or not, doesn't make any sense because the only people that feel any sense of debt to the Black church are the liberals. Not coincidentally, they are the Pro-LGBTQIA+ and Pro-Social Justice wing of the Post-Modern UMC Movement. This is akin to a White mainstream corporate slumlord in the Black inner cities and Black rural areas, getting an award for being 'Developer of the Year' because his properties elsewhere in suburbia and gentrified areas are so outstanding. This is how the new liberal Pro-LGBTQIA+ church treats the Black United Methodist Church; like slumlords overseeing their domains with masses of non-growing Black churches on the dole, and dependent on what used to be 'equitable comp' and handouts from the White mainstream UMC. A UMC now with 35% of its largest, strongest, Whitest, and most prosperous churches having left the apportionment system entirely. The White UMC liberals can't afford to pay their Negro wards the handouts that they used to. What is altogether worse, Black United Methodist Churches get saddled with ancient irrelevant pastors that can't afford to leave the system and can't grow a church, so their parishes are stuck with them until they die or the whole edifice collapses in dysfunction. Quite often they indeed collapse in dysfunction when apportionments cannot be made. Then your White liberal UMC friends, so eager to sacrifice all for their socialist-atheist LGBTQIA+ social justice friends, will step in and sell your 100-year-old church out from under you and use the money to continue their legal battles and 'Holy Conferencing'. Again, the current United Methodist Church, hemorrhaged of dang near 35% of its life's blood and many of its more financially and ministerially successful churches cannot afford to keep dysfunctional Black churches on the dole, urban or rural.

Part II

But let us stay out of church politics and administration for a moment and rest our deliberations upon one principle; God is stable. God is stable because God is stability. God is the stability. A church anchored in Jesus and the Father God of the Bible must by default be stable. The only way the church, a church, any church can become unstable is by abandoning its rock, for the sake of passing worldly trends. In our post-modern example for which the United Methodist Church, along with The Presbyterians, the Anglicans, and yes, even the Catholics are similar examples of the same phenomena; it is a 'woke' church that uses 'woke' standards and trends to guide itself instead of scripturally based standards and trends. Thus it presents itself meaningless; a giant contradiction in terms; a giant pitiable oxymoron of imbecilic and degenerate trends. A church that is mocking itself and its God into oblivion by having the nerve to suggest that it has the answers to the human predicament, and yet does not know what a man and a woman are; (after millions of years of mammalian evolution) and cannot explain it in English or Spanish...to Bishop Holston's Hispanic maid or landscaper without resorting to socialist-atheist LGBTQIA+ sexual algebra, and social justice warrior terminology and propaganda. Bishop Holston can't explain what a man and a woman are, but the United Methodist Church pays him $250,000 to interpret scripture and 'pontificate'.

Bishop Holston, one of our famed and vaunted 'Ebony Bishops' (now a dime and dozen, mostly female, riding Harleys and such) challenges us to 'Become who God needs us to be". What a theological nightmare. It is an oxymoronic statement of near Euclidian geometric precision. Who does God 'need' us to be? How would Bishop Holston know what God 'needs' us to be? Has he discerned the mind of God (and yet does not know or would not care to take the chance answering what a man and a woman are)? Presuming 'this' (G)od would tell you what he needs, you don't think it's at all relevant to what he has already written in his word in Black and White. He has told us what a man and a woman are. But because that definition isn't good enough for you or your socialist-atheist LGBTQIA sexual algebra friends, you presume to go into corporate prayer, fasting, discernment, Holy Conferencing, etc., about the need for God to change his mind and find better terminology to be more inclusive and welcoming, and apologize for the pain God has put that community, or the Blacks, or women through? I find it hard to believe in a God that doesn't know what a man and a woman are, and needs to be corrected by Bishop Holston, Bishop Sue, Bishop Sharma Lewis, the host of Ebony Bishops, the other DEI Bishops, the Council of Bishops, all the lawyers working for the current UMC and the UMC official Communications Office. If all of them and the hosts of heaven and hell were all added together and weighed, it would not move the scale on God.

Does a created being correct its God, and if it does so is its God, God. Nietzsche famously reported that the God of the Western Mind is Dead. He was wrong in one sense. 19th century science, psychology, technology, weaponry, mass production, and post-enlightenment invention didn't kill (g)od. Yes, with these powerful forces of man's nature, the forces of modernity (like post-modernity) would have killed (g)od had it been able. But they realized religion's value as an opiate of the masses; a kind of placebo...because of course they don't really believe in God, and even if they did, the idea that he should tell them what to do is repugnant. So, they do their best to impugn and mock God, and suggest that God doesn't know what a man and woman are, and that he needs correcting. Thusly they allowed this weakened (g)od to limp on defeated, wounded, carrying his cross, all the while scourging Him, insulting Him and wounding Him. This weakened God they mock and say needs correcting, by the most erudite of Bishops, Bishops Councils and Committees of Holy Conferencing to re-write Holy Scriptural mandates in a way that conforms more to man's nature as it presents itself to man. Man's nature as it presented itself to God must be corrected or put on the socialist-atheist trash heap of history as old and as antiquated, as making the mistake of saying 'Father God' around a group of 'woke' Methodists of the current age. A God you must correct about such a fundamental thing as what a man and a woman are ain't worth a 'hill of beans' and furthermore, nothing else this ignorant God could possibly say would be of much import either. Therein lies the rub, and the predicament of what was formerly known as American Post-Modern Christian Orthodoxy.

Part III

"Delegates urged to 'restart' church with less" –

United Methodist leaders challenged General Conference delegates to chart a brighter future for the denomination — but to do so with significantly less funds and fewer bishops.

At the first gathering of the policymaking body since a quarter of the denomination's U.S. churches left, the delegates heard sobering news about the financial state of The United Methodist Church.

Before the delegates is a proposed denomination-wide budget that would be its lowest in 40 years. It also represents the biggest budget drop in the denomination's history.

"This is a General Conference that must send clear signals to the local church," said incoming Council of Bishops President Tracy Malone, "that we are keenly aware that the loss of membership and the decline of sustainability has a direct influence on the amount of funds available to support ministry."

United Methodists can't support ministry at the general-church level in the same way they have in the past, the East Ohio Conference bishop said.

"Delegates to General Conference were urged to restart with less." That makes sense, only if we completely ignore the fact why we all have less, and that is the schism created by some people desiring a God that needs and tolerates correction, and others desiring a God that doesn't. What is altogether worse, is that the liberals decided there was something more important than traditional doctrine and that was 'being a woke church' and reflecting the amended values of an amendable God, who corrects himself and goes around righting his own wrongs? Balderdash! How can the creator God, a just God, who does no injustice, but measures every man and woman in the life of this world and the next (and the previous world), exactly in His just measurement, be accused of ignorance or powerlessness? This we trust, and it is central to faith. No matter what it looks like to me God is fair, God is right, God loves me, God is doing what is best for me, God has been good to me, and if I am sad in my misery God will give me joy amid misery in my Love of Him. In this world and the next. If it were even possible for God to do a man wrong in the life of this world, making him suffer over and above for his good deeds, 'per Jesus', in the misfortune of God allowing you to be killed for 100% Blind obedience to Him and doing Good to His Creation...to the extent God would even owe that 'man', God would raise him up from the dead to give him his reward at his right side in Heaven. This is a God that needs not be corrected (in any matter). Glory to God! Glory to God! Glory to God!

There are multiple times in the First Five Books of Moses and elsewhere that God not so casually mentions the fact that he is a jealous God.

Exodus 20:5-6 5 Thou shalt not bow down thyself to them, nor serve them: for I the LORD thy God am a **jealous** God, visiting the iniquity of the fathers upon the children unto the third and fourth generation of them that hate me; 6 And shewing mercy unto thousands of them that love me, and keep my commandments.

Exodus 34:14-16 14 For thou shalt worship no other god: for the LORD, whose name is Jealous, is a **jealous** God: 15 Lest thou make a covenant with the inhabitants of the land, and they go a whoring after their gods, and do sacrifice unto their gods, and one call thee, and thou eat of his sacrifice; 16 And thou take of their daughters unto thy sons, and their daughters go a whoring after their gods, and make thy sons go a whoring after their gods.

Deuteronomy 4:24 24 For the LORD thy God is a consuming fire, even a **jealous** God.

Deuteronomy 5:9-11 9 Thou shalt not bow down thyself unto them, nor serve them: for I the LORD thy God am a **jealous** God, visiting the iniquity of the fathers upon the children unto the third and fourth generation of them that hate me, 10 And shewing mercy unto thousands of them that love me and keep my commandments. 11 Thou shalt not take the name of the LORD thy God in vain: for the LORD will not hold him guiltless that taketh his name in vain.

Deuteronomy 6:15-17 15 (For the LORD thy God is a jealous God among you) lest the anger of the LORD thy God be kindled against thee, and destroy thee from off the face of the earth. 16 Ye shall not tempt the LORD your God, as ye tempted him in Massah. 17 Ye shall diligently keep the commandments of the LORD your God, and his testimonies, and his statutes, which he hath commanded thee.

Joshua 24:19-25 19 And Joshua said unto the people, Ye cannot serve the LORD: for he is an holy God; he is a jealous God; he will not forgive your transgressions nor your sins. 20 If ye forsake the LORD, and serve strange gods, then he will turn and do you hurt, and consume you, after that he hath done you good.

Ezekiel 39:25-29 25 Therefore thus saith the Lord GOD; Now will I bring again the captivity of Jacob, and have mercy upon the whole house of Israel, and will be jealous for my holy name; 26 After that they have borne their shame, and all their trespasses whereby they have trespassed against me, when they dwelt safely in their land, and none made them afraid. 27 When I have brought them again from the people, and gathered them out of their enemies' lands, and am sanctified in them in the sight of many nations; 28 Then shall they know that I am the LORD their God, which caused them to be led into captivity among the heathen: but I have gathered them unto their own land, and have left none of them any more there. 29 Neither will I hide my face any more from them: for I have poured out my spirit upon the house of Israel, saith the Lord GOD.

Joel 2:18 18 Then will the LORD be jealous for his land, and pity his people.

Nahum 1:2-8 2 God is jealous, and the LORD revengeth; the LORD revengeth, and is furious; the LORD will take vengeance on his adversaries, and he reserveth wrath for his enemies. 3 The LORD is slow to anger, and great in power, and will not at all acquit the wicked: the LORD hath his way in the whirlwind and in the storm, and the clouds are the dust of his feet. 4 He rebuketh the sea, and maketh it dry, and drieth up all the rivers: Bashan languisheth, and Carmel, and the flower of Lebanon languisheth. 5 The mountains quake at him, and the hills melt, and the earth is burned at his presence, yea, the world, and all that dwell therein. 6 Who can stand before his indignation? and who can abide in the fierceness of his anger? his fury is poured out like fire, and the rocks are thrown down by him. 7 The LORD is good, a strong hold in the day of trouble; and he knoweth them that trust in him. 8 But with an overrunning flood he will make an utter end of the place thereof, and darkness shall pursue his enemies.

Zechariah 1:14-15 14 So the angel that communed with me said unto me, Cry thou, saying, Thus saith the LORD of hosts; I am jealous for Jerusalem and for Zion with a great jealousy. 15 And I am very sore displeased with the heathen that are at ease: for I was but a little displeased, and they helped forward the affliction.

Zechariah 8:2-5 2 Thus saith the LORD of hosts; I was jealous for Zion with great jealousy, and I was jealous for her with great fury. 3 Thus saith the LORD; I am returned unto Zion, and will dwell in the midst of Jerusalem: and Jerusalem shall be called a city of truth; and the mountain of the LORD of hosts the holy mountain. 4 Thus saith the LORD of hosts; There shall yet old men and old women dwell in the streets of Jerusalem, and every man with his staff in his hand for very age. 5 And the streets of the city shall be full of boys and girls playing in the streets thereof.

2 Corinthians 11:2-4 2 For I am jealous over you with godly jealousy: for I have espoused you to one husband, that I may present you as a chaste virgin to Christ. 3 But I fear, lest by any means, as the serpent beguiled Eve through his subtilty, so your minds should be corrupted from the simplicity that is in Christ. 4 For if he that cometh preacheth another Jesus, whom we have

not preached, or if ye receive another spirit, which ye have not received, or another gospel, which ye have not accepted, ye might well bear with him.

God is a jealous God (by his own admission). In the school of 'woke', to be jealous is a negative, because it is a presumption of 'male patriarchy' (as though women aren't jealous). 'Woke' notwithstanding, a jealous God suggests that God is jealous over Himself, His Name, his power, and his prerogative. That is to say, he doesn't share. You share (what he gives). Does Bishop Holston share regular meals with his Hispanic maid and landscaper, and ask them to explain the variations of being saved by grace or works (in English)? One might argue OJ Simpson was jealous over his 'things' when he broke into that hotel with a gun and his White friends. Oj was upset that people were selling his 'things'.

Somewhere in my minds hyperbolic eye I see God saying, 'don't give His authority away'. Don't give it away to sexual trends and fads, don't give it away to AI, don't give it away to human reason, psychology, money, etc. Does the full moon make tides or perhaps devils, or does the God that put it there? While it doesn't take any man's authority and knowledge to be able to describe how the moon influences the tides, becoming 100% deterministic about it and leaving God out the equation is blasphemous. When the church emphasizes the 'means', more than the God who made the 'means', it is a corruption. But let us go on with exegeting General Conference, because I noticed in the Day 3 and Day 4 Summaries the foolishness of God's representatives (The Church) got even more intense.

Young people share fears, hopes for future church

CHARLOTTE, N.C. (UM News) — Speaking during the United Methodist General Conference, young delegates affirmed that amid the turmoil there is hope for reconciliation and growth. Alejandra of the Florida Conference told delegates that the younger generation is feeling the weight of the emotional, mental and spiritual trauma that comes with separation and disaffiliations.

I'd be scared about the future too if the people leading me act like they have absolutely no idea what a man and woman are unless they resort to LGBTQIA sexual algebra? This Youth told the General Conference of the United Methodist Church that the youth felt sad and traumatized because of disaffiliations and separation (akin to a bad divorce). Adult attendees sat there with false looks of concern and admiration on their faces...as though the separation and disaffiliations were a magic coincidence and not the result of some people desiring a God that needs and accepts correction. With well-fed smug looks on their faces no adult in Charlotte admitted their own fault in the conflict. Not a single one took responsibility, but instead blamed the conservatives for being racist, transphobic, and homophobic and thus driving a wedge in the official sexual Doctrine of the Church. Would it be sexual algebra, scripture and Discipline? The weird part to me is that DEI Bishops and Methodist Historians cannot understand the fact that there is a reason we call the governing Doctrine of the former United Methodist Church, The Discipline. It is not a book of suggestions. If you have that many new 'suggestions', start your own denomination. But the liberals know that won't work because no one in America or the world gives a craps-fart what their opinion on theology is...when of course they don't know the difference between a man and a woman without resorting to sexual algebra, completely deviant, and diametrically opposed from what the bible teaches. Even if a man and woman, stripped butt naked at General Conference, and the brought in a a post-puberty male dog, cajónes swinging, and a female dog in heat, our genius DEI Bishops and the assembled Prelates, officials, Elders, Deacons, and laity of the United Methodist Church would be forced from a new doctrinal position, to look at the butt naked human and animal specimens, and then agree that balls and penises, vaginas and breasts are just patriarchal social constructs, and as such have no meaning. They are magic coincidences, and the church should make no difference among them, resorting to 'sexual algebra' to try to explain the obvious differences. Sexual algebra is the construct, the part 'all in people's heads', the balls and penises, and breasts and vaginas you see are the reality. Even though the physical difference is staring them in the face, they will still double down on 'sexual algebra'. Furthermore at their confusion, and to prove to the public that there was no doubt, like Elijah at the showdown with Jezebel and 'prophets' of Baal, were I at the General Conference, I would demand that Bishops Bickerton, Sharma Lewis, Holston and any others in attendance that have any doubt go up and touch the penises, breasts, and vaginas of the butt naked dogs and humans that I would drag in there to try to prove to my denomination that indeed it was as the scripture said, and God did make us and many other mammals, animals and plant species male and female, all in his image. Of course, I'd do this in the hope that by touching these organs on stage at General Conference, it will bring a clarity that their eyes did not give them (even though seeing and touching their own sexual organs for what must be a lifetime, did not bring that clarity). Millions of dollars in combined salaries, fancy titles and robes, and we have people in high positions in the church that refuse to see the difference between men and women, and were they even to touch the naked man and woman, and male and female dog's sexual organs, would still be forced by their socialist atheist LGBTQIA ideology to say out loud to the UMC after Holy Conferencing, that there is not a difference between men and women an/or their physical sexuality and sexual identity is all in your mind.

Part IV

Adding speed and intensity to the whole oxymoronic tone and tenor of General Conference, is the fact that even though said Bishops wouldn't fain in the least to offer an opinion on what a man and a woman are that doesn't include socialist-atheist LGBTQIA sexual algebra, they made every attempt to convince the participants of General Conference that women were 'allowed' and told they could feel assured they could participate in deliberations without fear of harassment. Oxymoronic nonsense. How can a pro-LGBTQIA church make a place for just women? Women by what definition...the traditional definition? You don't know what a man and a woman are, but you guarantee the rights and safety of women? that is precisely why the church is complicit with Lia Thomas, swimming against women? Is a swimming competition with Lia Thomas in it a safe space for biological women? At General Conference there is a 'Women's Meeting Group' or Caucus, supposedly a safe space for biological 'women' and girls, and yet it will be filled with lust filled lesbians, and transgender women built like Ving Rhames. Is that a safe space for women? Is that a safe space for your daughter? A safe space for transgender women built like Ving Rhames and butch bull daggers is not necessarily a 'safe space' for biological women. Letting this socialist-atheist LGBTQIA sexual algebra identity theology' infiltrate United Methodist Church women's groups and organizations has not created 'Safe Spaces' for women. It has created the opposite. Here again, no wonder people are abandoning the church in droves with oxymoronic idiocy of that magnitude. Is queer/transgender reading hour a safe space for Christian children? A church that would promote such a thing is hell fire bound (granted amongst all the other things a church could be hell fire bound for)! How is putting your children in an environment where they are forced to act like they don't know what a man and a woman are a 'safe space'; a 'safe sanctuary'?

My 'favorite' highlight of General Conference is when the Asian American Caucus decried the 'Yoga' symbol on stage...not for theological reasons, but because it is associated with Narendra Modi and Indian Nationalism. No disrespect to the Asian caucus, but this is a perfect example (even for we Blacks) of why it is not good to go around comparing suffering. No disrespect to the Asian Caucus, but this is a perfect example even to we Blacks why it's not good to around comparing suffering. It has a weird way of bouncing back unpredictably. Is the impact of Pakistan (Islam) v. India (Hindu) as great as the 450 years or so of European domination in the Indian subcontinent, the middle east and Asia. When lines on a map move, and religions get jumbled and humbled for political, cultural and yes racial reasons, is one fallout really that comparable to the next? Did our Asian caucus get exposed to White European driven Christian United Methodism because God himself delivered it to them a la Mt. Sinai? Or did 450 years of European cultural domination give them their 'Methodism'? Saying Modi/Yoga don't deserve a flag or symbolism on the General Conference platform because the Asian Caucus is holding Modi/Yoga accountable for Hindu cultural nationalism is oxymoronic and disingenuous. Are the European Christian Masters now to be completely atoned for their legacy of crimes over the 500-1000 years of Western imperial, economic, political, military and cultural domination of the world, and now the United Methodist Church is going after 15 years of Hindu/Yoga nationalism, transphobia, homophobia, sexism (yet sex doesn't exist), and redefining the biblical/mammalian notion of male/female and suggesting that LGBTQIA sexual algebra provides mankind with a better sexual understanding? It is written:

Matthew 12:43-45 43 When the unclean spirit is gone out of a man, he walketh through dry places, seeking rest, and findeth none. 44 Then he saith, I will return into my house from whence I came out; and when he is come, he findeth it empty, swept, and garnished. 45 Then goeth he, and taketh with himself seven other spirits more wicked than himself, and they enter in and dwell there: and the last state of that man is worse than the first. Even so shall it be also unto this wicked generation.

White European Christianity, exhausted after World Wars, filled to the brim with the filthy lucre for which the United Methodists and its splinter groups are fighting over today, is no longer able to critique Humanity because it has decided to be complicit with and aid and abet every wicked trend in humanity. In that way it has mocked itself to death. It is as though the UMC were clowns. Literally 'Pagliacci', like the Italian Opera where there is a family/troop of clowns with a theatre act, and due to a love triangle, the title role clown, murders his wife and her lover (who not surprisingly or coincidentally is a clown in their troop). On stage! Watching General Conference 2024 was like watching a clown murder two people, and wondering whether it was part of the act or did two people just get killed. It looked very realistic, but camera technology, plastic surgery and hormones can simulate all kinds of things these days. How simple it was to this clown family, years ago when they first began clowning. Then the emphasis was on tricks that required skill and talent, like 70 clowns getting out of VW Beetle, transforming balloons into various animals and shapes, or doing magic tricks. Those acts no longer get the laughs they used to. So now the clown troop just gets up in front of an audience with no makeup or no gadgets, and amuses the audience by letting the audience insult it, hurl rotten tomatoes at it, accuse it of being killers and pedophiles, etc. Cue clown music. In 1968, the United Methodist Church was formed, 'swept clean' of its racism, the Central Conference, and its 'bourgeois' trappings. And as Jesus noted, thus having been 'swept clean', the original demon and 7 more of his demon friends worse than him, stormed in and took up happy residence. Presumably the crimes of European Christianity have been wiped clean because Post-Modern United Methodism is 'woke'? What if India/Modi/Yoga is 'woke' 100 years from now, will they be allowed to erase the crimes of their past and walk away, negating the purpose of the Asian Caucus in demanding the removal of Yoga/Modi symbolism from the stage and General Conference. Note that the Asian Caucus to the General Conference 2024 is not pissed off because of the theological implications of wondering is the God of the Bible, the same as the God of Yoga to justify symbolizing Yoga/Hindu Nationalism on stage at a United Methodist General Conference. White folks and our DEI Bishops aren't questioning that either. So what are they questioning? Whether or not they can fellowship with and be in communion with, Christians, former family members in the UMC that prefer the biblical and mammalian definition of what a male and a female are, to going around practicing LGBTQIA+ sexual algebra and teaching it to our children as normative.

This episode made me curious what the other symbols on the stage at General Conference were. I was not disappointed. It's rare that I'm overwhelmed. Let my New York Jewish readers empathize with me in saying 'Oy Veh' upon seeing the stage of symbols at General Conference. I was 'verklempt' (overcome with emotions). I was stunned to the point of near emotionalism. It was a stunned silence. I was watching a clown, sex, murder tragedy. A clown kills two people on stage, but we don't know if it's an act. On stage were flags and placards. Two were variations of crosses. I consider myself a funny dude, perhaps I could have even been a comedian; but I did not need jokes at General Conference 2024 because the thing in its entirety was a joke, a weeklong clownish joke for which the sad hilarity never stopped. In addition to the two crosses, whose difference was never explained, there was a silhouette of a dude facing left playing the saxophone. There is a placard of words in an African dialect (here again not explained). There was a placard of a lady silhouette dancing, with 'God' written at the bottom. There is a woman silhouette placard of a woman releasing a dove and/or in prayer and petition position releasing the dove. Unfortunately stuff like this screams "I am a joke"! They should have made one giant banner to go across the whole stage that said "We are jokes because we treat our God like He is a joke, an amusement capable of being wrong, that needs to be corrected or is somehow inappropriate. This God, the God of John Wesley is inappropriate and has made inappropriate comments that hurt people's feelings, and DEI Bishops need to correct him and apologize for him. And then you presume to go out and tell people they need this impotent weak God that doesn't know what a man and woman are and can't tie his own shoestrings (as it were). Can an omniscient God either not know what a man and woman are absent LGBTQIA+ sexual algebra, or have lied about it for 3700 years or so of biblical history and at least a few million years of mammalian history? Can an omnipotent God, not know you are mocking him when you make these assumptions about his fallacies and failures? What is worse, your claim that he is powerless to defend Himself, and his letting you do (tear the UMC up) proves you are right, proves you are wrong.

This is what current United Methodist authorities present to current and former Methodists as 'reality'; some pan-world concoction of ridiculous worldly symbolism and foolishness parading around as reasonability and openness. Bishops Tracy Malone, Bishop Minde Muyonba, Judy and Bickerton, Sharma Lewis, etc., these are your bus drivers and those placards behind them are the itinerary of where they are heading the church. Nowhere fast!

Chapter 2 - Ye shall not tempt the Lord thy God

Chapter 2 - Ye shall not tempt the LORD your God, as ye tempted him in Massah.

Exodus 17:1-7 KJG Exodus 17:1 And all the congregation of the children of Israel journeyed from the wilderness of Sin, after their journeys, according to the commandment of the LORD, and pitched in Rephidim: and there was no water for the people to drink. 2 Wherefore the people did chide with Moses, and said, Give us water that we may drink. And Moses said unto them, Why chide ye with me? wherefore do ye tempt the LORD? 3 And the people thirsted there for water; and the people murmured against Moses, and said, Wherefore is this that thou hast brought us up out of Egypt, to kill us and our children and our cattle with thirst? 4 And Moses cried unto the LORD, saying, What shall I do unto this people? they be almost ready to stone me. 5 And the LORD said unto Moses, Go on before the people, and take with thee of the elders of Israel; and thy rod, wherewith thou smotest the river, take in thine hand, and go. 6 Behold, I will stand before thee there upon the rock in Horeb; and thou shalt smite the rock, and there shall come water out of it, that the people may drink. And Moses did so in the sight of the elders of Israel. 7 And he called the name of the place Massah, and Meribah, because of the chiding of the children of Israel, and because they tempted the LORD, saying, Is the LORD among us, or not?

Deuteronomy 6:12-17 12 Then beware lest thou forget the LORD, which brought thee forth out of the land of Egypt, from the house of bondage. 13 Thou shalt fear the LORD thy God, and serve him, and shalt swear by his name. 14 Ye shall not go after other gods, of the gods of the people which are round about you; 15 (For the LORD thy God is a jealous God among you) lest the anger of the LORD thy God be kindled against thee, and destroy thee from off the face of the earth. 16 Ye shall not tempt the LORD your God, as ye tempted him in Massah. 17 Ye shall diligently keep the commandments of the LORD your God, and his testimonies, and his statutes, which he hath commanded thee.

Deuteronomy 9:17-22 17 And I (Moses) took the two tables, and cast them out of my two hands, and brake them before your eyes. 18 And I fell down before the LORD, as at the first, forty days and forty nights: I did neither eat bread, nor drink water, because of all your sins which ye sinned, in doing wickedly in the sight of the LORD, to provoke him to anger. 19 For I was afraid of the anger and hot displeasure, wherewith the LORD was wroth against you to destroy you. But the LORD hearkened unto me at that time also. 20 And the LORD was very angry with Aaron to have destroyed him: and I prayed for Aaron also the same time. 21 And I took your sin, the calf which ye had made, and burnt it with fire, and stamped it, and ground it very small, even until it was as small as dust: and I cast the dust thereof into the brook that descended out of the mount. 22 And at Taberah, and at Massah, and at Kibrothhattaavah, ye provoked the LORD to wrath.

Deuteronomy 33:8-11 8 And of Levi he said, Let thy Thummim and thy Urim be with thy holy one, whom thou didst prove at Massah, and with whom thou didst strive at the waters of Meribah; 9 Who said unto his father and to his mother, I have not seen him; neither did he acknowledge his brethren, nor knew his own children: for they have observed thy word, and kept thy covenant. 10 They shall teach Jacob thy judgments, and Israel thy law: they shall put incense before thee, and whole burnt sacrifice upon thine altar. 11 Bless, LORD, his substance, and accept the work of his hands: smite through the loins of them that rise against him, and of them that hate him, that they rise not again.

I urge the reader to come to his or her (sic) own conclusions regarding these matters and the propensity of the United Methodist Church to clown itself pretending like it is something it is not, like the drag Queens they celebrate so oft. Imagine, General Conference 2024 in Charlotte, consistent with being a barometer and thermometer of trends in mainstream society, politics and culture...and not a thermostat; The Bishops are at General Conference loudly and raucously protesting on behalf of Hamas and the Hezbollah.

The new UMC is a church of religious drag queen prelates, draped in Palestinian colors and flags and rainbow colors and flags. I think I read that six Bishops attended the pro-Hamas rally. I know they were probably DEI Black and brown and liberal on sexual and economic issues. Do you want to see a walking hypocrite, a hypocrite in person, of the same type as Jesus' condemnation of the Pharisees? These liberal Bishops out there protesting for Gaza and the Palestinian position deserve every bit of it! How is it they want to be in 'full communion' with everybody, except the 'conservatives' they've been in 'full communion' with since the early 18th century?

Matthew 22:15 15 Then went the Pharisees, and took counsel how they might entangle him in his talk.

Matthew 22:34 34 But when the Pharisees had heard that he had put the Sadducees to silence, they were gathered together.

Matthew 22:41 41 While the Pharisees were gathered together, Jesus asked them,

Matthew 23:2 2 Saying, The scribes and the Pharisees sit in Moses' seat:

Matthew 23:13-15 13 But woe unto you, scribes and Pharisees, hypocrites! for ye shut up the kingdom of heaven against men: for ye neither go in yourselves, neither suffer ye them that are entering to go in. 14 Woe unto you, scribes and Pharisees, hypocrites! for ye devour widows' houses (church property), and for a pretence make long prayer (Holy Conferencing): therefore ye shall receive the greater damnation. 15 Woe unto you, scribes and Pharisees, hypocrites! for ye compass sea and land to make one proselyte, and when he is made, ye make him twofold more the child of hell than yourselves.

Matthew 23:23 23 Woe unto you, scribes and Pharisees, hypocrites! for ye pay tithe of mint and anise and cummin, and have omitted the weightier matters of the law, judgment, mercy, and faith: these ought ye to have done, and not to leave the other undone.

Matthew 23:25 25 Woe unto you, scribes and Pharisees, hypocrites! for ye make clean the outside of the cup and of the platter, but within they are full of extortion and excess.

Matthew 23:27 27 Woe unto you, scribes and Pharisees, hypocrites! for ye are like unto whited sepulchres, which indeed appear beautiful outward, but are within full of dead men's bones, and of all uncleanness.

Matthew 23:28-29 28 Even so ye also outwardly appear righteous unto men, but within ye are full of hypocrisy and iniquity. 29 Woe unto you, scribes and Pharisees, hypocrites! because ye build the tombs of the prophets (John and Charles Wesley, Asbury, Whitefield, etc., and garnish the sepulchres of the righteous,

These liberal Bishops out there protesting for Gaza and the Palestinian position are the equivalent of political drag queens, draping themselves in the Palestinian flags and colors to prove how hip and with it they are. They deserve every epithet Jesus laid on the Pharisees; who say one thing with their mouths and then quite do another. With one side of their dastardly mouths, they proclaim trans rights, and LGBTQIA rights, and then with the other side of their mouths they proclaim Hamas and Hezbollah rights. One of side of their filthy mouths proclaims women's rights, while the other proclaims Hamas/Hezbollah Rights. And yet Islam is more rugged on homosexuality and transgender issues than nearly any conservative Christian church in America. A case is being made every day in the Middle East, but using Afghanistan as a prime example, women's rights are being trampled by the same people the Liberals in the United Methodist Church are championing. And Methodism pays these Bishops $250,000 a year?

9-11 anyone? Is the American historical mind so shallow that it forgot 9-11, Osama bin Laden, Al Caida, Isis, Isil (Obama's ridiculous construct), etc.? In France, England, Belgium even with all that weed, it seems every other week somebody with an Islamic ax to grind gets to stabbing or shooting. Anybody wanna look at Salman Rushdie and what happened darn near 35 years after the original Fatwah was given, and was lifted by Iran sometime later, only to be carried out by a dude who was hyped up on it anyway. These are the forces the United Methodist Church and its current crop of Bishops is celebrating? I am not anti-Islam. Far from it. I'm more or less in tune with their positions on basic sexuality, though not the repression of women. Much of Islam has its roots in Judeo-Christian values and history. I am against our current crop of Bishops because they think being on the right side of history is a substitute for being on the right side of the Lord. To believe whatever you want personally is a matter of choice and conscious, however to lead the UMC down that road is blasphemy and worthy of every condemnation Jesus gave the Pharisees and previous noted in this essay.

My favorite 'Political UMC' drag queen pro-Palestinian comment was by one of the participants that said 'the church can't remain silent when people are suffering'? What gall? What forgetfulness? Apparently the UMC is very picky about what it defines as suffering. Every week there is a sufferer of the week the United Methodist Church must speak up for. Gays, Blacks women, minorities, women in general, and yes the people of Gaza; those are the 'in crowd' sufferers right now, but long in the ascendency. If you are poor and White, male, conservative, etc., your suffering is minimized. Others are afraid of you and you are treated as though you deserve your exclusion by the stint of the fact that you ruled and have made all of the previously noted current 'in group' sufferers suffer years. Let the reader see these faults in logic for what they are, faults in judgement. By no means am I suggesting they have mental or intellectual problems, I'm arguing they have faults in their judgement as regards sexual issues and the church.

Psalm 111:10 10 The fear of the LORD is the beginning of wisdom: a good understanding have all they that do his commandments: his praise endureth for ever.

That is the problem with this motley collection of well-paid and well-meaning Bishops. Their fear of God is lacking. This I proved by arguing that you clearly don't fear a God you feel free to 'correct'. Perchance in your imagination, either God needs correcting or will gladly accept your correction, or provided this God is offended at your correction, He cannot punish you. Either one is a lack of the fear and reverence due God. To the point that you tell the world (and former members) with a straight face that your God was confused, did not know what a man and woman are/were, and needed Bruce Jenner/Caitlyn, Dylan Mulvaney, Ru Paul and the Ebony and liberal United Methodist Bishops to tell him. This upbraiding, presumably their God either took sitting down or found himself unable to respond even were he pissed off.

That basic lack of judgement has led to another collapse in logic by the liberal Pro-Hamas UMC drag queen defenders standing up where people are suffering. It is quite logical for us and the United Methodist Liberal leadership that leads us, to ask who the other people(s) and nations are that form the primary public and global support of the Palestinian/Hamas position. It's a valid question. Where does that trail lead us dear well-paid Bishops and the liberals that romanticize them but China and Russia. In their countries, and Gaza you and your religion are treated like the clowns and nincompoops you are. At best you and your Methodism are treated like a drug addict or the 'opioid of the masses'. At worst they will lock your 'Old Testament donkey' up faster than you can say 'I love Gaza' for proselytizing and evangelizing! Go to China, go to Russia, go to Gaza proselytizing draped in your rainbow flags and see what happens.

And yet the UMC is not protesting on behalf of the Uyghur population in Russia being oppressed and put into religious concentration/reeducation camps. 'Arbeite Mache Frei' doesn't it? The girl at General Conference protesting on behalf of the Palestinians said that the United Methodist Church should represent all people's suffering. How come some people's suffering is more timely, relevant, well connected in social media terms, and well paid while other suffering, even when known about, is not any Methodists radar screen.

And yet by so vocally supporting the Palestinians, we can't help but normalize the Chinese and Russians that support them. Indeed, 'the enemy of my enemy' is my friend, according to Winston Churchill right? Let us not forget, the Chinese and the Russians are in a current geopolitical struggle with America, that is already a tinderbox. There is presently a Russian submarine parked off the coast of Cuba. But there our DEI Bishops are legitimizing the geopolitical interests of the Russians and Chinese by appearing to identify with them regarding Gaza. The Chinese and the Russians are avowed atheists in political, theological, and philosophical terms. It seems our current post-General Conference 2024 church wants to be in 'communion' with everybody but us conservatives.

Our elite colleges campuses are a conflagration of liberal hedonism and narcissism masquerading themselves as a desire to 'fix' the world and transform the world into some kind of humanistic socialist-atheist perfectly equitable paradise. The Chinese, who have stolen more intellectual, pharmaceutical, military, and corporate copyrighted materials than a little bit, become a fetish of the young and dumb college crowd, who think traditional history is revisionist history, and revisionist history is 'The Traditional History' as a discipline. Do you think it is a magic coincidence the Tik-Tok debate is going on at the same time as this social disruption and dangerous pro-Palestinian protests? For the most part, American youth are saying they don't care who owns Tik-Tok, as long as they can make silly dance videos and do stupefying podcasts and videos about the best makeup to use and how to 'trick out' your Chevy truck. This is the default setting when a society and culture doesn't teach its own unified history, but in a boneheaded effort to prove how permanent it is, it allows itself to be critiqued, criticized, and nitpicked, all the while elevating the idiot making the critique. This it does in the mistaken notion that it is so powerful it cannot be defeated. It is like historians who don't know what was taught, only what the critiques of what was originally taught were. With that mindset, everyone elevates the critique. Imagine it is like purporting to know Automotive Engineering and Manufacturing, but all you have ever been around is shade tree mechanics. There is nothing wrong with shade tree historians; just don't be naïve enough to call them automotive engineers or manufacturers. It is like thinking Rick Ross loves cars and knows a lot about cars because he has a car show once a year that 15,000 attend.

And yet here we go jumping into bed with the Chinese and the Russians by overtly loving the same thing they love (in the Palestinian issue), normalizing them. Our youth are willing to tear up, deface and spray paint on the monuments of our noblest academic institutions because of the magic confluence of social media, and American history taught and defined by critics and criticism of it. And yes, a theological and religious history of America taught by Methodist, Presbyterian, Episcopalian, Anglican and even Catholic criticism and critics of it of it. And if our new best friends, the Palestinians and the people of Gaza, happen to have as their best friends Russia and China, well, more proof we are radical liberal Bishops and on the right side of history. $250,000 per year y'all.

The Chinese do copyright infringement, and technology and intellectual property theft at scales the world has never seen. The Russians kill their enemies in broad daylight in western countries. Putin, without reestablishing the Soviet Empire per se, or even any pretense to Communist and socialist humanism and ideals, even compares himself to the Empires of the greatest Tsars and wants to do something similar regarding Russian global power and influence today. This is even if he must drag his people along kicking screaming, drunk out their minds, and religious in a way only former atheists can be without having been transformed by the Holy Ghost, but transformed by the Decree of the Emperor (Putin or Constantine).

Part III

But let us get serious for a moment by dear Ebony Methodist brothers and sisters. Apparently we got invited to a party on October 7th. From what I am told there was techno music and the party was to last from Friday night to Sunday morning, nonstop. We came to the party. Others came to the Party. The Jewish techno ravers threw a party, but trust me, Hamas decided to throw a bigger party that night/day. We happened to be at the party, and because of liberal soundbite Tiktok Politics infiltrating the Church, there we are supporting Hamas and jumping in bed with the Russians and the Chinese by default because of our blind admiration for the suffering of Black and brown people...when it is conveniently at White hands. Black and brown people are dying in Chicago, Detroit, Atlanta, New Orleans, and chocolate cities across America, Haiti and Africa in ridiculous feats of mindless ethnic or gang violence. But that violence is not important enough to speak about because it doesn't come at White hands, and you can't sue or critique White folks and get paid like Ben Crump. Furthermore, protesting and tearing the city or university up, because of George Floyd, or what the Jews and academic institutions with high levels of Jewish participation in the student body, faculty and staff are doing to the Palestinians and the people of Gaza, while senseless mindless violence you can possibly control is going on in your backyard is insane, inane, and ridiculous. This is the kind of selective outrage I am talking about. There is footage of a New York subway full of protestors draped in Palestinian flags screaming like wild banshees for Jews and Zionists to reveal themselves, and I do not think it was so that they could congratulate them and tell them "Come on Down, you're the next contestant on 'The Price is Right". This happened in America, 79 years after World War II. If nothing else proves how dangerous allowing revisionist history to be dominant is, I do not know.

The October 7th party (rave) however, was not a wild, wooly, drug induced, drug fueled, sex filled, out of control party like the Israeli hipsters planned. Unfortunately, it turned into nightmare that has lasted months and months, and revealed cracks and kinks in the Democrat and Republican party as regards Antisemitism. The political toll on Israel has grown in exponential proportion to their securing of military victories and doing their will on the people of Gaza. Now the party started on October 7th but hasn't stopped since, is too much. It is going on, on the campuses of American universities, and yes, some United Methodist Bishops went out there trying to make statements about their discerning the 'right side of history'. Now that the October 7th party is way out of control however, we're stuck trying to figure out a way to get out of it before the police and the media come, holding people accountable, each in their own structural power ways.

Russian support for the Palestine/Gaza situation puts us in the bed with them at one of these Puffy style parties, filled with athletes, entertainers, socialist-atheists, people trying to 'find themselves practicing LGBTQIA+ sexual algebra'...and wait for it...there is TD Jakes (reportedly old 'Power-Bottom' himself. Whether TD is the power bottom he is reputed to be or not, his association with and affiliation with Puffy and Puffy's parties has come to haunt him and associate him with values that were he not such a hypocrite regarding the gospel, he never would have associated himself with.

The socialist atheist LGBTQIA left is playing the church and its theoretical good intentions like a fiddle. They know every time somebody hollers suffering, we will come running as long as the world has gone running ahead of us and before us. Thus we (the UMC) can follow the world, get there, and act like they were there the whole time. But by the time that has happened, the church will only clown itself again by realizing time, sentiments, and social media likes and dislikes have shifted again, and they must chase the world once more trying to catch up. "Fascinating, absolutely fascinating," as Dr. Edward Wimberly used to say.

Black people in Chicago, Atlanta, New Orleans, Detroit, etc., aren't suffering enough for a 'shot out' from the UMC church but folk in Gaza are? White folk in Appalachia OD'ing and dying in droves and numbers that fill rural morgues and funeral homes beyond capacity don't deserve a shout out at General Conference 2024, but the Palestinians and of course the LGBTQIA+ sexual algebra community gets all the shout outs and gets to dance in the aisles in their flags. Talk about a little leaven, the church of Almighty God has reduced itself to explaining sexuality by means of LGBTQIA sexual algebra, and teaching alphabet soup, sexual gumbo, sexual goulash style teachings. The UMC now teaches the idea that one should consider one's sexuality like he or she (not to wit) was preparing sexual fried rice without or without egg, vegetables, onions, etc., let alone beef, pork, chicken, shrimp etc.. This is what UMC church teachings about sexuality are now in complete contradiction to and diametrical opposition to biblical and mammalian historic truths about sexuality.

Black on Black absurd levels of violence, family instability, and the fact Atlanta Fulton-County can't build a jail fast enough to house all of the mostly Negro inmates that have been produced in 50 years of Chocolate mayors, chocolate Police Chiefs, Chocolate Fire Chiefs, Chocolate city Councilmen, Chocolate School Boards, Chocolate Superintendents, and yet our Ebony DEI Bishops are not concerned about any of that, and none of it gets a mention. They are worried about making sure Hamas and the LGBTQIA+ community get their chance to dance in aisles at the vaunted General Conference 2024. To add insult to injury, none of that Black internal violence is worth students at Columbia and Harvard tearing the campus up over, but Hamas and Gaza is? Hamas and Gaza had a party Oct 7th. They were so excited about the party that they filmed it themselves, and put it all over social media. Short films of them killing people in the most horrific of ways. That party was justified but Jan 6th wasn't? Black Lives Matters and Antifa antics are justified, but a militia of poor White men with high school diplomas, so desperate for self-esteem they select confederate and Nazi imagery to represent themselves, they are not suffering. No sympathy for them (per the soup nazi Seinfeld episode)! Extreme suffering, or the sense(s) of extreme suffering lead to outbursts, but some people's outbursts are tolerated and welcomed by the UMC hierarchy but others are not. Materialism, broken families, and the suffering caused by those processes, the UMC hierarchy has not commented on, but the 'sufferings' that they can chase the secular world behind (transgender rights, homosexual rights, Hamas rights, are exalted. These are the ones they adopt and imitate.

John 13:15 15 For I have given you an example, that ye should do as I have done to you.

The way this issue is causing a fissure in America is evident on college campuses across America. Instead of our Ebony and liberal bishops representing a position of moderation and erstwhile stability, they have chosen to rabble rouse along with the rabble rousers. What other indignities must God's church suffer. Clearly this is our cross we bear in these times. As Jesus was mocked on the cross, so the liberals mock him, saying "I'm going to tell God what a man and a woman are." And the coup de grace my dear respected Christians is that the average Muslim and Jew for that matter, thinks we are polytheists. The concept of the trinity is an ideological anathema to them and a matter of grave suspicion. Were they in the ascendancy over us, they just as surely would tell us so. But of course, we no longer know what a man and a woman are so any other pretenses to universal knowledge notwithstanding, must be rooted in folly. What the liberals would fain have us believe, is that the same God in the person of Jesus, that was raised from the dead, presumably by his own wits, or his Father's, doesn't know what a man and a woman are? In human terms and spiritual terms, it must take way more knowledge to circumvent death, than it would take to know the difference between a man and a woman, and/or have a simple and reliable idea what a man and a woman are...but yet this is what our new post-General Conference 2024 DEI and assorted liberal bishops want us to preach. Preach insanity. What lows must we be reduced to.

Did not the UMC find itself going through the same thing Lucasfilms has gone through after the Acolyte (no pun intended)...only the UMC has been going through it 50 years with the culmination being a complete alienation of the original fans. Were that not tragic enough, the very communities, the new 'Woke' Star Wars nominally are supportive and acceptive of have not shown any great interest in the franchise by all its patronizing of the feminist LGBTQIA sexual algebra communities. So the ratings of tanks. Women outnumber men. If women liked the new pro-LGBTQIA sexual algebra 'woke' Star Wars, women could singlehandedly change the 'rotten tomatoes' and all the other scores by simply overwhelming the platforms. But they do not. They don't even like it. This is what happens when design your whole agenda and theology by what only 10% of the population on a good day, on the best of days will admit to? Why would a franchise as important as Lucasfilm's do it and why would any sane denomination do it...ergo our present post-General Conference UMC. Lucasfilm sacrificed all canonical consistency, and nearly all consonant storytelling arcing, all to tell a new story of lesbian space witches, who have been discriminated against; because of course, the universe and the Jedi oppress them and hate them, thus they have to hide out in space mountain, without the roller coaster...a flammable space mountain...unless those mean nasty Jedi used the force to set a mountain of lesbian witches that had the power to have 12 year old sized twin baby girls? This is the type of absurdity George Lucas has been reduced to...and trust me, God is way madder than George Lucas at the corruptions going on in the UMC to his original themes.

Part II

Instead of urging America to slow the rhetoric down on both sides of the debate, our DEI Bishops have made a decision to 'get on the right side' of socialist-atheist revisionist LGBTQIA+ sexual algebra history and go full 'woke'...and as the saying unfortunately goes, and you can ask Bud Light whether or not this is true, when you go full 'woke', you go broke. Reminds me of that famous scene in the Ben Stiller movie

Tropic Thunder, where Robert Downey's character describes the difference between an actor 'going full retard' and 'half retard' and how going 'full retard' can be damaging to one's career. Our liberal DEI bishops have decided to go 'full retard'. They have made a decision to accept the forces of chaos, trying to be hip and follow their socialist-atheist LGBTQIA+ sexual algebra social justice warrior friends, they are so enamored of in spite of all the Lord, or the entity formerly known as The Lord God has done for them and humanity. Let the reader and the church in America go to the throne of grace in a kind of prayer.

79 years after World War II, and Treblinka, Dachau, Buchenwald, etc., and the intervention of America and Western Europe, and generations of Jews prior, during and after the holocaust finding refuge in America from Pogroms and expulsions look at what happened on elite college and universities in America. With survivors of Auschwitz and the like still alive in America, and certainly their near relatives still alive in America, they can see United Methodist Churches draped in Palestinian flags (if not Yoga/Indian Nationalist) flags. Bishops of the UMC church will talk the same rhetoric as the pro-Palestinian liberal social justice media talking points. What must it be like for the Jews of that generation to see their children, grandchildren, and great grandchildren involved in collegiate and post-graduate academic life at the so-called best universities in America get hounded, harassed, and called murderers and worse in antisemitic rages and rants.

Perhaps on a human level you might be sympathetic to that argument. I certainly hope so. But if that is not enough, consider American history. Consider what was lost in American lives and the leveraging of national resources to defeat Naziism, Imperial Japan, and in the Cold War. 79 years after World War II this sacrifice of individual and political blood means nothing to supposedly the best and brightest minds at American Universities, to the extent they are rioting on behalf of Gazans ostensibly, but ultimately doing the bidding of Russia and China. It is shocking how the current Arab-Israeli conflict is revealing deep fault lines and fissures in American culture. This debate is also revealing how Black America can be manipulated. One day I'll have the courage to tell Black people my rationale about the quality of our academic, theological, political, and intellectual discourse (or lack thereof). Was it just the power of Tik-Tok, Facebook, and other social media that took Black people overnight from the point Jews were our allies during the Civil Rights movement, and pre-Civil Rights oftentimes the only way we could get comparative products in our communities because White folk certainly were not going to deign to come into the Black community to sell us the things they would sell themselves, to Jews being identical with the White mainstream. the fact they are for all intents and purposes European, that is to say Ashkenazi, as opposed to Sephardic or African. Of course post-1917 and post 1948 settlement in 'Palestine' was largely dominated by Ashkenazi and quite often secular Jews from Russia and Central Europe for which the strong tradition of socialism and socialist-atheism as a social 'construct' were powerful forces in the development of Jewish settlement and politics. For whatever damage it did to the development of modern Israeli politics and history, it also had the effect of locating Eretz Israel quite squarely in the secular European Philosophical tradition, even though of course Hassidism was equally as strong, but it was not a dominant. Of course from that sprang nearly all the forms of Judaism current in America from variations on reform, to Orthodox, to Hassidic, to whatever else. Hereagain, on the surface all White. It didn't take much propaganda from Russia, China and a long tradition of American Black Muslims and radicals to view Jews, at least in their overtly irreligious and overtly physically and culturally White forms to, as being inherently against Black people and we run slam into the 'opponent of my enemy, is automatically my friend'. Only in Churchillian lips does it make any sense, oratorical or otherwise. Quite often, quite because of your 'new friends', it can get you in the wrong place at the wrong time doing the wrong thing. Thus via bots, spam, and paid social media accounts, Black people are encouraged to do all kinds of things, such as not vote, dislike Jews and Israel, support reparations, etc. By the same means, American and European Jews were so identified with White mainstream cultural and economic dominance, that to see an Ashkenazi Jew is to all but see a White man from rural Mississippi with a Confederate flag on his truck, and an anti-immigration bumper sticker blasting I'm proud to be an American.

Of course, this 'brainwashing' is in complete ignorance of the fact of the Jewish presence and support in the Civil Rights Movement. This is in complete ignorance of the fact that quite often what appeared to be the exploitation of Black communities by Jewish shop owners, was due to outright bans on Black ownership. White people wouldn't let us have functional official legal businesses (accessing banks, lending, etc.) and they darn sure weren't going to deign go beneath themselves and actually provide the Black community with standard products and services (that is to say treat them equally). Who was left but the Jews who could obtain the legal and credit means to open businesses serving Black communities standard or something that resembled standard products and services. It wasn't long before 60's rabble rousers pointed out the 'magic coincidence' of Jewish ownership in Black communities, necessarily framing it in exploitive terms. These rabble rousers had just as much antipathy towards the Black church and its presumed Cadillac driving preachers, and 'pie in the sky' mentality. Essentially in one stroke these rabble rousers blamed Jewish shop owners and the Jewish race, as well as traditional Black denominational Christianity for 'exploiting' and 'retarding' Black political and cultural development, and not being more radical.

I don't mean to suggest that there are not critiques that should and could be made of The Black Church historically, and even White Jewish economic, cultural, and political engagement vis a vis African America. I only mean to say that history is complex and filled with nuances which cannot be oversimplified by draping yourself in a Palestinian flag and hollering about a UMC that hears suffering. In such meaningless political drag queen posturing these Bishops no doubt feel they (via self-reporting) are on the right side of history. This is the kind of stuff children do not Bishops. History is not as simple as being on its right or wrong side and neither is the God of history. These bishops would fain believe that they 'know history' when they see it, and are quite capable of ascertaining which side is the right side to be on. Only when they joined the UMC side as candidates for ordained ministry, the right side of history was anti-LGBTQIA, but of course now...just now...they are going to tell us lowly Methodists and God what a man and a woman are (or aren't). So, this is two clear examples of them being on the wrong side of history, and both times they swore (literally) that they were right. Ladies and gentlemen of Methodism, that is insane foolishness fit for children and adolescents who of course are convinced they know what the world needs, thus they are intent on protesting and making a stink until adults see how smart they are.

Only when a man or woman (sic) hits 30 or so, one realizes that half the ideas you had at 21 were wrong, and the other half were silly, vain and inconsequential. This combination of youth, silliness and wrongness is cute in adolescents and teens, but in 50-, 60-, and 70-year-old Bishops, it is dangerous to their souls and the church. Dangerous like if a lunatic doesn't know how to drive and has no experience driving at all. But some kind of way, he has convinced you (the supposed adult in the room) that he merely needs experience, and that he has quite observed people driving all his life and thus is certain he can do it. So with no license and no experience, you (the supposed adult in the room), give him the keys, because of course, everybody deserves a chance, even a lunatic. Let the lunatic drive. Let him drive your children to school because he deserves a chance. Let him drive the church van. He just needs experience. He got stigmatized as a lunatic for 2000 years (as though that's what held him back, not being a lunatic), but now give him the keys and let him drive the Mercedes. Or I'll do one better, see if the current Bishop of N. Georgia gives her motorcycle keys to a lunatic because he has been stigmatized all his life and just needs a chance to ride motorcycles. Therein lies the rub, that there is a significant possibility he kills him or herself, a possibility he or she kills others, and a possibility he or she destroys the vehicle, Mercedes or Hyundai. That is the current position of the UMC. We are at the will of DEI bishops who have never driven, but have convinced themselves they deserve a chance to drive a high precision automobile because they have watched others drive and are convinced, they can do it better simply by having watched others and they come from formerly marginalized groups. They believe they should be given the keys to the Mercedes, not just the Hyundai because they have been stigmatized all their lives as non-drivers and the system owes them the right and power to drive. I'm not taking sides. I'm pointing out facts.

Chapter 3 - The Cost of DEI Bishops to the Church

Chapter 3 - The Cost of DEI Bishops and Elders to the Black United Methodist Church

Yes, I am going to make the argument the DEI Ebony Bishops in many regards helped catapult the UMC into schism, dysfunction, and division. As bad as that is in the annals of history, there is the much, much worse impact of DEI Bishops on the Black American Church. At a time when Black communities are reeling from violence, underperforming schools, and a family and community structure that has been devasted in the past 50 years, the Black United Methodist Church writ large, our Ebony Bishops, and our Ebony denominational elites have been strangely silent. Apparently, they have had bigger fish to fry, like fighting transphobia, homophobia, anti-union forces, and racism.

Our children are running the streets in every major urban chocolate city killing each other darn near indiscriminately, and this is not as big a problem to our Ebony Bishops than Li'l Johnny being able to cut his penis off at 11 and li'l Suzie being able to take hormones and cut her nascent breasts off at 11. Transphobia, sexism, racism, homophobia they are against...God phobia, they are not against. God phobia (fear of God the Father), they are not against. God Phobia they encourage by telling people theological idiocy like if they are not comfortable using the term Father God or relating to God in that way because of how they have been traumatized on earth by the earthly fathers, its quite ok to use any other term that makes one more comfortable. In this line of thinking, they are not comfortable with their Father God because it has masculine and patriarchal connotations and denotations.

Here again, that line of reasoning is the direct result of teaching a (G)od whose Bible is like an etcha'sketch toy. Time you get displeased or want to change something in the picture, you just shake it hard enough to erase whatever was in the picture. This is how you get to a God that can and needs be corrected every so often, supposedly by well-meaning liberals and humanists. This God can't save himself, how can a church ideologically constituted as such, preach that God can save others...as in the old famous evangelical line...“Jesus Saves!”. Really UMC? He can't save himself from getting corrected about what a man and a woman are by liberal socialist-atheist LGTBIA+ sexual algebra, but he can save me, a poor sinner man. My righteousness comes from Him and his word, and now it is ‘etcha-sketched’ away by academically trained liberal ecclesiastics into oblivion. Make no mistake about it, the Liberals are imminently proud of new ‘etcha-sketched’ language that takes the LGBTQIA movement into full communion and with no restrictive language all.

The tragedy of DEI Bishops is that they have destroyed the witness of the Black church. First of all, in the old days, one made Bishop by distinguishing him or herself at previous levels of ministry and leadership. Typically, a man or woman of character and ability, would go into a church or community and ‘grow’ that church, its members and its ministries, beyond what it was when he or she got there. That is now considered an old-fashioned way. A better way to pick people to rise is that they have friends in high places, the right social principles and politics, and they can check off all the right DEI boxes (minority, female, gay, etc.) to fit in the new UMC political and administrative structure. So a lot of these Bishops don't ‘preach’, they certainly don't preach Jesus, and would fain shoot themselves before they preach God the Father and his stern word. They preach a God of liberal social justice principles to make everybody feel happy, welcome, and included. The problem is that it is so welcoming and affirming, like a homeless shelter, because everybody and anybody can get in, no one wants to be there, not even homeless people. Many homeless people claim that not only is it safer on the streets, but the homeless shelter itself exposes them to predators, and then forces upon them the shelter's rules. Sounds a lot like the current UMC to me.

The Pharisees, excuse me, DEI Bishops have created churches just like that. They can't get enough of telling the world how open and welcoming the new UMC is, only to face the hard cruel fact that fewer and fewer people (of any stripe) want to be there. They preach openness and welcome, but just like a homeless shelter, which is the definition of openness and welcome, but no one in their right mind wants to go there unless they are forced by necessity. They'll sleep at the Atlanta Hartsfield Airport before they go to a homeless shelter. The homeless shelter is open, presumably the airport isn't, and one is liable to expulsion or arrest...but homeless people prefer the airport or the streets instead of the homeless shelter (the new UMC). At the homeless shelter there are rules like no alcohol, no drugs, be in by 8pm and out by 8am. In the supposedly open Methodist church, the new rules, supplanting the old rules that were theologically based are the rules that one can't be transphobic, homophobic, or express traditional sexual male and female norms. What was it Jesus said:

Matthew 23:13 ¶ But woe unto you, scribes and Pharisees, hypocrites! for ye shut up the kingdom of heaven against men: for ye neither go in *yourselves*, neither suffer ye them that are entering to go in.

Matthew 23:14 Woe unto you, scribes and Pharisees, hypocrites! for ye devour widows' houses, and for a pretence make long prayer: therefore ye shall receive the greater damnation.

Matthew 23:15 Woe unto you, scribes and Pharisees, hypocrites! for ye compass sea and land to make one proselyte, and when he is made, ye make him twofold more the child of hell than yourselves.

They make up rules for themselves and then rules for everyone else. They know quite well that if they were out one night and saw a transgender woman with smeared make up, one high heel, and drunk out of his mind, they'd cross to the other side of the street not show all this 'love of neighbor' they preached about at General Conference. But if you, were to do that, or it got to their knowledge or attention that you humble UMC members crossed the street to avoid a Trans-female drunk man with one high heeled shoe on, our DEI Bishops would lambast you and call you homophobic, transphobic, racist and everything else social justice warrior lingo has taught them. The DEI Negro Bishops love going around hollering about racism and poverty, but I guarantee you not a single Bishop's residence is in the projects or the American inner city. What these DEI Bishops mean, is that you lowly UMC members and White people need to do something about poverty and racism, not them.

Part II

$250,000 per year in salary and not a single Ebony Bishop is competitive as a TV preacher, evangelist, or a revivalist. None. Zero. Dead weight. Is this a coincidence? Coincidental or not is it good for the church, evangelism and outreach to have a host of dead weight Bishops? Can it possibly be good for the Black church, which has a history of fiery spirit-filled oration?

Romans 10:13-17 13 For whosoever shall call upon the name of the Lord shall be saved. 14 How then shall they call on him in whom they have not believed? and how shall they believe in him of whom they have not heard? and how shall they hear without a preacher? 15 And how shall they preach, except they be sent? as it is written, How beautiful are the feet of them that preach the gospel of peace, and bring glad tidings of good things! 16 But they have not all obeyed the gospel. For Esaias saith, Lord, who hath believed our report? 17 So then faith cometh by hearing, and hearing by the word of God.

All these dead weight Ebony Bishops should count themselves lucky they make good money, because if they had to get by on preaching and honorariums, they'd be as broke as the urban and rural small membership Black churches they supervise. These DEI Bishops don't write.

They don't even pontificate and combine all their 'real', 'honorary', and 'imaginary' doctorates together, such that I doubt if they can produce five academic papers worth their weight in salt. They'd be happy to go somewhere and talk about social justice principles or wrap themselves in a Palestinian flag, or talk about how dangerous homophobia, transphobia, racism and sexism are...something no one would deny mind you. But to expect a high academic quality paper out of them, good luck (and I don't believe in luck). Go investigate the academic careers of our DEI Bishops and I guarantee you will find plagiarism and other academic crimes worse than anything Claudine Gay submitted to the Trustee Board at Harvard. I don't mean to attack them, but if you are a Bishop and you don't excel at the preaching graces, is it not natural to think you would excel at the academic or administrative graces, and the walls of many good United Methodist Homes would find one or more of your books?

Nope, Pharisee-ism and dead men's bones is all they have to offer. When you have hired a bunch of Negroes who if the White man didn't give them something they wouldn't have anything, that is not good for the Black UMC or the White mainstream UMC. Many of our DEI Ebony bishops in no wise could make it on their own, like certain breeds of Bulldogs whose jowls are so big they can't survive an independent existence apart from man. Similarly, our DEI Bishops are like domesticated turkeys after generations of human breeding. Through human intervention, the breasts of living female farm to table turkeys, grow so fast, and are so big that some full-grown turkeys drag their breasts along the ground, thus virtually ensuring they would not be able to escape from predators and predation in the wild. Similarly, our DEI bishops are out there defenseless on the street corner trying to preach a God that has no idea what a man and a woman are or lied about it for 2000 years.

So goes our DEI Ebony Bishops. If the White man threw them out of their bishoprics and the episcopacies, there is no way they'd survive 'in the wild'. If they had to rent a building, musicians, and preach every Sunday they'd be closed 6 months after their largest White patron gave up. They'd be closed in months had they to depend upon themselves and their own preaching, evangelizing, and administrative resources. They already know no one wants to hear that crap they are preaching, because no one wants to hear it even with the $250,000 per year platform they currently have. Methodists don't want to hear it and neither does the world.

A good question to ask is how Black United Methodism got here with all this dead DEI weight in high places that is of absolutely no use to the wider American and global community, nor even the Black United Methodists they purport to serve and represent. Dead weight. I call them Dead weight but do not think I am being mean spirited. They are dead weight. Ask them what a man and woman are, and they will not be able to tell you without resorting to socialist-atheist LGBTQIA+ sexual algebra, and the drivel they will spew will make you wonder if you or they are developmentally disabled.

A baby's eyesight is very poor at birth, but they know their mother's voice is at a higher pitch than their father's. Constant repetition tends to be reinforcing, such that stereotypes eventually do become truths. As with eyesight, completely consistent with the phrase 'blind as a bat', a baby knows the difference between the smooth face of their mothers and aunts and the stubbled faces of their fathers and uncles by touch. Faith, not by sight, but by sound and feel. And then our Ebony bishops come along and tell him his baby senses lied to him, and Bishop is going to tell him what a man and a woman are, or aren't, and what your father and your mother are, or aren't! Ah true faith, for even a baby could not be convinced intellectually and academically what a man and a woman are short of his senses of sound and touch. Even a baby would not completely discount what he or she knows by sound and touch, to believe some LGBTQIA+ sexual algebra our DEI Ebony bishops are preaching. No wonder Black Bishops can't preach. Out of the mouths of babes.

Matthew 11:25 25 At that time Jesus answered and said, I thank thee, O Father, Lord of heaven and earth, because thou hast hid these things from the wise and prudent, and hast revealed them unto babes.

How be it so, babies know the difference between a man and a woman, and cannot see or reason, but our Ebony DEI Bishops do not. Women, men, older kids and adolescents love to carry and play with babies because they are cute and lightweight, even if they are not potty trained. The Black UMC and the White mainstream liberal UMC has been carrying Ebony Bishops, lugging them around like the transportable versions of the Oracle at Delphi, and they are 'dead weight'. Dead weight can be simply defined as being a grown human being, with a clear biblical mandate, leading the Church of God, but you either really don't know what a man or a woman are absent LGBTQIA+ sexual algebra, you don't care, or you are willing to lie and talk the talk of anybody paying you. Which one is it Ebony bishops?

How did we get here with this dead weight? Some people think it is a conspiracy theory. They think Whites are so desperate to hold 'us' back that they serendipitously planted the seeds for future Black incompetence and failure by promoting all these dead weight DEI Ebony bishops. This conspiracy theorists believe, occurs by intention as the White UMC power structure, purposely hired and elevated incompetent Black people, because incompetent Blacks are not only more likely to not make waves, but they will also retain in their little Negro minds that the only reason they make $250,000 per year is because the White man elevated them. The implication of that fact being that they're not capable of attaining all that independently on their own merits; and so they will sense themselves beholden to the White UMC power structure and be obedient to and anticipate its every whim and fancy like forgetting or seeming to forget what a man and woman are.

But conspiracy theories are meaningless with a 100% sovereign God. A 100% sovereign God knows what a man and a woman are because he made them. The socialist-atheist LGBTQIA community, and the Ebony Bishops found out after the fact, that there were men and women. That's why it took them 200-300 years since the age of enlightenment to come up with something they think makes sense and can 're-place' the polar understanding of male/female throughout nature and the Bible. God knew there were men and women because he created them to be so. Glory to God, you found out after the fact you are alive, and much of what you know is only what your parents told you. How can you dictate what happens in a place you didn't even know you were in? Be a well-paid Ebony Bishop. A 100% sovereign God doesn't consider Himself to need correction. Nevertheless, we can map out some late 20th century social phenomena that I think gets to the point of why we have dead weight DEI Bishops that are of no use to the Black community, the Black United Methodist Church, or the wider United Methodist Churches.

Part III

The Methodist Church unified in 1968. My first day of elementary school was in a newly integrated school and a community transitioning because of White flight. Everybody had the greatest of intentions. And yet we were in the deep south. Brown V Board of Ed was in 1954 and integration was a difficult slow process, further complicated by the fact that there were some aspects to how integration played out that had negative effects on the Black community and Black institutions. In elementary school I began having White teachers. Typically, even though the teachers and staff were integrated, the teachers that taught 'the best' students with the highest test scores were usually White. With parents that were both educators in the Metro-Atlanta public school systems, I tested well on standardized tests and so typically went to these White teachers as I progressed in grade level.

Everybody had good intentions. The White teachers had good intentions, but I noticed some things. Imagine being a White southerner and from 1955 backwards in time, you, your grandparents and your ancestors were told that you were superior to Blacks (or any other race), and that they deserve to be treated as such. Most of my White teachers just went off my test scores and affirmed me, like they would any other student (thank God for standardized tests). But a few, one in particular, seemed to enjoy opportunities to put smart Black kids in their place. This she would do in a slick somewhat patronizing and insulting way that she wouldn't do to the dumbest White kids. As much as I read and have read all throughout my life, my memory regarding certain words and concepts is pretty well developed and started so at a young age. I'm not bragging. I'm dang near retarded in many other fields. I was in the fourth grade, and I memorized the questions and the answer, quite accidentally. After reading the material a few times, I did not even interpret it as intelligence or memory that I could memorize chunks of the questions and the answers, let alone that it might be interpreted as 'cheating' to relate it almost word for word. Even at a young age it was quite common for me to memorize little chunks and passages, if I were really interested in a subject. 'Humiliated and horrified' I was, (cue my Yoda voice), when my teacher accused me of cheating. I have never cheated and still haven't. Either I know the material, or I don't and take the consequences. I don't care enough about outcomes to cheat, and it is a quality that has served me well, if in an irregular fashion academically irreverent way.

That is so much the case that in Mrs. Bailey's Algebra II class later at Douglass High in Atlanta, I got the mimeograph sheet with questions and space for the answers on the front. The back was blank. I answered the few questions I could, and promptly flipped the paper over to the blank side a drew a picture of my conception of a 'city block' of the future using recently acquired skills learned in my mechanical drawing class. Gosh, I wish I could look at that drawing today. What a Rorschach test. Mrs. Bailey gave it back to me with a fat zero on it, and it is lost to history. That is what I would do before I decided to look on my neighbor's paper or even plan to cheat by sneaking in test assistance materials.

I was accused of cheating. The very same thing happened in the Candidacy process to become an Elder in the UMC. But let us continue the story before reflecting upon such matters. Another funny thing that happened in the same 4th grade class under the same White teacher (who let me not seem to say that she did not have good intentions, and was I'm sure doing her best, she was not unpleasant). In that class we'd have Field Day once a semester, or twice a school year. There are races and competitions and a little talent show. I was blessed to grow up in a neighborhood amongst older boys who were athletic, so in school, an integrated school mind you, I tended to excel for my grade level.

In the 4th grade I sensed it as a kind of peer pressure to be athletically successful based on prior success. Cue violins, Simone Biles, Coco Gauff, Naomi Osaka et al, talking about their mental health issues stimulated by the increased expectations that come with success, and the sense of not being able to live up to them. Quite often it is called 'imposter syndrome' and inhabits the minds of even the greatest athletes and entertainers. But I was in the fourth grade. I loved to be competitive and play with the older boys and quite often they picked me on their pickup teams above dudes their age. I enjoyed the camaraderie and sense of accomplishment inherent in athletic contests. At the same time, I did not want to come off like I was purposely dominating my grade level White friends, who my identity was different than it was with my Black friends and the older athletic Black boys. The first semester at field day, I smoked my age group, white, Black and all. The 2nd Field Day after having White friends and associates whose homes I had been to, and parents I knew, I was not so interested in smoking them. I threw the 2nd Semester Field Day grade level race so I could share the triumph with my White and Black friends.

But a strange thing happened. All the older boys came up to me immediately after the race. They asked me what was wrong. They acted disappointed and said that they thought I would have done better, what happened? I tried to make some kind of excuse, but it didn't matter. Thus, I learned in the 4th grade on Field Day to be 'dang near' 100% self-motivated. You're not going to make everybody happy in any case. Don't do what you do, to make others happy or sad. You must take a very utilitarian view of your own talents. By this I mean that one should not generally put one's talents at others' disposal. Get it from God and do it. You may make others happy, but never entirely happy. And you may make others unhappy, but hopefully not entirely unhappy. This book is not me being provocative. It is me being self-motivated to say what I have to say, and sit down like Rev. Dr. Clarence Thrower Jr., taught me. God knows all things best. You never seek to make others happy or unhappy, and to the extent you do, it is of no concern to you as regards your art. You cannot afford it to be. The moment you play to the crowd, is the day you end on the 'American Idol' of religion(s), playing yourself to the point of mockery as the world judges your 'talent' (when you should be judging the world).

This teacher, the gifted teacher, was steeped in the 1955 Jim Crow Southern racism like a tea bag for 50 years before she ever was around Black 'picki-ninny' children. Absent standardized test scores, she would have 'handpicked' students for the 'Gifted' class based on her prior 'Jim Crow' notions and conceptions of what 'good Negro children' and 'smart Negro children should be like and what opportunities they deserved. She resented my athletic prowess, resented my academic prowess and I learned a rough lesson in the 4th grade that had the negative effect of turning me off on 'performing' for teachers and 'performing' for grades. She resented a 9-year-old boy's talents, but I cannot blame her, and I am not mad. She carried the assumptions Jim Crow and Segregation taught her, and the only other ideas she had about Black people were as entertainment, sports, and demeaning caricatures of stereotypical Black behavior. She did not have ideas of Blacks competing on equal footing with the 'best' of White culture. Here again, thank God for standardized test scores, which even they cannot ignore for cultural reasons.

Earlier I alluded to the fact that on Field Days, after events, we would have a kind of talent show until dismissal. I was an only child that read all the time, thought all the time, played by myself a lot, and made-up stories and games all the time. The one advantage in such circumstances is that you learn early and often how to entertain yourself. This is pre-phones, video games, computers and of course I lament the way post-modern children are raised with pads or games in their hands at all times; connected to social media 'influencers' at all times, etc. I played and made-up games and stories from being alone so much. My mother and father surrounded me with books and musical instruments in a very casual way such that I got to it when I got to it. I'd get to it and go for hours on some fanciful, rhapsodic, or whimsical tangent.

I didn't enter the talent show 1st or 2nd semester. In all fairness to Mrs. Jones, My 4th Grade White teacher, she was not a racist. Nor do I consider it her fault and her responsibility, that she behaved like that. Mrs. Jones loved little black children, and 4 to 6 perfectly average or slightly less than average black kids in her class of 20 was no problem. Even two somewhat above average Black kids, provided they are manageable and know their place can get love too. But the exception to her roots in the Jim Crow South, is the smart talented little Negro with natural intelligence, athletic abilities, and genuine leadership traits. That is the one you resent subconsciously and thus restrain and undermine instinctively; per 50 years of life in the Jim Crow South. That little Negro is a threat to whatever it is White people might attain.

With that thought in mind one might see how without a smoking gun slam dunk conspiracy theory, the history of slavery and racism would have effects even in integrated settings that were supposed to be 'safe spaces' for children, integrated settings that were supposed to be the solution to inequality and every other socio-economic issue. But let us return to the talent shows in the 4th grade. I did not want to participate. I had self-esteem issues stemming from father issues, long before I got in Mrs. Jones class. I wanted to have fun and be 'that nigga' (for lack of a better phrase), but I felt any success I got I didn't really deserve. Indeed, what a crime for a child to be able to 'effect' and 'project' being exceptionally good at something, only to go home and cry about what he or she doesn't have, in their situation with their father and family. Consequently, the last thing I wanted to do was get into a talent show. But of course, subconsciously I was fascinated by such an idea, and in watching others, I started coming up with things that I would do, given the chance if I did perform.

I was happy to opt out with the other wall flowers, the ne'er do wells, the thugs, pimps, and hustlers (who hung out with Jephthah); who would rather display their talents in the shadows, the cuts, the fades, the traps. I sat back comfortably assuming that I would opt out of the talent show. However, Mrs. Jones said no one could opt out, and if you had no talent, just get up and talk about yourself for 30 seconds. In hindsight it was a beautiful exercise for children and whatever limitations Mrs. Jones may have had, she probably was one of the better teachers at the school post-integration.

My little Negro mind got to racing, to have something to say when I was called, because of course I wasn't going to volunteer. I remembered that Steve Martin's 'Wild and Crazy Guy' routine was popular, and there was something about it I liked and entertained myself with in solitary moments where bored kids used to imitate their elders. Over time (alone), I put the physical motions with it and talked it like Steve martin as best I could. Well, after hemming and hawing a little bit, I went into a crass imitation of Steve Martin's 'Wild and Crazy Guy' in my 4th grade 1st semester talent show. I started killin! It was one of the most fascinating and memorable moments in my life because it showed me what audience approval and an audience with you really feels like. The wide eyes, the smiles, the interest, the laughs, and them hanging on your every word...I felt it for the first time in the 4th grade. That sense and kind of immediate approval resonated with me as an only child. Plus, it showed me in the 4th grade that my interior life, could be entertaining to others or something that others saw humor and value in. That was the first Field Day Fall Semester.

Spring semester, the high I was on after the fall performance, which I won, was long gone, and the old me, filled with low self-esteem and doubt was back. I figured I can't do the same thing, but maybe I can. Maybe doing Steven martin was the thing, and the fact it was me doing it was not so important. That is to say, maybe me acting like Steve Martin is more entertaining than me acting like me, or anyone else or anything else I could think of.

Sufficiently scared, my first intention again was to opt out. Ironically, Mrs. Smith would have been happy to see me opt out as she resented (through no fault of her own) my success. But my peers, Black and White did not want to see me opt out, and had furthermore convinced themselves that I had something special in the works. The pressure came back, as I again waited to be called up. I was not going to volunteer, and they had convinced themselves that I was to go last because of course I'd have something special and be so entertaining. The pressure was mounting. I watched others fail, succeed, and sorta succeed. I assumed that if I get out there and act like Steve Martin at least I couldn't do any worse than I did before.

After being called upon, I got up and went into the Steve Marin Wild Crazy Guy spiel and schtick, and it fell completely flat. The deflated faces of my former admirers startled me. A sense of dread overcame me as feelings of fear and embarrassment overwhelmed me. Time slowed like molasses in winter weather, the stares of my classmates like darts and spears. I distinctly remember my sense of panic. But I had a couple advantages. Having watched everybody else perform I could refer to them in some way, imitate them in a way that didn't mock them, and include my impressions of their performances in my act. In addition, I did physical humor type things, grand sweeping over exaggerated motions, that often took on a life of their own. And periodically, I'd go back into my Steve Martin Wild and Crazy Guy Schtick. I won the talent show again second semester, but the second was different in that I learned the hard way, that you must have different material and have to be thinking and able to improvise all the time, even when you can't. The experience of being in front of a crowd and sorta winging and improvising their entertainment had a great impact on me that made me a great fit later for worship leading and participating in the order of service at various Churches when I started serving the Lord and His UMC.

I learned another interesting lesson that stuck with me as well. Once again Mrs. Smith was loathe to see me successful, but I was surprised by another group's 'hating on me' to use a phrase. The second time Mrs.

Smith and the Cool kids publicly loved it, but the ne'er do wells, reprehensibles, pimps, thugs, and hustlers, from the land of Tob with Jephthah, I had previously been on good terms, with came up to me after the performance somewhat disappointed. They told me in no uncertain terms that I was not really that funny, it was a schtick, but that it might work other places besides the streets and with street Negroes. In the 4th grade mind you.

Why did I divert the reader with such mundane matters? First off, the next time I got up in front of an audience and presumed to educate, entertain and encourage them it was as a seminary bound candidate for Ordained Ministry in the United Methodist Church. 2ndly White people, White institutions, knee deep in White supremacy unwittingly have done the same to the Black United Methodist Churches for generations. It has accepted the mediocrity and even failures of Black Churches because it fits the stereotype of the Black church needing perpetual help and leadership from their White mainstream counterparts in United Methodism. Meanwhile when real Negro talent even fain come into the official system, and dare raise its head, it is seen as a threat. Something must be wrong with it. It is cheating in some regard.

And yet they must prove they aren't racists. So they must hire some Blacks. The Blacks they hire they pull from that pool of mediocrity, of those who can't do anything on their own, and are dependent upon White mainstream promotion and leadership.

Part IV

Much of the part that gets unspoken is that many of these Black female DEI hires get foisted upon Black and White local churches that bear the burden of the sins of the forefathers. DEI progressive White liberal Bishops who know dang well a White southern church can't grow and expand into the wider White mainstream communities surrounding them, with a DEI Black female hire do it anyway (pound foolish and penny wise). They do it anyway, presumably to be on the 'right side of history'. It burdens the White local churches because all they do is pay their DEI hirelings and survive, as opposed to really having a chance at growing and thriving. DEI mandates are quite often 'not a good fit' mandates. But there these DEI and White progressive Bishops go sticking DEI hires down the throats of local churches like some kind of social justice medicine that quite often happens to taste terrible. And they must put these DEI hires in churches that can afford them, and they are mostly White, in order to do social justice, socialist atheist style redistributing the wealth and largess of the church to those minorities who hitherto have not shared in the proceeds and power. So the White mainstream appoints complete DEI nincompoops to high offices in the church that don't know what a man and woman are, but demand social justice for the practitioners of LGBTQIA+ sexual algebra. They demand justice for radical feminists willing to promote women's issues and rights by hacking their breasts off, and taking enough male steroids, hormones and testosterone to make a female horse grow a foot-long beard and testicles. That is the current UMC and its DEI Bishop's conception of the doctrine of the church of Jesus Christ.

1 Timothy 3:10 - 4:3 10 And let these also first be proved; then let them use the office of a deacon, being found blameless. 11 Even so must their wives be grave, not slanderers, sober, faithful in all things. 12 Let the deacons be the husbands of one wife, ruling their children and their own houses well. 13 For they that have used the office of a deacon well purchase to themselves a good degree, and great boldness in the faith which is in Christ Jesus. 14 These things write I unto thee, hoping to come unto thee shortly: 15 But if I tarry long, that thou mayest know how thou oughtest to behave thyself in the house of God, which is the church of the living God, the pillar and ground of the truth. 16 And without controversy great is the mystery of godliness: God was manifest in the flesh, justified in the Spirit, seen of angels, preached unto the Gentiles, believed on in the world, received up into glory. KJG 1 Timothy 4:1 **Now the Spirit speaketh expressly, that in the latter times some shall depart from the faith, giving heed to seducing spirits, and doctrines of devils; 2 Speaking lies in hypocrisy; having their conscience seared with a hot iron; 3 Forbidding to marry, and**

commanding to abstain from meats, which God hath created to be received with thanksgiving of them which believe and know the truth.

How do we know DEI Bishops are manipulated, and no good to the Black, White or global UMC? We know because the very same values and Discipline they swore to uphold when they were seeking ordination and acceptance as Elder in the UMC, they have said along with Nietzsche that 'god' they swore to is 'dead'. The God they 'swore' to in fancy ordination robes and events is 'dead', and only survives because human DEI bishops corrected Him and put a cast on His 'brokenness' so that this new 'god' (a caricature of the old angry jealous God of the Bible) limps along on the crutches of human reason, or on some theological version of a socialist-atheist LGBTQIA sexual algebra 'deity life support machine'. Our DEI Ebony Bishops are so smart that along with their White counterparts, they have to tell a supposedly omniscient God what a man and woman are...and they feel no shame that they are just repeating what post-modern social-atheist LGBTQIA+ sexual algebra teaches, and uses the exact same terminologies in imitation of 'the world'. Instead of His testimony, God's testimony, they accept the testimony of this world about something as basic to mammalian reality as what a man and a woman are. How in the hell (literally) can anything else they have to say be meaningful?

Chapter 4 - The New Paganism

Chapter 4 - The New Post-Modern Paganism
Let us go further in our analysis of the disastrous General Conference 2024. The funniest thing to me is that the God they worship is not the God of the Bible. It would be like following a random man home because he looks kinda like your father only to find out he is not. I know it sounds rough to accuse Bishops and Prelates of abandoning the God of the Bible, this is not a time for being soft spoken. My lips are uncircumcised and I'm going to give the UMC church I grew up in 'the business end' of these unholy lips. I haven't been in their 'Holy Conferencing' but I can guarantee that if my lips are uncircumcised, their ears and lips are just as uncircumcised based on what/whom (socialist atheist LGBTQIA philosophy) they have been listening, and spouting that ideology with their mouths.

Jeremiah 6:10-11 10 To whom shall I speak, and give warning, that they may hear? behold, their ear is uncircumcised, and they cannot hearken: behold, the word of the LORD is unto them a reproach; they have no delight in it. 11 Therefore I am full of the fury of the LORD; I am weary with holding in: I will pour it out upon the children abroad, and upon the assembly of young men together: for even the husband with the wife shall be taken, the aged with him that is full of days.

How can the reader tell from General Conference that the current UMC Church does not worship the God of the Bible? Ask it? Ask them? Ask the Bishops, Prelates and Communications offices what they exalt and are proud of, and it is their acceptance and promotion of secular social justice, socialist-atheist, LGBTQIA+ sexual algebra values not biblical ones. Ask them what kinds of Methodists get a chance to 'dance in the aisles' draped in their rainbow flags doing same sex kissing and which one's don't? Ask them which Methodists get photo ops draped in Palestinian flags, and which ones in American flags don't? I don't have to prove it. The liberal DEI Bishops and the global UMC communications office proved it for me. Look at the placards they had on stage! One was of a silhouette dude playing the saxophone, another a woman dancing, one had words in Swahili (perhaps). None of that has any biblical precedent whatsoever. That goes without even speaking to the issue of what a Yoga (apparently Hindu Nationalist symbol) is doing at a United Methodist General Conference where the church is being rent and cut asunder like old laundry scraps of fabric.

Saints, it is time for the big guns. This posturing by the UMC amounts to Neo-Paganism. The God of the Bible is quite precisely restrictive, on purpose. The Neo-Pagan God, like the Roman and Greek conception, is non-exclusive to the point of being and tolerating Pantheism. That is to say, seeing God in everything is one thing, but seeing little gods capable of justifying themselves independently or based on human reason is quite another. It is one thing to serve the God of the Bible by seeing Him in everything, it is quite another matter to deem every and any old god you run across as equivalent and the same as the God of the Bible. I already told the reader, our God is jealous. Take him or leave him (and many have chosen to leave), He is a jealous God.

Exodus 20:1-7 KJG Exodus 20:1 And God spake all these words, saying, 2 I am the LORD thy God, which have brought thee out of the land of Egypt, out of the house of bondage. 3 Thou shalt have no other gods before me. 4 Thou shalt not make unto thee any graven image, or any likeness of any thing that is in heaven above, or that is in the earth beneath, or that is in the water under the earth: 5 Thou shalt not bow down thyself to them, nor serve them: for I the LORD thy God am a jealous God, visiting the iniquity of the fathers upon the children unto the third and fourth generation of them that hate me; 6 And shewing mercy unto thousands of them that love me, and keep my commandments. 7 Thou shalt not take the name of the LORD thy God in vain; for the LORD will not hold him guiltless that taketh his name in vain.

This kind of Neo-Paganism is exemplified in the interest groups and various caucuses' that petition the UMC and its Prelates like the worst influencers and influence peddlers on K Street in Washington, DC. The UMC should have just called the City of Charlotte and the environs of the General Conference K-LBGTIA+ Street. For they have certainly made it a home for any two-bit theological hack, hustler, and lobbyist for some social justice grievance cause or another. This political Neo-Paganism in the church, akin to kissing the rings of prelates and kneeling at their feet hoping for favors, power, and position is grotesque and sickening to any Bible based Christian. If you think I'm being rough, look at what our UMC Church said itself as it summed up Day #3.

There were LGBTQIA activists and lobbyists, Fossil Fuel Free Divestment activists and lobbyists, and earth day services and celebrations at First UMC in Charlotte. There was a 'Love your Neighbor' event and lobby supporting Palestine. And an organization of activists and lobbyists was there from and for 'Mission Together' for the Global Methodists to advocate from the Congo and the Philippines. Do you see the leaven? Do you see Christian and biblical theology and practice being transformed into this kind of amorphous, nebulous mass of social principles and acceptance doctrines that is quite precisely pagan. Post-General Conference 2024 views and attributes are conducive to the world, and completely opposed to the idea of the 'jealous' God of the Bible.

The pagan or socialist-atheist says there are no absolutes and everything is relative. Anything one feels or feels oneself attracted to, or that makes him or her 'feel' spiritual is the experience of God, and it is just as valid as any traditional theological construct. Watch the leaven. A church without biblical sexual standards is pagan, and after endorsing shacking up, busted families and gay parades, this is a pagan view of sex and sexuality. It is not to be believed but to the present DEI Bishops, the remedy for the church's sins in the past, is going completely to the extreme in the other direction and taking out all the rules. This is like believing that the cure for asthma is simply to stop breathing. We have church leadership, that thinks with a straight face that repenting for past mistakes, can be accomplished by totally embracing pagan, socialist-atheist LGBTQIA+ sexual algebra extremism. This is why I call their policies and the policies of this General Conference suicidal.

The most vicious form of this Neo-Paganism that has infected the UMC is this obsession with race and color coding. In the old days, pagans feared 'familiar spirits', 'unfamiliar malicious spirits', witches, demons and things like that. It is probably not a coincidence that the devil, demons, and Sam Smith Grammy performances are associated with red and flames. Colors carry symbolism. Certain days or celestial occurrences are seen as harbingers of prosperity or evil. Science now tells us the "how's" behind the phenomena of this past May's Solar flares and observable aurora, but to the pagan mind, it could take on angry or destructive overtones. To the pagan mind. And there in Charlotte upon that prayer mountain one of the Ebony Bishops unleashed a thing on an unsuspecting UMC public called 'Thursdays in Black'. This is supposedly as a response to the idea in many cultures that Black is a symbol of mourning, evil, or malevolence, but Bishop Latrelle Easterling wanted the UMC to redefine the world 'Black' as a symbol of strength and resistance. America is falling faster than Rome, and our Ebony Bishops have launched a campaign to not only reclaim the world Black, but to use it as a platform to speak out against the oppression of not just coloreds, but women. Legal, safe, and accessible abortion is a personal and medical choice; however, living in a society and culture that treats abortion as a tool for women's liberation and freedom, is just as pagan a notion as Roman citizens throwing unwanted or inconvenient children off a cliff into the city dump. Christianity came into the Roman world, like Judaism, opposed to those kinds of pagan practices. **Now the Neo-Pagan UMC approves of them.**

Forgive me, but people making $250,000 shouldn't be known for saying silly things in their professional capacities. Silly childish, childlike things, and asinine things; things that with all the problems in the world make absolutely no sense at all...unless you are a pagan convinced that color associations define reality, not God. Bishop Latrelle wants members of the UMC at General Conference to wear all Black one day as a symbol of calling attention to rape and violence against women...if that's not pagan...neither is...(wait for it)...the power of one, the power of two, the power of...MANY!

Mark 5:1-20

King James Version

5 And they came over unto the other side of the sea, into the country of the Gadarenes.

2 And when he was come out of the ship, immediately there met him out of the tombs a man with an unclean spirit,

3 Who had his dwelling among the tombs; and no man could bind him, no, not with chains:

4 Because that he had been often bound with fetters and chains, and the chains had been plucked asunder by him, and the fetters broken in pieces: neither could any man tame him.

5 And always, night and day, he was in the mountains, and in the tombs, crying, and cutting himself with stones.

6 But when he saw Jesus afar off, he ran and worshipped him,

7 And cried with a loud voice, and said, What have I to do with thee, Jesus, thou Son of the most high God? I adjure thee by God, that thou torment me not.

8 For he said unto him, Come out of the man, thou unclean spirit.

9 And he asked him, What is thy name? And he answered, saying, My name is Legion: for we are many.

10 And he besought him much that he would not send them away out of the country.

11 Now there was there nigh unto the mountains a great herd of swine feeding.

12 And all the devils besought him, saying, Send us into the swine, that we may enter into them.

13 And forthwith Jesus gave them leave. And the unclean spirits went out, and entered into the swine: and the herd ran violently down a steep place into the sea, (they were about two thousand;) and were choked in the sea.

14 And they that fed the swine fled, and told it in the city, and in the country. And they went out to see what it was that was done.

15 And they come to Jesus, and see him that was possessed with the devil, and had the legion, sitting, and clothed, and in his right mind: and they were afraid.

16 And they that saw it told them how it befell to him that was possessed with the devil, and also concerning the swine.

17 And they began to pray him to depart out of their coasts.

18 And when he was come into the ship, he that had been possessed with the devil prayed him that he might be with him.

19 Howbeit Jesus suffered him not, but saith unto him, Go home to thy friends, and tell them how great things the Lord hath done for thee, and hath had compassion on thee.

20 And he departed, and began to publish in Decapolis how great things Jesus had done for him: and all men did marvel.

Beloved, who in the hell over the past course of 2000 years of Church history has intimated that the church condones or encourages violence against women. The liberals love going off like Cervante's hero Don Quixote. Only in the post-modern Neo-Pagan church the windmills they are constantly running off to fight are sexism, racism, homophobia, and transphobia. How in the world is the church complicit in violence against women? If she didn't call the police, how the hell is Rev. Jones supposed to? Said differently, is the church complicit in every social and political malady, from wars, to poverty, to social injustice etc. Was the church responsible for the fact those forms of oppression existed long before it! Did Stalin, Hitler, Genghis Kahn, or Tamerlane need the Biblical God to co-sign on their reigns of terror? And trust that when the church was complicit, the pure church was long gone, and it was inhabited by Bishops, Vicars, Prelates, Cardinals, and Popes that had long before adopted worldly interests and values, long before they aided and abetted political and economic leaders in oppressing 'the people'.

Is a Black woman making $250,000 per year in a country that held her ancestors in abject chattel slavery, going to stand up in 2024 and make the argument the Bible, patriarchy, and church silence are the reason western women are suffering and held back today, such that every minute they run around hollering 'girl power', 'girls run the world', and 'Black girl magic'. And they must do this (including being gay, fatherless, husbandless, and/or childless), in some kind of Mao like 'permanent revolution' so they can take back their power as women? And this is what the UMC leadership and DEI Bishops are saying with a straight face!

Reader I am no genius. The church has gone full circle and is now embracing pagan roots so deep it is not unheard of to find Black and White Christians in Europe and America elevating Gaia, Isis, Athena, Aurora, Brigid, Calypso, Calliope, and Chandra. Please do not get me wrong, I have no problems with embracing those concepts, my problem is someone telling me that is supposed to be the new 'drill', the new Discipline in the United Methodist Church. Supposedly, women consider stuff other than God their Father affirming because of all they have suffered in Post-Modern America...out pacing men in higher education and income, taking over positions traditionally held by men, and acting like they no more need a man to help with child rearing purposes and what he could possibly contribute to a child's mental and physical health, than she needs a hole in her or her child's head. Let them that have ears, hear.

Here again, I'm not making the argument the church has been perfect. But the idea that the cure is to run blindly and aimlessly in the opposite direction is ludicrous. Latrelle Miller Easter Epps, Baltimore-Washington Delaware area. Thursday morning of the conference she stood before the delegates and talked on the damage done when the church is silent on violence against women, transgenders, homosexuals, etc. Immediately I thought of Trump's reaction as Elijah Cummings and John 'Good Tubba' (good trouble) Lewis got up on the Senate floor lambasting Trump for one thing or another that no one, not even liberals can remember. Trump said Cummings and 'Good Tubba' John Lewis need to go back to their districts with large numbers of broken homes and academically underperforming, and economically underperforming districts and work on those problems before you go around fixing the world 'Don Quixote' style.

Lawd, Bishop had the nerve to mention that she was standing up for indigenous women that end up missing. There is a lot she left out in that. She, even though she makes $250,000 wouldn't pay a dime of her salary to the protestant churches crimes in America and the Third World. They want us to pay but they will not, nary a dime. Can an incompetent DEI Bishiop, apologizing on behalf of a dysfunctional church with one foot in the grave and the other on a banana peel, make up for the indigenous and American, Canadian, and Australian Aboriginal children, sent off to learn Christian values, in boarding schools and with 'good' White Christian families in boarding schools in order to foster their assimilation into a White culture that perpetually views them as inferior and is indoctrinating them with the same idea? Does a Negro DEI Bishop's apologies on behalf of White European Christian Manifest Destiny and White men who abandoned the UMC Church in droves when separation became legal, absconding with most of the money, going to ease the pain of a broken UMC? Really Latrelle?

This brings up a fascinating question. Which one would be worse in theory and reality, getting taken from your family at 8, being grilled on catechism and Protestant Christian doctrine, and told how you and your indigenous culture were inferior and worthless. Or the same church officials (150 years later) telling 8-year-old indigenous children that if you feel like a girl, we'll encourage and help you live like it, and help pay to get your penis and breasts surgically removed. Both are crimes that need to apology for! In the old UMC Protestant set up, aboriginal kids gave up their theological cultural heritage. In the new UMC set up a child might lose a penis or sex organs. What is unimaginable, is that our new DEI Ebony Bishop Easterling thinks this new way is a great improvement over those old 'White men' forcing their beliefs on the 'developing world'. Our DEI Bishops are the White man's new Buffalo soldiers except that instead of collecting children to be deposited into reform schools, and stealing land on behalf of the White man, now the new DEI Buffalo soldier Bishops steal the penises and breasts of young confused male and female children. But let us go one step further, if you think this UMC sponsored hacking off children's penises and breasts is not a pagan monument as bad as any statue of the like we find in Africa and Asia of phallic symbols and fertility statues/symbols/cults with amble hips and breasts you are being naive. Yes, the UMC is now in the business of making public totems to cut off penises and breasts. That is what the rainbow flag at General Conference represented, hacked off breasts and penises, (blood sacrifices to a new LGBTQIA+ idol god). See how they danced in the aisles like some pagan celebration.

They may as well do like the Sons of Jacob. What was Shechem's penalty for defiling Dinah? Leah was Dinah's mother. The reader might remember that Leah played 2nd fiddle to Rachel, as Jacobs primary wives. To say this caused intergenerational and interfamily conflict would be an understatement. It seems everyone in Jacob's life sensed who his favorites were and who they weren't, and this made tensions and machinations inevitable. This culminated in Joseph being sold into slavery. But before that we have Leah's sons, Dinah's brothers, determined not to let their sister be disrespected as though if Rachel had a daughter and it happened to her, Jacob would allow such a thing to be tolerated. Dinah's brothers were

Genesis 29:31-35 31 And when the LORD saw that Leah was hated, he opened her womb: but Rachel was barren. 32 And Leah conceived, and bare a son, and she called his name Reuben: for she said, Surely the LORD hath looked upon my affliction; now therefore my husband will love me. 33 And she conceived again, and bare a son; and said, Because the LORD hath heard that I was hated, he hath therefore given me this son also: and she called his name Simeon. 34 And she conceived again, and bare a son; and said, Now this time will my husband be joined unto me, because I have born him three sons: therefore was his name called Levi. 35 And she conceived again, and bare a son: and she said, Now will I praise the LORD: therefore she called his name Judah; and left bearing.

Let us go further into the 'mystical crimes of patriarchy' and men (even brothers) owning women's bodies and chastity. It is these same brothers that are complicit in Joseph's later tragic mysterious disappearance and being sold into slavery.

Genesis 37:17-25 And **Joseph** went after his brethren, and found them in Dothan. 18 And when they saw him afar off, even before he came near unto them, they conspired against him to slay him. 19 And they said one to another, Behold, this dreamer cometh. 20 Come now therefore, and let us slay him, and cast him into some pit, and we will say, Some evil beast hath devoured him: and we shall see what will become of his dreams. 21 And **Reuben** heard it, and he delivered him out of their hands; and said, Let us not kill him. 22 And Reuben said unto them, Shed no blood, but cast him into this pit that is in the wilderness, and lay no hand upon him; that he might rid him out of their hands, to deliver him to his father again. 23 And it came to pass, when Joseph was come unto his brethren, that they stript Joseph out of his coat, his coat of many colours that was on him; 24 And they took him, and cast him into a pit: and the pit was empty, there was no water in it. 25 And they sat down to eat bread: and they lifted up their eyes and looked, and, behold, a company of Ishmeelites came from Gilead with their camels bearing spicery and balm and myrrh, going to carry it down to Egypt.

The ring leaders were Reuben, Judah and Levi, Leah's sons and naturally the sons of Leah's handmaid would have gone along, no doubt resentful from a lifetime of feeling like 2nd or 3rd class citizen sons after Joseph and Benjamin were born. But back to Dinah.

Genesis 34:1-7 KJG Genesis 34:1 And Dinah the daughter of Leah, which she bare unto Jacob, went out to see the daughters of the land. 2 And when Shechem the son of Hamor the Hivite, prince of the country, saw her, he took her, and lay with her, and defiled her. 3 And his soul clave unto Dinah the daughter of Jacob, and he loved the damsel, and spake kindly unto the damsel. 4 And Shechem spake unto his father Hamor, saying, Get me this damsel to wife. 5 And Jacob heard that he had defiled Dinah his daughter: now his sons were with his cattle in the field: and Jacob held his peace until they were come. 6 And Hamor the father of Shechem went out unto Jacob to commune with him. 7 And the sons of Jacob came out of the field when they heard it: and the men were grieved, and they were very wroth, because he had wrought folly in Israel in lying with Jacob's daughter; which thing ought not to be done.

Genesis 34:8-15 8 And Hamor communed with them, saying, The soul of my son Shechem longeth for your daughter: I pray you give her him to wife. 9 And make ye marriages with us, and give your daughters unto us, and take our daughters unto you. 10 And ye shall dwell with us: and the land shall be before you; dwell and trade ye therein, and get you possessions therein. 11 And Shechem said unto her father and unto her brethren, Let me find grace in your eyes, and what ye shall say unto me I will give. 12 Ask me never so much dowry and gift, and I will give according as ye shall say unto me: but give me the damsel to wife. 13 And the sons of Jacob answered Shechem and Hamor his father deceitfully, and said, because he had defiled Dinah their sister: 14 And they said unto them, We cannot do this thing, to give our sister to one that is uncircumcised; for that were a reproach unto us: 15 But in this will we consent unto you: If ye will be as we be, that every male of you be circumcised;

Genesis 34:22-31 22 Only herein will the men consent unto us for to dwell with us, to be one people, if every male among us be circumcised, as they are circumcised. 23 Shall not their cattle and their substance and every beast of theirs be ours? only let us consent unto them, and they will dwell with us. 24 And unto Hamor and unto Shechem his son hearkened all that went out of the gate of his city; and every male was circumcised, all that went out of the gate of his city. 25 And it came to pass on the third day, when they were sore, that two of the sons of Jacob, Simeon and Levi, Dinah's brethren, took each man his sword, and came upon the city boldly, and slew all the males. 26 And they slew Hamor and Shechem his son with the edge of the sword, and took Dinah out of Shechem's house, and went out. 27 The sons of Jacob came upon the slain, and spoiled the city, because they had defiled their sister. 28 They took their sheep, and their oxen, and their asses, and that which was in the city, and that which was in the field, 29 And all their wealth, and all their little ones, and their wives took they captive, and spoiled even all that was in the house. 30 And Jacob said to Simeon and Levi, Ye have troubled me to make me to stink among the inhabitants of the land, among the Canaanites and the Perizzites: and I being few in number, they shall gather themselves together against me, and slay me; and I shall be destroyed, I and my house. 31 And they said, Should he deal with our sister as with an harlot?

The men of Shechem & Hamor were greedy and that convinced them of the merits of circumcision, but we must believe the bible when it says, Shechem's 'soul longed for Dinah. Furthermore, I'm a little suspicious of the Bible using the phrase 'Dinah went out to see the daughters of the land'. Not too long that after we find Judah himself having his own 'going out to see the daughters of the land' and ending with a woman named Shuah.

Genesis 38:1-6 KJG Genesis 38:1 And it came to pass at that time, that Judah went down from his brethren, and turned in to a certain Adullamite, whose name was Hirah. 2 And Judah saw there a daughter of a certain Canaanite, whose name was Shuah; and he took her, and went in unto her. 3 And she conceived, and bare a son; and he called his name Er. 4 And she conceived again, and bare a son; and she called his name Onan. 5 And she yet again conceived, and bare a son; and called his name Shelah: and he was at Chezib, when she bare him. 6 And Judah took a wife for Er his firstborn, whose name was Tamar.

We could exegete that story at another level too. It is also interesting to note that the Bible does not reflect Dinah's protests at the situation. Assuming she was raped she would have naturally protested to her brothers. This is not recorded, plus we might have a hard time believing that Shechem's heart went out for and his very soul longed for a woman who he knew dang well hated him. What we know is that neither her brothers nor her father reflects upon her opinions or wishes either. Whether this was because they were all sexist patriarchs, so it didn't matter, or it was because she loved Shechem as much as he apparently loved her and unfortunately Shechem wasn't good enough for Jacob or her brothers Levi, Simeon, and Reuben. Furthermore, for grown men, who very well knew the pain of any mishaps in one's crotch, to agree to be circumcised is a lot, and agreeing to be circumcised for a woman you raped and that you know hates you would be even more difficult to believe. When Judah 'took' Shuah, were taking to always mean rape, would he have had two more children with her? Of course, it is easy to see how the economics and sexual politics of the day may have forced her into dependency on a man she possibly didn't 'love', but would Judah have 2 more kids with a woman if it were sexually or physically unpleasant or repulsive. Suffice it to say here in a patriarchal sense, that the penalty for 'defiling' Dinah, was them weakening themselves as men (in the circumcision process), and in the very moment of their greatest physical weakness Reuben and Levi killed them, and then the other brothers spoiled the city, taking women, and children and probably selling them into slavery.

Other than my exegetical prowess, the only reason I cited the Dinah story is because I believe the Ebony Bishops are putting themselves in the stead of the Son's of Jacob and the price for not only the possible sexual abuse issue, but the privileges of patriarchy in the disposal of women's bodies and men's sole definition of the 'honor of women's bodies' is that a man/men must afflict his manhood to the point that he's weak, and then they rob him and all the men while in their weakened state. Thus they make men go around apologizing all the time. They make men in general and annual UMC conferences all over the world condemn themselves for the past crimes of patriarchy. We men must admit how patriarchy is institutionalized and corrupts the freedom of women. Men must remove themselves off boards and leadership positions and DEI some women into those 'positions of power' as a humiliating punishment. To these DEI Bishops, the idea is that Men don't deserve to be on certain committees and the like. Men don't deserve to have a voice. If men do want a voice these DEI bishops will let them, but only if they sexually mutilate themselves by cutting their penises off and being coming transgender. Then you can rule with the women.

Or perhaps these social justice warrior Ebony Bishops are more like David. King Saul understood the allure of his wealth and power. David wanted it. What man wouldn't want to be the Kings son in law. Men have long time been going around disposing of women's bodies in whatever way was convenient to their own power. We find recorded in the Book of Judges how Caleb swore that whatever man conquers Kiriath-Sefer, he would give his daughter in marriage. Feminist/womanist theologians stop there screaming and hollering bloody patriarchy! But were they to read just a little further, they would see that Caleb's daughter Achsah boldly went to Caleb with her own and new family's interests in mind and asked Caleb to give them the lands around the initial property too. No, in their exegetical minds, women are always victims in the text. Nevertheless, Saul said he didn't want a dowery, he wanted...

1 Samuel 18:22-27 22 And Saul commanded his servants, saying, Commune with David secretly, and say, Behold, the king hath delight in thee, and all his servants love thee: now therefore be the king's son in law. 23 And Saul's servants spake those words in the ears of David. And David said, Seemeth it to you a light thing to be a king's son in law, seeing that I am a poor man, and lightly esteemed? 24 And the servants of Saul told him, saying, On this manner spake David. 25 And Saul said, Thus shall ye say to David, The king desireth not any dowry, but an

hundred foreskins of the Philistines, to be avenged of the king's enemies. But Saul thought to make David fall by the hand of the Philistines. 26 And when his servants told David these words, it pleased David well to be the king's son in law: and the days were not expired. 27 Wherefore David arose and went, he and his men, and slew of the Philistines two hundred men; and David brought their foreskins, and they gave them in full tale to the king, that he might be the king's son in law. And Saul gave him Michal his daughter to wife.

I would possibly make an argument, that anytime the Bible (or DEI Bishops) use requests about men's sexual organs and the freedom to use them as means of exchange, there is some kind of trickery involved. How does one prove one is a hero, nay, even a martyr and freedom fighter, to our new crop of Pagan DEI Ebony Bishops, be brave enough to cut your penis off and be transgender! Go get us some hacked off penises and breasts by approving, supporting and even encouraging that kind of lifestyle, and then you might get the wealth, power, position and privilege in the UMC.

If that is not enough Neo Paganism for you, let us look at the vaunted prayer room, so ubiquitous at our North Georgia Annual Conferences. The new Neo-Paganism roots itself in body, blood, sex, and race, not the Bible nor the God of the bible. First of all, why would you even pray to a God, you don't think knows what a man and a woman are? That's insane and bad evangelism. Furthermore, according to the liberals, assuming God hasn't merely been lying to us about the matter for 2000 years, God had no idea he was wrong until liberal theology and the Ebony Bishops got here to correct Him in 2024. God was wrong for billions of years, completely unaware what a man/male and woman/female are or misinformed what a man and woman are, until liberal socialist-atheist LGBTQIA+ sexual algebra theology exposed Him?

That is a pagan god. Only pagan gods need correcting. Pagan gods have human desires and characteristics (including ignorance) like the Greek pantheon of gods. It is a pagan conception to have an anthropomorphic god, a god rooted in human fallibility and frailties, like capriciousness and being wrong to the point of needing correcting by your creation. Hindu and Japanese cosmological systems have gods that have all sorts of mutable qualities and characteristics, or powers that they appropriate to themselves, represented and portrayed in color, diversity and intensity. The God of the Bible proclaims himself jealous. This is not the place for a treatise of comparative religion. Hopefully the present discussion has been sufficient to describe the neo-paganism that has infected the UMC church and its DEI Ebony Bishops in particular.

The prayer room at General Conference is already a ridiculous notion because its insane to ask a God that doesn't know what a man and woman are anything else. How could you trust that god's opinion on anything else? Plus, it wouldn't matter because you feel free to contradict Him at will and correct him. What is that to base a prayer life on? Truthfully speaking, I have somewhat fond memories of the 'Prayer Room' at North Georgia Annual Conferences in previous years. Its quiet. There were candles and low lights lit. There were scriptural prompts and prayer prompts along the walls and exhibits. There was something like a maze drawn on the floor, and as one went through different paths, it ended at a central location representing finding 'God' upon completion. A God that doesn't know what a man and a woman are must by default be lost. If he doesn't know where he is, how can He be at the center of a UMC prayer room spiritual maze. The new god of the UMC, who ever needs correction and Bishops to apologize for him, might not know what planet earth is, where it is or he may have forgotten how to get here. Let's pay some Ebony Bishops $250,000 a year to tell God where he is, and not coincidentally, what a man and a woman are. God might be sitting around twiddling his thumbs because either he doesn't know what to do, or he needs UMC DEI Ebony Bishops to tell him where he is wrong and how to atone for himself with those he has hurt through sexism, racism, homophobia, transphobia, and the wage and prosperity gap. That's not only the God they serve, but that is the one they are teaching the unsaved world and children is worthy of worship. It's as bad as UMC Bishops teaching them Zeus makes lightening, not nature and certainly not the biblical God that created nature.

Considering this, God might need therapy, secular therapy or therapy from one of our DEI Ebony Bishops so he can get himself together (as it were). What if God is so confused, he doesn't know why he's alive or has suicidal feelings of low self-esteem because every time He turns around, the clay on the potter's wheel is there trying to correct him and tell him how much misery and pain He is the cause of and must apologize for. Oh my, the god of liberals is confused. He needs help. He can't communicate his intent himself and/or the world He created, and thus needs secular philosophy and DEI Ebony Bishops to tell him, and give him a language to talk in (LGBTQIA+ sexual algebra). This god is like Joe Biden, unsteady on his feet and sometimes he forgets where he is, thus he must have aides and interlocutors in DEI aides like our Ebony Bishops. They must speak for him and make sure he uses the right pronouns and terms and doesn't do or say anything old fashioned and accidentally offend someone he has hurt through his patriarchy.

It is sheer insanity to pray to a God like that. Even our slave ancestors in the 'Invisible Church' had no notions of such a god as that. In the middle of being 'slaves' (a terrible fate), even they never sought out a God that would apologize to them, and that they could berate for putting them in a 'slave' situation. Quite the contrary, they were quite fond of the phrase 'God is a mind regulator'. How can he be powerful enough and/or wise enough to 'regulate' your mind when he himself is confused? How confused? In theory post-modern western humanity acts like it doesn't know what a man or woman is, but practically speaking going in the 'wrong' bathroom will get you locked up and other people traumatized. Presumably, if God doesn't know what a man and woman are after 13 billion years of earth's existence, how can he regulate anything else. If you really thought another human being didn't know what a man and woman are, of any race, nation, culture, or even age outside of infancy, you'd call him and his god ignorant and insecure. Our DEI Ebony Bishops know dang well that if I came in a public women's restroom at General Conference while they were taking a dump or just primping in the mirror, the last thing they would do is have a gender affirming conversation with me about how the Methodist Church is a safe space. No, they'd call security first and let security and the police department of Charlotte figure out my gender, not God or the new policies of the UMC.

The United Methodists, amongst other things, wouldn't hire me because I had a felony weed conviction in 98', and other charges common to Negro males that grow up and experience adolescence with absentee fathers. Who knew however, that if I dress up like a woman and have gender affirming surgery, I'd have an easier chance of teaching Sunday school, getting ordained, and pastoring a church in the new 'Rainbow Flag Brokeback denomination UMC. Surprise, I could even be an Ebony Bishop, the first transgender Ebony Bishop. That would be funny if it were not so sad.

...either/or 'Either you hold fast to me unconditionally in everything, or you—despise me'. If God should—or could—speak of himself as though he were not the only one, unconditionally everything, but merely some sort of a something, someone who had hopes of perhaps being included in our (human) consideration—then God must of course have lost himself, lost the notion of himself, and would not be God.

Soren Kierkegaard, The Lily of the Field and the Bird of the Air

Chapter 5 - Whoopin Old Testament Donkey

Chapter 5 - Whoopin 'Old Testament Donkey' like my name was Dad

Honestly the first week, I thought 2024 General Conferencing, purported holy conferencing was over. I certainly had hoped it was over, because when I woke up Monday and Tuesday, imagine my surprise to see more summaries of General Conference Daily Events from the UMC Offices of Communications (the ministry of propaganda). After viewing these news items, all my hopes that things couldn't get any worse were dashed. General Conference 2024 had the appearance to me of being like a car stuck in the mud, spinning its wheels, desperately trying to get out. But it's been stuck so long spinning its wheels, that it is not only digging itself a deeper rut, making it harder to get out; the car has been revving its engine so long, that in trying desperately over and over to get out of the rut, it has now or is about to soon run out of gas.

Thus, as I was reading this morning, I had a Wesleyan experience of 'feeling strangely warmed'.

In the evening I went very unwillingly to a society in Aldersgate Street, where one was reading Luther's preface to the Epistle to the Romans. About a quarter before nine, while he was describing the change which God works in the heart through faith in Christ, I felt my heart strangely warmed. I felt I did trust in Christ, Christ alone, for salvation; and an assurance was given me that He had taken away my sins, even mine, and saved me from the law of sin and death. (Journal of John Wesley)

But my 'warmth' was not from a 'borned again' experience I was having. Mine was anger and indignation rising upon me for which I well knew the cause. My 'professional' experience with the UMC left me a lot of 'church hurt', anger and resentment, and about $180,000 in student loan debt. But anger and resentment for a believer, intellectual or academic, is not enough to write great essays and sermons on, though quite often anger and resentment are a powerful inspiration and motivation. I didn't care, I'll write out of anger and resentment. At my age, career opportunities dwindling, anger and resentment are all I have left.

Thus, in my reflections on what I was seeing from the UMC reflecting General Conference 2024, I was 'warmed', not quite in the Wesleyan sense, by an overriding desire to write and pontificate in such a way as to kick the post-modern UMC's 'Old Testament Donkey'. In the projects, low-income working-class areas, and petty bourgeois Black communities that spawned me, we have many euphemisms for what I want these essays to do. You can hardly be Black in America and have never heard of an 'Old Testament donkey' whooping. As a matter of fact, that phrase represented a threat, and accompanied much of our childhood and youth. When we got to adolescence it was not uncommon to hear that some individual got his or her 'Old Testament donkey kicked'. Young adulthood introduced me to the concept of someone getting the 'brakes beaten off them'. When I began reading the British euphemisms for kicking 'Old Testament donkey', I was sufficiently motivated and inspired for today's task of critiquing the 2024 UMC General Conferences. There I was reminded of phrases like...to 'thrash', to 'clobber', to 'work over', 'lay into', and 'put the boot in'! My personal favorites are 'beat the living daylights out of' and 'beat or knock seven bells out of'. Duly motivated, dear reader, let us begin today's task of whooping the post-modern UMC, and praying that it's not too late to save it from mocking its God and itself to death.

Part I

One reason the Pharisees nit-picked Jesus and tried to 'bring him down to size' was because they felt what he presumed to do (forgive sins), was blasphemous because only God could forgive sins. Of course, Christian doctrine teaches us that is precisely the point, of Jesus being God the Father manifest in the flesh; and thus able (enabled) to forgive sins. Yet let us add another element to this discussion. Jesus could forgive sins because he was God manifest. His disciples, we are taught, inherited similar power, as being able to 'loose and bind' things in heaven and on earth.

Matthew 18:18 18 Verily I say unto you, Whatsoever ye shall bind on earth shall be bound in heaven: and whatsoever ye shall loose on earth shall be loosed in heaven.

It is thus perfectly reasonable and theologically possible for UMC DEI Bishops, the representatives of the Pope, et al., to 'loose and bind', and as it were, forgive sins. Presuming Jesus metaphor is correct, and they are in the vine, attached to the branch, attached to the trunk, within the trunk, within the roots, and that presumably is how the fruit even 2000 years later could still be ripe, and have the mark of the manifestations of God, and thus forgive sins and loose and bind on heaven and earth. But a critical question must be raised. What if the post-modern ecclesiastic fruit is detached from the vine and the branch? What if it looked like ripe fruit still because it takes a while in the natural for things to rot. The yellow banana bunch we see at the grocery store was picked green upwards of a month ago. But detached and left to its own devices all the bananas can do is rot, no matter how green, yellow, ripe and healthy they look at any given moment after being detached. Suppose the UMC Church is that 'fruit', however it is detached from the vine and completely in 'the world' dying, no matter how green or ripe it looks at any given moment? If that were the case, no matter how bright, shiny and technologically adaptive the structure of the post-modern UMC and its communications office appears to be, it is all but dead. Even if the fruit still seems sweet, and like fine wine, seems to get better with age, it is still dead.

I'm reminded of a troop of ape primates, as presented by the Discovery Channel or some other such channel. The 'Discovery Channel' in Post-Modernity is filled with such mythological gems as, 'Naked and Afraid', 'Ghost Adventures', and 'Deadliest Catch'. On similar 'education themed' channels here in Post-Modern America, there are shows on Aliens, Real Housewives of This or that town, and other media effluvia. These monkeys knew the growing seasons, and had long inherited migratory patterns based on heredity, the seasons of the year, and which plants, fruits, shrubs are in season or not, at what times. There is a fruit tree, but the branches are too high for these terrestrial monkeys to get. So unlike the Giraffe, they must wait until the fruit gets really ripe, and falls off the tree on its own. As the fruit falls and lands to the ground, it begins to decay and rot. But as it does, natural fermentation takes place and has the effect of intoxicating the little monkeys. For days on end, as long as it lasts, in a Bacchanalian feast, worthy of the party the King of Persia threw in the Book of Esther they eat this natural fruity wine. It is a plus because they get calories and fiber from the fruit itself, calories from the fermented alcoholic content, and intoxication to boot. It's an ape/monkey fantasy land...or is it. Days on end, as long as the party lasts, the apes revel in a Dionysian ritualistic yearly haze of chaos and confusion. They stumble around drunk, carousing in ways considered inappropriate sober. The hierarchical and sexual order breaks down, resulting in conflict and brawls. They exhaust themselves and fall asleep; only to wake up rearing to go do it all again, as long as the fruit lasts. But the fruit is in limited quantity and time takes its own toll. And what once was varying levels of fermentation and sweet taste, is now putrid, rotting flesh, as abhorrent to the taste as the same thing was once delicious. And when the food, beverages, and refreshments are gone, the apes move on too...the wise females and big males heading off first.

Brothers and sisters (sic). This is like the current UMC Church Post-General Conference 2024. Not only is it completely 'detached from the branch', it is rotting and putrefying with all the dizzying effects of rapid change, turning church tradition, polity, and policy around 180 degrees.

It's intoxicating effects pervade the media, which pats our representative (and thus wise) DEI bishops and prelates on the back, but they and everybody else move on when there is nothing left that is not disgustingly rotten. All the monkeys move on, leaving your rotting once flowering fruit's carcasses on the ground scattered to and fro, for scavengers even lower than the monkeys and apes to scavenge. Let them that have ears, hear.

Part II

Ergo General Conference 2024. Being fruit detached from the vine, you still 'feel' and 'want' the power to 'forgive sins' and 'loose and bind', but you are detached. Jesus says that this power comes from being 'in him'!

John 15:1-8 KJG John 15:1 I am the true vine, and my Father is the husbandman. 2 Every branch in me that beareth not fruit he taketh away: and every branch that beareth fruit, he purgeth it, that it may bring forth more fruit. 3 Now ye are clean through the word which I have spoken unto you. 4 Abide in me, and I in you. As the branch cannot bear fruit of itself, except it abide in the vine; no more can ye, except ye abide in me. 5 I am the vine, ye are the branches: He that abideth in me, and I in him, the same bringeth forth much fruit: for without me ye can do nothing. 6 If a man abide not in me, he is cast forth as a branch, and is withered; and men gather them, and cast them into the fire, and they are burned. 7 If ye abide in me, and my words abide in you, ye shall ask what ye will, and it shall be done unto you. 8 Herein is my Father glorified, that ye bear much fruit; so shall ye be my disciples.

The vine, the branch, the limb, the trunk, the stem, the roots, are all rooted in God's word, and a concept of an eternal, omniscient, and omnipotent God that doesn't need correction.

Numbers 23:19 19 God is not a man, that he should lie; neither the son of man, that he should repent: hath he said, and shall he not do it? or hath he spoken, and shall he not make it good?

...This fruit detached from the vine has no respect for God's eternal word and feels it needs to correct God on matters of basic mammalian fact! It is preposterous to think God doesn't/didn't know what a man/ male, and woman/female were when He inspired the bible? He had Moses, Elijah, Isaiah, Jeremiah, and Jesus deluded to the point that what they thought a man and woman are, are not, and it takes post-modern LGBTQIA+ alphabet soup philosophy to give us a better example and working model than what the biblical and mammalian model provides? This is what our DEI Bishops are selling us! And our DEI Bishops want the power to 'forgive sins', 'to loose and bind in heaven and on earthy'! Such that when our DEI Bishops say what the bible says is a sin, is no longer a sin, God himself must follow them! Such that when 'they' say 'shacking up', is no longer a sin, God must follow their lead. Such that when our DEI Bishops say 'stealing and behaving disrespectfully in the name of social justice' is not a sin, God himself must follow! The very nerve of these people. Anyone who falls for such logic is drinking the 'cool aid', enjoying the now decaying, fermented, rotting, fruit of what was once a powerful force for righteousness and bourgeois protestant Christian values in American culture. What once was fruit (the UMC), however now detached, is just an intoxicating chaos breeding force in families and societies, just like our previously mentioned drunken monkeys.

This is also probably why intoxication is such an off resorted to condition of humanity when dealing with feelings of shame, anxiety, sin, and suffering. All the great Dionysian nihilist tendencies and celebrations of current and past modernity are ever infused with massive amounts of alcohol and drugs. If I'm not mistaken, the United States consumes about 70% of the intoxicants produced on the planet.

The Post-Modern 'woke' UMC brings its own intoxicating libation, purporting to be or masquerading as 'liberation'. With one stroke of a Bishop's pen, homosexuality is not a sin anymore. Shacking up, not a sin. Greed, profligacy, not a sin. There are no more discouraged behaviors to be ashamed about publicly or privately. Imagine my bewilderment when reading Rabbinic Commentary on the book of Joshua to see what worship of the god 'Peor' entailed. Reference Joshua 22 and Numbers 25. I am quoting:

"The worship of Peor, involved defecating in front of the idol...The bizarre service of Peor is based on the body's ability to separate and absorb the nourishing content of food, and expelling the waste, and was thus meant to symbolize the human responsibility to distinguish good from evil, and spiritual from material." Artscroll The Rubin Edition Prophets

The reader knows dang well that you could get on the internet with that kind of theological and spiritual non-sense logic and get half-a-million followers if you were sincere, earnest and entertaining in your delivery (get it, delivery).

Can you imagine that Hebrews that knew Joshua, knew of Moses, and certainly knew the Torah traditions of slavery in Egypt and subsequent deliverance at the leadership and miracles of God, could possibly fall for such a thing? You'd have a hard time imagining yourself falling for such a thing as going to some kind of shrine, altar and/or deity figurine, saying some ritual mumbo jumbo, squatting down and dropping a load in front of the deity while it is looking at you. But indeed, stranger things have happened; perhaps even entire denominations, 'brokeback' denominations, pretending 'en mass' like we don't know the difference between men/males and women/females. But guess what, Rabbinic scholars suggest that when Jewish men did the ritual of the worship of Peor it was with good intentions and to appease Moabite women. But that is a story we might take up another time.

Leave people to the will of justifying their animal natures, by wrapping it up in Christian theology. Churches become like clubs and social organizations. It is no coincidence that the most prestigious clubs and social organizations have lots of rules and pre-requisites. Once a club or social organization gets rid of the rules in some misguided attempt to appeal to the masses, it has virtually mocked itself into destruction. Who wants to be something everyone else can do? What 'elites' and their bourgeois imitators would want to join organizations like 'skull & Bones' and varying elite university fraternities and sororities if they found out Drake, Kendrick Lamar, Rick Ross, Gary Bussey, Meg tha Stallion, and the guy that played Bozo the Clown were in it. You certainly would rethink whether it was really an elite organization (no disrespect to the above-mentioned Negro celebrities). The prime motive in the human existential reality is to distinguish oneself by joining some club or group. When we are talking about the Crips, The Bloods, the Alphas, the Omegas, Jack and Jill, and/or the Boule, the whole point is to submit to the highest standards, requirements and prerequisites to get to an elite level. Theoretically there could be an organization of broke, homeless, and insane people with no jobs that started a club for other homeless people to join...but even they would have to have some rules. And now in the current state of Post-Modern American United Methodist Civilization, it would be easier to get put out of an organization of broke, homeless, insane, deranged people with no jobs that started a club for other homeless people to join than it would be to get put out of General Conference for heresy. We have gone out and created an organization no sane person would want to join. No one wants to join any old organization that accepts any old body because it has no rules.

After two or three years of seminary and run arounds in the UMC, I googled what it took to be, or to call oneself, an ordained minister in general. The rules and laws vary so much, as to be all but irrelevant. But the UMC and the wider Denominational churches had rules and discipline. In exchange for accepting the rules and discipline, one had attained a higher standard of operations. No matter what and where you come from in the past, if you uphold the rules and the discipline, the church and community would accept your bourgeois aspirations at face value. And let me reiterate, no matter where you came from, whatever bad background, how bad your parents were, your criminal history, what race you were, the bourgeois denominational church in American history would accept you as precisely that, a bourgeois middle class citizen family man/woman. Our church cannot sell that anymore; thus no one is interested, and membership and evangelism is collapsing.

The UMC and other 'demonimations' (sic) have shot themselves in the foot by rejecting what used to be presented as common-sense bourgeois middle class values. Many immigrants to America were dirt poor. They were indentured servants, slaves, and former slaves. Having a respectable character, family, values, standards, a respectable role in the church and community, this was an aspiration for Americans of all races. Sadly, this is no longer, as America today has degenerated into the politics of what other people and the government owe me (Black, White and others claiming to be so marginalized in the freest country in the world). It is like now we have a God who is an 'ambulance chaser' God (religion), who is only worth something because he can convince worldly authorities that somebody else is the reason for our suffering and make them pay reparations. This God they sell is a genius at proving that everything and anything is not your fault...and thus somebody owes you. This is what our current UMC DEI Bishops are selling. Where once the denominational church uplifted values, morality, business and professional standards in America, now it has over moralized itself into a socialist atheist nihilist theological think tank, that thinks that it needs to apologize for its own 2000-year-old values. These are the same values that for 2000 years have provided a guiding light of civilization in the Middle East, Europe, Africa, and Asia etc. Babies and bathwater are not equivalent.

Part III

Equally fascinating is that there is a part of me that thinks it is possible to have sincere motives to go around forgiving sin in general, and by the stroke of a Bishop's pen forgiving sin. It is quite possible, that this delusion, inspires DEI Bishops and other liberals to like Don Quixote, go around chasing windmills of sins to forgive and things to loose, on earth and in heaven in the form of the LGBTQIA+ social justice socialist atheism; and bind on earth like homophobia, transphobia, sexism, racism, etc. I will give our Ebony Bishops and the wider post-modern

UMC the benefit of the doubt and argue that they have good intentions, and their hearts are in the right place with all this forgoing and forgiving of sin by a few strokes of the bishops' pens.

What I will not forgive them for is forgiving themselves of their own sin in detaching the UMC Episcopacy and the UMC Discipline from the vine, to wing it on their own 'reason', 'ration', and sense of 'fairness'. In this bizzarro parallel universe our DEI bishops and the liberals that enable them inhabit, the church doesn't offer help to human beings in an unstable world of confused values and shifting values, and materialism. Quite the opposite, every moment they get in front of a mic, they are apologizing on behalf of the church and God for the damage done to women, the LGBTQIA community, the Black and brown community, the Hawaiian community, etc., ad infinitum. Every problem in the world they make the church and God either apologize for, or apologize for being a silent witnesses to. They think that is effective evangelism and creates a warm welcoming environment. Problem is, the people they are apologizing to are not flocking to the UMC, the same way women and the LGBTQIA+ community did not flock to The Acolyte Stars Wars TV show just because it was inclusive. Similarly, our DEI ebony bishops and the warm inclusive environment they supposedly created for minorities, is not attracting large numbers of African Americans or 'brown people' back to the UMC, or to it at all.

It seems noble and righteous to ask forgiveness for the church's historic 'roles' in racism, slavery, discrimination, sexism, classism etc., and the church's collusions in those socio-economic forces. But it is merely a hustle. It's also insulting, which is why there is never a resurgence in membership in ANY of the communities the UMC apologizes to for historic crimes. No one cares about our meaningless and insulting apologies. Imagine the audacity and hubris of the White western world in thinking that the worst thing to ever happen to any indigenous society or civilization was them, and the White western world still has that much control over their lives than to be singlehandedly capable of increasing the global quality of life and self-esteem merely by apologizing and paying some sort of western derived monetary compensation. Are they not somehow confusing God's affirmation with liberal White people's selfish hubristic need to think that their affirmations actually mean something to people? It is as though former deplorables the world over, were waiting on White folk's apologies all this time before they can have any self-esteem or dignity in themselves; like Black women weren't beautiful before, and aren't beautiful unless Vogue, Elle, and all the big fashion houses have Black and brown models or Lizzo on the front cover.

Imagine if I just walked up to a handicapped person in a wheelchair and said I'm sorry for your pain, I'm sorry for discriminating against you, I'm sorry for calling you crippled and using derogatory terms in the past. I'm sorry for marginalizing you, I'm sorry for not recognizing intersectionality and your human dignity. And I'm sorry for the church being complicit in your pain because they have not made it a 'safe space' for disabled and 'differently abled' people. Is all of that really supposed to make him or her feel better about themselves? What if I said all that in front of people; would it not have the effect of being kind of embarrassing to the handicapped person? The average handicapped person out and about in the world would be offended. Most of us in that position would react with indignity. "I'm doing fine without your self-righteous pity, save it for someone who needs it!" Would it not be a further insult to give the handicapped person with a profession and self-esteem, a $5 handout for his or her historic pain. Self-respect would demand they tell you they don't need your money. Unfortunately, this is the Global Strategy of the UMC, apologizing all the dang time. General Conference 2024 was a prime example of that insulting and thus destined to fail strategy that believes you can ingratiate yourself with people merely by apologizing to them and throwing money at them. This is also my central problem with reparations as a concept for African Americans. But that is a nearly entirely different discussion.

Part IV

Another tragic sinful variation on the theme of the dangers of apologizing all the time can be seen in children's apologies. I certainly would not dispute that 'the art of the apology' is a good lesson for children to learn, as it is a rule of life. However, have you ever noticed the moment in a child's existential life (self-consciousness), that he or she realizes the phrase 'I'm sorry' is like a magic abracadabra or magic linguistic talisman that absolves the perpetrator of guilt and quite often punishment. The scolding parent says, "you pushed your li'l sister down, trying to get to the mashed potatoes, tell her your sorry!" You tell your li'l sister you are sorry, not because the childish offender really understands the pain they caused, but because that is the only way to make the parental fussing go away. In the end, the kid really did want some mashed potatoes bad, and his sister was in the way. In that way, ethical or moral liability is a later phase of apology, than the immediate responsibility to verbally apologize. To sense moral liability, is to be motivated to apologize. But when we teach young children that they must verbally apologize for quite willful acts, the words coming out of their mouths do not carry the actual weight of moral responsibility, lest no one would have to tell them to apologize. That comes later. This childish ridiculousness is the position the UMC is in, throwing apologies around like dollars in a strip club, sticking them anywhere they can in the native's G-string grass skirts and coconut shell bras. Like saying 'I'm sorry', is a magic talisman that makes all the adult fussing go away, the UMC is apologizing again, and again, abracadabra-ing its way to repentance and healing. In some ways it's a weird reversal of the 'saved by faith' or 'saved by works' argument. The one verbally apologizing, clearly believes he is 'saved by works' (the act of apologizing). However, presuming he or she is genuinely repentant, and has a kind of silent faith in the desire not to make the same mistake again, and combines that silent faith, with 'acts meet for repentance', as John the Baptist would say, needs not make verbal apology at all.

Matthew 3:1-8 KJG Matthew 3:1 In those days came John the Baptist, preaching in the wilderness of Judaea, 2 And saying, Repent ye: for the kingdom of heaven is at hand. 3 For this is he that was spoken of by the prophet Esaias, saying, The voice of one crying in the wilderness, Prepare ye the way of the Lord, make his paths straight. 4 And the same John had his raiment of camel's hair, and a leathern girdle about his loins; and his meat was locusts and wild honey. 5 Then went out to him Jerusalem, and all Judaea, and all the region round about Jordan, 6 And were baptized of him in Jordan, confessing their sins. ***7 But when he saw many of the Pharisees and Sadducees come to his baptism, he said unto them, O generation of vipers, who hath warned you to flee from the wrath to come? 8 Bring forth therefore fruits meet for repentance:***

Apologizing is like saying Abracadabra and making the li'l childish 'oopsies' and 'boo-boos' magically go away. In a similar vein the apologies of the UMC uttered at General Conference are just hustles to absolve themselves of guilt and look religious. That is to say, forgive themselves of their sin. They have become their own God, they are forgiving themselves of the sins of the UMC since the mid-18th century. Thus forgiven of sins, they want to walk Holy with fancy emblems, robes, and titles. They want to step forward a new 'Holy' Church because they have absolved themselves of sin through highly ritualized 14-page apologies, spells, and abracadabra incantations read by DEI Bishops.

But it is like a good friend of mine named Mbaba Hakeem. His father was a UMC District Superintendent in Delaware in the 80's. His mother was one of the few Black Delegates at the General Conference of 1968 that created the UMC out of the Methodist Church and the United Brethren (sic, how ironic). As interesting as all that is, for now I will limit myself to a discussion of that couple's son, Mbaba. His father's rise in the post-1968 UMC is fascinating, however.

Hakeem (not his born name but his adopted name reflecting his Afro-centric revolutionary interests and tastes) came of age in the 1960's graduating from MIT in 1974. With the politics of race during that time, his father's United Methodism was unappealing, however proud he was of his father's achievements in the United Methodist church. He made up for the 'spiritual vacuum' in his life created by rejecting his father's values, no longer going to church, no longer accompanying his mother on saxophone or flute as she played the piano or sung hymns or led directed the choir, by getting heavy into the Black Panthers, The New African Revolutionary Movement, Martial Arts and Tai Chi.

I am recounting the story of Mbaba Hakeem merely to use him as an example of what our Ebony DEI Bishops are doing by going around forgiving the White church by apologizing to the world on its behalf in a ridiculous series of statements, intended purposes, principles, mission statements, and ideals, all aimed at apologizing. To do that, I shall cite my second favorite Mbaba Hakeem story, the favorite being the time, he and a friend wanted to go see Nina Simone in concert, but the concert was sold out. They showed up to the concert in full Black panther/Black radical/Afros, etc., and demanded to see Nina and her manager. When they made it backstage, they informed Nina and her manager that there were death threats against her that they had been informed of, and that they were there to provide extra security. Nina and her manager promptly gave them two tickets near the front row center and thanked them. They fabricated the death threats. Considering Ms. Simone's later mental health issues, in hindsight a harmless prank may have had more profound consequences than Hakeem and his buddy could have imagined. But those are stories for another time. It's my 2nd favorite Hakeem story however, which corresponds to the behavior of our DEI Ebony Bishops and the wider post-modern church. That story goes as follows.

According to Hakeem he is a 6th degree Black Belt in Karate or some other martial art. Of course that is very impressive. Yet he qualifies his 6-degrees of Black belt excellence with the following statement. Degrees 1 thru 4, he got through study with a 'master'. The 5th and 6th degrees he conferred upon himself after independent study. It could indeed be possible that after reaching the 4th degree, he couldn't find a master on a higher level, so he trained himself through study, discipline, YouTube videos etc., and got to a level for which he knew he could perform at the 5th and 6th degrees. Obviously, it would have been slightly better to have trained under a master from a higher level, but in that the possession of the skillset of the 5th and 6th degrees speaks for itself, it must be allowed to speak itself.

That would have been enough for me to assume that his capabilities at the 5th and 6th degrees were valid. But that was not the end of the story. No sooner had Hakeem told me about the curious nature of how he made it to the 5th and 6th degrees, than he told me that he was drunk when he made the decision to confer upon himself the 5th and 6th degrees. Not only had he gone from the 5th to the 6th degrees from his own study, his own comprehension, his own merit, but also from his own drunkenness.

Because I'm sure enquiring minds want to know, I'm sure the reader is wondering just how drunk he was and might that have impaired his physical abilities or his thought process. It could be possible, he had a sip or two, or was tipsy and being somewhat unusual, he interpreted tipsy as drunk thus his judgement neither his balance was impaired during the workout session where he assessed his skills at the 5th and 6th degrees.

No ladies and gentlemen (sic), Hakeem said he was sloppy drunk during these proceedings. And to me, that is how DEI and Ebony Bishops are made, and how they end up going around with theological degrees of belts teaching classes to unsuspecting ignorant youth and the misinformed. But like Claudine Gay, something about their rise is problematic.

DEI Bishops, a symbol and token of a repentant church, or a liberal White mainstream church that hides its agenda behind Ebony DEI Bishops that are apologizing on their behalf, begging for forgiveness from the world. We owe God. The Christian owes God. We don't owe the world, BLM, the LGBTQIA, the socialist atheists, etc. We owe God. To Him is due all our apologies and repentance. Any other definition disconnects us from the vine, the branch, the limb, the trunk and the root. False apologies, the apologies of children still wetting their diapers and beds, for whom biblical wisdom, morality and ethics are a convenience and utilitarian.

Part V

General Conference 2024 "Let the Apologies begin". The Church in Africa gets 2 more Bishops, new Map, but they wanted 5. The Russian and Central European Church was allowed to split off...amicably.

Ah dear brothers and sisters (sic), how many times have the representatives of White mainstream power gathered to dispose of the affairs of their colonial subjects? Have we forgotten the Berlin Conference (1885), where the powers of Europe unilaterally decided to regulate colonization and trade in Africa. Oh, do such things not smack of the Sykes-Picot (1916) agreement where France, Brittain, et. al, agreed to spheres of influence in splitting the rotting yet geographically important rotting corpse of the Ottoman Empire. From the Raj to the East India Company, oh how Europe and the White mainstream loves its ('holy' conferencing), where they delve into the domains, affairs and psychology of their coolies, niggers, chinks, spics, etc., and what is best for them. How could the developing world be so insensitive to LGBTQIA rights, as the western church liberal's claim developing world churches are 'backwards' regarding post-modern trends in human sexuality? But the post-General Conference UMC leadership doesn't recognize in the least their own post-modern Western ideological and cultural Imperialism and holding 'natives' accountable to western pro-LGBTQIA+ standards which are presumed to be better than indigenous cultural and religious values. But no, let the UMC apology for past (White man run) religious and cultural imperialism in the developing world be true. Let it be faithful and true, a gift to the natives, for their recognition of the powers of the White Western Denominational world to unilaterally control what the definition of a 'sin' is, even if it is in complete contradiction to scriptural integrity and 2000 years of church tradition. Is it reasonable to think the sexual imperialism of our current DEI bishops is any better than the theological imperialism of the expansion of White western Christianity in the development of the church in the new and developing worlds during the age of Colonialism and conquest.

The impact of Islam, Catholic Christianity, Protestant Christianity, post-modern materialist socialist-atheism, and technology has been incalculable on the developing world. To suggest that they are hardly any better for it today should be self-evident in requiring more than an apology from DEI bishops. For all the developing world evangelizing and philanthropy done by European and American whites (much of which ended up self-serving), many indigenous cultural forms and systems (good and bad) were wiped out. The effects on traditional indigenous philosophy, religion and praxis, of participating in a White mainstream dominated Euro-American denomination has often had deleterious effects on indigenous and developing cultures. It affected indigenous views of 'God', 'White people', White culture and their sense of the value of their own indigenous race and character. Do you think the same thing is not going on when Kamala Harris and our DEI Ebony Bishops lecture the African and developing United Methodist world on how they need to accept the LGBTQIA+ sexual algebra? Dr. Livingstone presumed his version of Christianity was right in the orthodox sense, justifying forcing it on natives and beating them over the head with it; just like Kamela and our DEI Bishops and the impacts of their browbeating kind of sexual algebra imperialism on the Methodist churches in the developing world, which are largely conservative. Here again, these effects have been incalculable on indigenous societies. The effects of religious colonization have been incalculable. The Methodist church in the developing world, no matter how you 'whitewash' it, is the precise result of generations of natives bred under the 'de facto' superiority of European and western Christianity. Our DEI and Ebony bishops are comfortable with acknowledging that crime (because it was perpetrated by the White male patriarchy); but the crime of imposing the LGBTQIA agenda on the post-modern natives certainly does nothing to prove anything has changed in the assumed superiority of Western values! Thus, the current DEI 'powers that be' in the UMC church do not understand the true value of the crime, or who they need to repent to, rendering all of the apologies coming out of their mouths completely meaningless babble like the children they are. The debt owed to these indigenous cultures is not calculable to apologies, material renumeration (reparations), and to assume so is even more insulting than the original crimes during the colonial age.

But now the White people called 'Methodist' have absolved themselves of all that guilt simply because they have DEI Ebony Bishops and placards of apologies at General Conference. These DEI Bishops do incantations and draw ups, write odd sounding papers, and statements of apology, acknowledging the 'terrible crimes' of those (White men) that preceded them in the offices of the episcopacy. I suppose that is one way to hide a crime; committing an even bigger one...in the name of Jesus (who not coincidentally didn't know what a man and a woman were until post-modern theology); yep, that Jesus had his whole church wrong, deluded for 2000 years...how insensitive of an omnipotent and omniscient God. How many native African, Native American, Aboriginal Australian, etc., dialects and tongues have been erased because of the religious, commercial, military, and legal foundations of the European languages and Arabic as they descended into Native life? Is the UMC apologizing for all that? Hell no! They can't, and that is precisely the problem with going around forgiving yourself of your sins and expecting others to embrace you because of it. Not coincidentally, that is the problem going around telling people you are a 6th degree Black belt, but you self-approved yourself in a drunken state to your last 2 degrees.

Part VI Hawaii

An apology was made for the UMC and its role in Hawaiian politics and history. The Europeans didn't want Africans, Indians (far east), the Arabs, Native Americans, or the Chinese to consider their inherent human worth and capabilities in the world valid, or worthy of respect and dignity. This allowed Whites to consider native bodies and their lands to be completely at the disposal of Whites. Europeans possibly could have felt motivated to treat the above noted peoples with respect and dignity upon first contact, but the economic and geopolitical temptations of manipulating and enslaving them outweighed any ethical or theological considerations. The only 'considerations' of note were the competition between European powers to develop the military and political capacity to rule and dominate native populations. And we know from church history, even with 'introducing' natives to Christianity and converting them, this still did not confer upon the native a degree of respect commensurate with that shown to European peoples. To my secular atheist friends that blame the church and religion for every human (all too human) crime, nothing in the European secular humanism of the time conferred any degree or respect upon the native either. Oddly enough, we can be assured that at the same time White folk didn't know what a human being was (vis a vis chattel slavery), they were very assured what a man/male and a woman/female are. When Europeans were colonizing the world and bringing it under the sway of their version of Greco-Roman Orthodox and Protestant Christianity, I know the colonized and enslaved peoples of the world would have much rather that the White man was somewhere locked in Holy Conferencing, behind the closed doors of their monasteries at the Vatican debating what a man and a woman are and the relative merits of sexual algebra, instead of debating what a 'human being' is and whether or not they should colonize the non-White natives. Of course, the definition of 'fully human' was 'fully White'. My God how the past 1500 years of church history and geopolitical history would look different if Europeans had been debating what a man and a woman are instead of what a human being was. Their conclusions as to what a human being was, destroyed many a culture along the way to promoting a Eurocentric version of Christianity, that they don't even believe in anymore. Europe is all but atheist, and America has lost the battle with the world in terms of adapting the Christianity to fit the advancements of socialist-atheist LGBTQIA+ styled materialist liberalism. But when Europe was traipsing the world under the pretenses of 'manifest destiny' and their inherent superiority, the Bible, the literal word of God was not in dispute, neither was there a dispute as to the fundamentals of what a man and a woman are. Not only does the developing world have something to gripe about in terms of White folks' deliberations and Holy Conferencing and the value of them, add Mother Nature Herself to the entities that wish White people would have debated the benefits and drawbacks of industrialization and commodification on the environment and ecosystems.

Next the UMC will be apologizing to Mother Earth, if they haven't already. When I call Post-Modern American Christianity Neo-Paganism, I am neither exaggerating nor being hyperbolic. But back to the Hawaiian apology. It seems the denomination had a role in the overthrow of the Hawaiian Monarchy in 1893. One of the early White Methodist Pastors, the once Right Reverend, once Right Honorable, Rev. Harcourt W. Peck played a role in colluding with Sugar Plantation Owners and Interests, and not coincidentally the US Marines, in order to steal Hawaiian lands and make indigenous rule all but impossible. During the fight (if you can call western organization, tactics, and equipment against natives a fight), our UMC pastor Rev. Peck distinguished himself as a sharpshooter and senior aide to the U.S. Military commander. The petition at General Conference for the apology also noted that even presently, Native Hawaiians like Native Americans and Blacks, continue to suffer disproportionately from economic issues, homelessness, and poor health. Here again, this is an exercise and tactic by our hypocritical DEI Bishops in the politics of forgiving yourself of sins. These apologies are wrong on so many levels besides their patronizing nature.

Do you know how pompous and arrogant you must be to think your apologies should mean something/anything to the people in question 135 years after the catastrophe? I robbed you blind, and then my descendants, living comfortably playing golf on your lands, and surfing your beautiful scenic oceans, apologize to you. You're still broke and must do the hula dance and make leis for tourists to survive, but in addition to an apology from the United Methodist Church, you natives have the benefit of Oprah and the Rock being your neighbors. The Jews and Palestinians remember their 'Nakbas', and their holocausts at the barrels of guns and increasingly sophisticated bombs. The Hawaiians, Native Americans, Africans, get apologized to, while the 'victors' keep the best spoils for themselves and have the Natives on perpetual welfare. Think of the Hotels, superstar villas, resorts, golf courses, etc., in Hawaii, and wonder which one would you rather have. One side has the villas, the hotels, the resorts, golf courses, luxurious palatial estates and the like, and the other side gets apologies, welfare, and token representation, cleverly disguised as reparations and good will. And there our ebony DEI bishops go apologizing for crimes of this magnitude on behalf of the current White mainstream power structure and the geopolitical resource possessions of the perpetrators.

These DEI bishops are criminals. Not only did they destroy a denomination, in the process, they were absolutely of no worth at all to the Black UMC, which is the even greater tragedy if we consider that the 'Local Church', is The Church, not episcopacies, administrative structures, budgets and judiciaries. It is criminal for them to stand up in front of the Hawaiian delegation and people, and apologize on behalf of White European colonization, 135 years or so after White folks unilaterally turned their 'paradise' into the White man's paradise, and this priced natives off and out of their own paradise. It is as if White folks gentrified dang near the whole entire island chain and made every native (more or less) homeless and dispirited. Can you replace what they lost to European contact with apologies, reparations and DEI Bishops? How insulting to native peoples.

I don't care how big a financial reparation is, can it cover the cost of a 'dream deferred'? Can it cover the cost of millions of 'dreams deferred'? What was lost in the negation by European rule, of what 135 years of independent native economic, political, and cultural development might have looked like? What might 135 years of natives evolving their own theological insights and practices, either without exposure to Eurocentric Christianity at all, or exposure to it on their 'own' cultural terms instead of 'at the barrel' of a proverbial gun, have looked like? Are then White folks simply to apologize and come up with some sort of affirmative action, reparation figure, that in the African American context, suggests $250,000 for each descendant of enslaved Africans.

A monetary figure can't be attached to that any more than guessing a man's future wages when he died in a car accident, and his family sues for damages. He might have died the next day? Either way it is cold comfort to his loved ones and family. They'd certainly rather have their loved one than $250,000...or not. What will an apology do? How do you sufficiently apologize for hundreds of years of African, Native American, and Hawaiian deferred dreams, and Europeans monopolizing 'the hell' out of anything they had of value in terms of culture, traditions, and geographic and natural resources. How do you put a monetary value on that, or even pay for 'therapy' (European therapy no less) for entire groups of people that for 400 years have been told they are ugly and fat, or had slanted eyes and bucked teeth, etc.? How do you pay for enough therapy for an entire group of people that for 400 years was told their culture was inferior, their gods are inferior, their minds are inferior, etc.? And then to add insult to injury, the same people who told you that you were inferior for 400 years, now apologizes to you and wants to give you reparations? It took 140 years of Methodist history in Hawaii for the UMC to chastise itself for traipsing the world and calling every people, every culture, and every religion they encountered (even Judaism and Islam) inferior to White western European Christianity! Is the current United Methodist Church still so arrogant as to think that sending DEI Bishops to Hawaii and letting them recreate some hocus, pocus, 24-page letter of apology, will absolve them of their sins? Here again, we are witnessing people relying on the power of the pen and their own vain imaginations to absolve themselves ('loosing and binding on earth and in heaven') of sin and guilt.

They arrogantly absolve themselves and forgive themselves of sins, and believe it in their power to do so, the same way many of the same DEI Ebony Bishops used the power of the pen and their own vain imaginations to with a stroke of the 'bishops magic pen', call a thing God originally called a sin, perfectly fine. To that they add the audacity of thinking they not only have the authority to do so, but others should magically accept their apologies, and forgive and forget all former sins, and immediately adopt your LGBTQIA+ position in the face of 2000 years of church doctrine and history. How can you accept the apologies of a God that doesn't know what a man and woman are? Is He sane? Is that God in 'His' right mind if he lets you (the clay) tell Him what a man and woman are? You send DEI representatives of that 'God' to Hawaii, to apologize on behalf of the UMC. But that 'God' is so out of His mind He either no longer knows what a man or a woman are, or he is sufficiently confused, deranged and/or deluded about it, as to be in a state of dementia and needs human DEI Bishop interlocutors to speak on his behalf. This is the level of insane paganism, the church of Jesus Christ in the form of Methodism has been reduced to...some bat boo-boo crazy God that goes around apologizing for having ever called something a sin that humans (the clay) found inconvenient. What kind of God is this the UMC is now selling to an unsuspecting world! What kind of God is this that so feels he needs to justify Himself and provide reparations for his past 'mistakes', that he wants to share 'filthy lucre' and token titles and positions in a weak Denominational church with the natives he hurt. This God can't bless people supernaturally, he must pay them in the natural! This is quite precisely a pagan notion of God. What in the world?

As for apologies from the Europeans. Perhaps there are good motives and intentions towards Hawaii and other natives, but no consideration is taken as to what cultural, political, or spiritual significance was lost. We know very well how White folks have appropriated various American lands and geography. But little is known in terms of how the Native Americans thought about Malibu, the Rockys, Yosemite, and other landscapes of their heritage. Apologies, welfare, token representation and reparations apparently are a just reward for Native American tragedies and labors. Yes, don't worry, the UMC is going to Jesus like, sacrifice itself on the cross of worldly secular opinion, to absolve itself of all the guilt for a patriarchal God and his crimes. Like Jesus, the current UMC will take up its cross, the cross of socialist-atheist LGBTQIA+ and crucify itself, sacrificing itself on that cross as denominational dysfunction and chaos flows like blood from its wounded body. This God must be apologized and atoned for because he makes mistakes like giving boys that don't want one a penis. Crucify Him, this God commits crimes against humanity like standing by silently as lands are stolen from Natives and they are enslaved and oppressed, and standing by silently as women are abused, oppressed and treated poorly. Crucify Him! Oh, the irony of the same God that told White folks that manifest destiny was their right, now the White man says that God doesn't know what a man and a woman are? For that matter, to the current UMC, John Wesley doesn't know what a man and a woman are either. You believe in his theological speculation about the church and the unseen, but you think John Wesly was completely misinformed about the seen (penis/vagina). You know Wesley's story. Considering that not only was he married, but in a sad marriage, we must presume he had some familiarity with what a man and woman are…that is unless you are a current UMC DEI Bishop. If you are a current UMC post-General conference, John Wesley is as ignorant as your god.

Let me close the matter of this false apology hocus pocus, and insulting notions of reparations on this wise. Wallowing in sins and perpetual self-flagellation is not a solution to sin, in oneself or others. Look what you, they, did to me is not the proper attitude of a Christian. What is New Testament 'forgiveness'? Jesus preached radical forgiveness to individuals, but we do not preach forgiveness to races and groups of specific people. DEI Bishops absolve historically oppressed communities from forgiving their enemies and empower them to go around wallowing in the politics and theology of 'look what happened to me', 'look what they did to me' and 'look what the world owes me/us'. We can go around suing people with some kind of social or economic justice (atheist) mumbo jumbo divorced from work and 'works', and centered on entitlement.

That is not what Jeus taught and is further evidence the Post-Modern UMC is fruit that is completely detached from the branch, the limb, the trunk, the stem, and the root. Thus, all we are offering is the intoxicating sweet smells of a God that owes you money (as though that were the only thing He has of value to you), and a god that owes you an apology for the mistake of having made you Black, White, male, female, poor, rich, etc. Whatever you come up with that you hate about your life or dislike about your life, this god will appease you and apologize for it, and justify whatever crimes against your own body or the bodies of others you commit because you are merely reacting in pain and anguish to the mistake god made. A god that doesn't know what a man and a woman are is oxymoronic. Frankly it would indeed take a god that ignorant to pay DEI Bishops and prelates $250,000 per year to go around offering insulting false and fake apologies to anyone that demands an apology from God. God owes us an apology for being alive? We're picking characteristics (sex), after the fact, and then blaming God for having made us not what we currently want to be. What ever happened to being happy and thankful to be alive in any circumstances! This is how the slaves made it. Of course they were not happy to be in slavery, but they had hope and faith, knowing who they were on the inside, and when they got in their 'invisible church' ring shouts and brush arbors to worship, they sang and danced in therapy to relieve their pains yes, but also in thankfulness and thanksgiving for the blessings they had and could perceive. They dang sure didn't have time to complain about being born a woman or a man. That was perhaps the least of their worries. And now we are told we serve a God who makes mistakes, and happens to create some people slaves, poor or in the wrong sexual body, and thus He and his DEI bishops who must speak for Him owe us an apology for our sufferings? Or He and his DEI Bishops must justify our crimes against ourselves and others we do to self-rectify what God seemed to get wrong? This is complete nonsense theology ladies and gentlemen (sic).

You'd think because of all the apologies, to the gays, the Blacks, the women, Polynesians, Africans, etc., this would endear the mass public to the UMC. But of course, like all counterintuitive logic, the exact opposite is true. Even though we accept anybody no matter what they do sexually, masses of LGBTQIA+ are not flocking to the UMC, now that it so open. People are still leaving faster than they are coming, DEI Bishops or not. The UMC is faced with ever dwindling numbers, and dwindling relevance to anybody other than the former people they hurt and have put on the DEI dole.

Reconciliation and restoration are not one-way streets where the 'powers that still be' apologize and monetize the reconciliation process, as though the process were 100% dependent on the UMC Church and its grand high fallutin judiciaries and holy conferencing. The natives are no more a part of the process now than they were when holy conferencing and manifest destiny sent that 'Methodist Pastor/Sharpshooter' to be complicit in the White American occupation of Native Hawaiian Islands. But the natives should not worry. In exchange for everything they lost, they have a hocus pocus apology, presented by Ebony DEI Bishops that prove there is a seat at the table for everybody.

Let us take the example of the biblical ancient Hebrews and conservatives of all ages. When the children of Israel faced a national catastrophe, the immediate response was to declare what God owes you. We assume we are good people, his people; we were made this way, we have been winning and ruling, it is always supposed to be like this, we will always be on top. This attitude only serves to deepen the crisis. As the crisis and chaos deepen, and the losses stack up, it becomes apparent that clearly, the 'God owes us' approach is not working. This precipitates a readiness for the counter argument, which is that the reason we failed and are failing is because of our sin, not because God owes us something. If we stop sinning and do it God's way, God will restore and redeem our fortunes and our feelings. The call and the focus are to double down on our repentance and decision to do it God's way, not what God owes us. Repentance and piety focus on what we owe God, not what God owes us.

The Post-Modern UMC's god, is the god Dorothy found went she went looking for the Wizard of Oz to help her. Only when she got to the Wizard, promises of his power, were reined in by the fact that his displays of power were caused by machine contraptions, smoke and mirrors, and dramatic deep voices, hocus pocus spells and incantations, pronounced over lights, camera, action, CGI, AI General Conferences. It is still going on and I will give further commentary on the events, briefings, and horrifying proceedings.

Chapter 6 - Brokeback Denomination

Chapter 6 - Brokeback Denominationalism

At General Conference 2024 a Women's association celebrated past, present and the future 'United Women in Faith'. The obvious lunacy of this should be self-evident to the reader. If you don't know what a woman is, how can you create groups just for women? If the only way you can explain what a woman is, is to resort to LGBTQIA+ sexual algebra, how can you create a group...just for 'women'? Having done so (in name only), is it still 'for women' if transvestites and former men participate? If the transvestites and former men have an opinion (assuming it is nominally a democratic institution), are their 'opinions' worth the same weight as biological women? I worked as a janitor at a middle school (after seminary graduation mind you). Part of my duties were to clean the 'Boys' and 'Girls' restrooms late at night after the school was closed. I developed an entirely new appreciation for what girls/women go through. When I cleaned the sanitary napkin disposal bins out, the bloody, stringy, clotty mess I saw literally scared me, and put the fear of God in me.

I began to wonder what my thoughts and feelings might be if at 13 years of age, all that came out of me once a month, for up to an entire week accompanied by cramps and abdominal pain! Go ahead UMC, put Ru Paul and Dylan Mulvaney et al in the 'United Methodist Women in Faith'. Oh lawd, I just realized 'United Women in Faith' was a name change from 'United Methodist Women'. More smoke and mirrors, being sold as good ideas, like the Obama administration using the term ISIL as opposed to ISIS for the terrorists in Iraq.

You might also question the 'activities' of gay women in such organizations that are nominally for 'women'. It's better than trans-women (or is it), and that is just from a biological and philosophic perspective. A gay woman is still a biological woman, even if she is attempting to be a transgender man. But of course, unless a gay woman is doing the equivalent of cruising the singles bar, why would she want to be in an organization filled with 'traditional' biological women, who are mothers and wives. Is she trying to 'break up homes', will she inadvertently 'break up' homes.

II

A bear got hit by a car yesterday in Gwinnett County. The media asked how it happened, amongst other questions. The woman said, he (the bear) "came out of nowhere" and that she couldn't figure out how he got there. Really? This bear died but I had an angelic visitation from him, whereupon I interviewed him for this present essay. He said:

"She came out of nowhere with blinding lights, at speed. My ancestor bears, mama them, brothers and sisters, cousins, etc., had been in that area for years. We had a pretty good relationship with Native Americans, with the rise of 'The White man', this gentrification of formerly bear neighborhoods and boroughs just won't stop. The Natives respected us, as evidenced in Native Folklore. There are traditions of maternal instincts being so fierce in bear mothers that they adopt human babies. Bears were also respected clan symbols for the Creek and the Chippewa, Algonquin tribes, Huron and Iroquois all represented themselves by varying symbolism of the bear. We'd laugh as watched their bear dances, and were honored when warrior wore bear claws around his neck or torso, or when the Native Holy men used bear claws in their clan rituals to symbolize power and strength. Yes, those were the good old days. Lately however, the 'Germs, Guns, and Steel' have gotten to be too much."

He closed his remarks with "I think I'm going to join the United Methodist Women in Faith."

III

"Full Communion with Episcopalians gets closer."

I guess if there are other 'brokeback denominations' who serve a God that doesn't know what a man and a woman are, you may as well join them. As in, if you can't beat em, join em. That is indeed how one gets bigger. Here I will insert Nietzsche's other famous dictum, "if you want to get bigger and more popular, add zeroes." Add zeroes to any number. How impotent are the UMC and Anglican Church? In this one case I think Marxian logic is very helpful. Suppose for a moment, religion is the opiate of the masses. That would mean that the Anglicans and UMC are offering a placebo as opposed to God (as opiate). A God that doesn't know what a man and a woman are can hardly be said to produce a real 'opiate' like effect on people. It was like when I was a teenager, every once in a while, in an effort to buy marijuana, we would buy kitchen 'oregano'. As I keep repeating, an omnipotent and omniscient God, real or not philosophically, will have an opioid-like effect and make one able to endure all manner of suffering and pain because of the narcotic like presumption, God knows what is best for me and if I am suffering, it is because 'He' is refining me in the process. Or, 'He' will not put any more on me than I can bear. But a God that doesn't know what a man and woman are, probably doesn't know what you can bear or what is best for you. This god that needs correction, cannot be omnipotent or omniscient, and so the 'power' of his opioid like high, enabling the endurance and tolerance of the 'suffering' humans endure is way less. This might be the reason faith and denominationalism are so weak in America today. Real sufferers/addicts need high power exotic weed, while the UMC, Anglicans, and Presbyterians are selling homegrown. Real sufferers need uncut strong cocaine from South America, while the UMC, Anglicans, and Presbyterians are selling cocaine cut with large amounts of baking soda or even rat poison. Real sufferers drink high power alcohol, 80-120 proof. The UMC, Anglicans et al, sell completely non-alcoholic cocktails (mocktails), where the alcohol content is so low, you must drink a 'whole heap of it' to even get a buzz. Let them that have ears, hear.

IV

I think the question for the UMC General Conference 2024 is to ask itself whether a gathering of hitherto known born biological women, called the 'United Women of Faith' (formerly known as the United Methodist Women) can call itself a 'safe space' for women (sic) with the participation of 5% transvestites and 5% transwomen in varying stages of medical transition? How is that a 'safe space' for women? A young adolescent girl at a YMCA somewhere in the Midwest got traumatized twice. She was in the 'women's dressing room' at her local YMCA and saw a transwoman that had not completed the process of physical transition. Thus, his penis was showing in some regard. Like children, 'from the mouths of babes', she immediately ran to the YMCA management. But instead of getting an award, she got traumatized again by the YMCA staff that lectured her and treated her like she was 'wrong' for feeling uneasy in the presence of a 'ding-a-ling' in the 'Women's Restroom'. They told her that her unease was all in her mind, and she should carry on with her business. The current UMC policy is capable of such horrors, and I ask the question is this a 'safe space' for Women, as our DEI Bishops proclaim? Have they fully integrated the bathrooms at General Conference to such an extent that transvestites and transwomen can waltz into the Women's (sic) bathroom. Is that a safe space for women or a safe space for little girls? As I was thinking on these matters my mind wandered to the technology that now exists, where fake monkeys, fake birds with cameras and sensors on them, can be placed around wild habitats to video record transactions (natural animal behavior) and transmit the video and data on what the actual members of that species do. Interactions between animals and the robotic camera deep fakes, can be observed in species and between species. At best, perhaps this is benign transvestitism and transwomen at a gathering for biological women. They are mere silent, robotic observers, with

$500 worth of makeup on, $500 worth of medical and hormonal surgical technology to look fake, documenting real biological women's lives with camera lens of their eyes and through the colored shades of their minds. Perhaps I will grant that when these robotic deep fakes are silent, the General Conference 'United Women of Faith Prayer Breakfast' may not be unduly disturbed by the presence of transwomen. But if your 4-year-old daughter's response upon seeing a 'woman' formerly known as a man, is to start singing the Aerosmith song 'Dude Looks like a Lady', is that a safe space for women or your daughter? Would you chastise your child or call her a genius for noticing? Would you criticize your child the way we quite often criticize children for being too honest? We all have been children, and we all know children who being presented to adults with any 'abnormality', will immediately ask about it. "Jr, this is Mr. Jones, say hello to Mr. Jones". The child responds, "Hello Mr. Jones why are you so fat", quite precisely because the child has never seen a man that fat. Whether adults admit it or not, many toddlers and children, begin to stare at trans men and women, who don't look quite like the stereotypical men and women. Is there something wrong with that. A child with a dog, certainly knows his dog has a masculine name and the name corresponds to his penis. To call your child wrong for noticing that a transwoman doesn't look 'right'...well...that is why our children have record levels of mental health issues. We keep telling them their eyes are deceiving them, and they should pretend like biological sex and gender, are all in people's heads. Well, if sex is in people's heads, what else simply exists in people's heads? If we legitimize a reality where everybody can walk around believing that what's in their head is 'decisive', that is the definition of chaos, masquerading itself as 'freedom'. If she and her mother go to the women's bathroom at General Conference 2024, and the 'Dude', that 'Looks Like a Lady' is there, is that a safe space for women? Really United Methodist Church?

There are further questions we might ask, now that our DEI Bishops have told us that such situations should be considered normative at public events and conferences. As I said, perhaps I will grant that when these 'plastic, surgically altered, robotic deep fakes are silent, the General Conference 'United Women of Faith' Prayer Breakfast may not be unduly disturbed by the presence of transvestites and transwomen. But the moment they begin interacting, sharing, voting, and even 'leading', it is a violation of the rights of biological women. It is 'mansplaining' writ large, as former men, explain to biological women, what biological women 'need' emotionally, politically, or culturally. Can a transwoman define womanhood? Does a real understanding of something come merely from imitation of it. To revert back to our example from the natural world, the moment a human designed robot animal with a camera begins interacting with the other animals in the habitat, man is manipulating the situation for his own reward even if man thinks he is being good, benign, or beneficent to the animal(s) he thinks he is to some extent fooling by using a deep fake robot animal to surveil with. Surely the more man knows about animals, the more he can protect their habitat, etc. But is that presently the case. Today we know more about the natural world and the universe than we ever knew before, and it rarely to never made animal habitats and ecosystems any better because man has stuck himself into them as its ruler and master.

My favorite example of the complexity of these issues involves a show on one of the Discovery, Science or Nature styled shows. Scientists put a robotic gorilla with cameras in Gorilla habitat to observe gorillas in their habitat and see how they interacted with 'a strange' foreign gorilla. It looked almost like a child's toy gorilla, but it was designed by scientists to be as realistic as possible. It was a plastic-hairy small juvenile sized Gorilla, like a toy, with cameras for eyes and in the neck, sensors to detect touch, and mechanically, at least while the battery was running, it could raise its arms and turn its head in reaction to prodding or contact. When a group of real Gorillas encountered the robot camera and sensor laden fake gorilla, the Silverback immediately went to check it out, presumably to see if it was a threat or not. He neared it, sat down and stared at it, as if to stare it down. Of course it could stare back, but it was an empty stare, its fake eyes either cast in one direction, or going back and forth mechanically, like a panning camera. As the Silverback stared it down, he moved closer and closer, thinking it would probably run. Finally, he sat very near to it, staring as though waiting for it to make an aggressive move. In imitation of Theodore Roosevelt, he grabbed a stick, and sat nearer still. A few minutes later he began prodding and poking the fake gorilla with the stick. It didn't move, except to raise its arms mechanically. He poked and prodded some more, finally hitting the gorilla with the stick and then running away, looking back to see how the fake gorilla would react. The fake gorilla raised its arms mechanically up and down, producing that grinding mechanical sound that accompanies nearly all manmade machine products, robotic and industrial. Immediately the Silverback backed away from it a distance and sat continuing to stare at it. A few subordinate males came over and began poking and hitting the robot with sticks as it sat raising and lowering its arms. One of the subordinate males poked the robot gorilla too hard and it toppled over, unable to right itself. But the cameras were still recording and transmitting. The gorillas were all startled when the robot accidentally toppled over and wondered if it was going to get up and be angry or violent with them. It did not.

They poked it some more on the ground, as juvenile males came over and started throwing rocks at it or hitting it with a stick. Noticing it didn't attack the juveniles, the females and even infant gorillas came over to investigate the robot monkey. The childish adolescent gorillas wanted to play with it and mocked its robotic motions. But the robot gorilla did not play back, other than raising and lowering its arms, now on the ground. All of which was being supervised by the big male. After a while the big male moved on...his lieutenants following, the adolescent males and women following not far behind. The last to leave were the children and juveniles who continued to try to play with the fake robot, until seeing their parents and the troop move off in the distance, finally scrambled hurriedly to catch up; leaving the $10,000 super realistic fake gorilla camera, data storage and transmission center behind. Let them that have ears, hear.

Part II

Another quick interlude about 'safe spaces for women' and whether General Conference 2024 was such a space. For over 20 years I have been thinking about the fact that women on their menstruation in the Old Testament days were seen as impure and unclean, and put outside the camp during that time (of the month) with other similarly indisposed women. Of course, feminists and LGBTQIA alphabet soup types reject this automatically. Theologically and practically, they deem it as not only unfair, but a sign of the patriarchal tyranny of men. They suggest it downgrades, devalues, and dehumanizes women. Beloved brothers and sisters (sic), there are many things to keep in mind here. Before the invention of sanitary napkins of any mass reliability, it was a difficult thing to manage for a girl or woman. During my job as elementary school janitor, existentialist philosopher, and theologian that I am, I wondered how I would feel as a girl, at 12 or 13 years of age, getting a period for the first time. Psychologically I would think I was dying. The only time a child sees that volume of blood is like watching adults slaughter animals for food preparation or on television. Quite often there are physical pains associated with menstruation like cramps and abdominal pains. Menstruation can be accompanied by headaches, soreness, and other generalized aches. And then it happens once a month, regularly like clockwork. It makes it harder to function in regularized 'normal' activities during that time of the month (to use a phrase). To begin to deal with such issues as a 12- or 13-year-old girl seems quite traumatic. Nay, even perhaps as the feminists say, unfair for a patriarchal God to demand such things of a female child. She is bleeding off and on regularly, and I am told from commercial television that there are even 'spurts'. But as horrifying as that was to me, it must be equally horrifying to a 12- or 13-year-old girl experiencing it for the first time. Is being around former biological men in the Women's Bathroom at General Conference 2024, who have never experienced such a thing, a safe space for girls?

I'd rather my daughter be 'outside the camp' with the other menstruating girls and women, her mothers, her grandmothers in a long tradition of feminine energy and power. There she is with the big girls 'outside the camp'. Now my little girl is a woman with the other women, because her body is now demonstrably fertile. The first period is a kind of Holy Bat Mitzvah specifically between a girl and her God. Only God knows the exact timing. The smartest scientists, male and female don't know the exact timing, and can only narrow it down to usually between 12 or 13 years of age. There in the company of other similarly disposed women, she can experience true feminine camaraderie. There she can learn from the older girls and women to normalize the experience, foods to crave (tied of course to nutritional needs like iron), etc., linking the experience with the ancient God given privilege that only a woman has, to open the matrix and birth human children, the crown of God's creation (so far). But our God (the God of the Old Testament) quite often requires sacrificial blood for his privileges.

In Old Testament times He required the blood of lambs, rams, goats, and cows. In New Testament times he required 'the blood', of 'the lamb', Jesus Christ. The privilege granted to man at Sinai in the form of the Torah required blood. The privilege granted to non-Jews to be grafted into the Abrahamic tradition, required the blood of Jesus. And dearly beloved, the privilege given to women to house and birth the human choice fruits of God's creation requires a monthly blood sacrifice, from our sisters, mothers, aunts, daughters, etc. totally without her consent, volition, or will. Thus, no man, I repeat, no man can artificially replicate the experience of having a period. I'm reminded of when Dylan Mulvaney posted pictures of himself in a local drug store, purchasing sanitary napkins because he wanted 'the experience' and to see what it was like. Apparently, he assumed that the worse thing about a 'period', was how people look at a woman in the store when she purchases sanitary products. Dylan Mulvaney and our DEI Bishops think God owes Dylan an apology for making him a male at birth! And yet, even with our sympathetic liberal DEI Bishops promising even more 'inclusion', Dylan has not become a United Methodist! Even after we welcomed him and others like him with open arms, you don't hear Dylan,

Sam Smith, Ru Paul, Billy Porter, Billie Eilish etc., running down to their local United Methodist Church to get some of this newfangled liberal DEI 'religion'. Someone needs to tell our DEI Bishops we should not be in the business of proclaiming and evangelizing the idea of a God that must make apologies for his behavior, and who and what he creates.

Oh yes, and while women were outside the camp they 'gossiped' and talked about what it was like to be married, and to have sex. They talked about what childbirth was like. Girls were not thrown to the wolves or looking on the internet trying to figure out their sexualities and how to express their sexuality on their own. No, they were guided by older girls and women who passed down traditions and sayings from their mothers and aunts. Some of these traditions would have gone back to the most ancient of times, and in those times of womanly seclusion a girl would be exposed to them and her older sisters in a therapeutic way. This is the true heritage of femineity, not dressing up like men and Mad Max Furiosa-like beating up hundreds of 250-pound men built like football players. Is menstruation womanhood, or is Ru Paul's definition of crass womanhood with $500 dollars' worth of makeup, a $1500 dress, a $1000 wig, $30,000 worth of plastic surgery, and the 'Sashay Shante' soundtrack on repeat, womanhood? And of course, is using feminine pronouns and going to the Woman's bathroom at the United Methodist General Conference 2024 a better definition of 'womanhood' than we got in the mammalian and biblical forms?

The socialist-atheist LGBTQIA+ sexual algebra community wants to take all the old-fashioned notions about what a 'woman is', i.e. a period and breasts to breast feed, and tell women that acting like a man, automatically results in the liberation of women. How in the world can imitating someone else be freeing to you? They tell women that they should be ashamed of their periods, disguise it, hide it, doing your best to carry on like a man, like normal, like men appear to do. The socialist-atheist alphabet soup communities, say take testosterone and other male hormones, even going so far as to encourage girl children to cut their breasts off. Why is post-modernity telling our girls these are liabilities and will keep you from living a fulfilled academic and professional life. Thus if you want as fulfilling a life as men (appear to have), you better take testosterone, cut your breasts off and go around seeking some kind of competition with men. Marriage precludes the time required for academic and professional success, abandon them. You don't need a man, not even for children these days. This, socialist atheists tell us means freedom for women. if you don't want your breasts or your penis, cut them off. Beloved I can't emphasize enough the villainy and the treachery the church has fallen into against its own men, women, and children.

Part II

Speaking of presumably 'safe spaces' for women (Clearly not General Conference 2024), let us ask the question can modern and post-modern feminism and womanism create safe spaces for women? Is a space where you feel you must act like and be competitive with men, automatically a safe space for women? Is completely ignoring men unless you are recounting the horrors of patriarchy and male privilege, automatically a safe space for women? Is an environment where abortion is encouraged (not just a perfectly available legal safe medical procedure which I am for), automatically a 'safe space for women'? Is it a safe space for children? Seriously, is a society where abortion is not just free, legal and available, but encouraged as a means of women's liberation and controlling their sexuality, a safe space for children?

Stacy Abrams, whose mother and/or father were Methodist preachers had the nerve to suggest during her campaign for Governor of Georgia, that the ultra-sound heartbeat that parents hear while their child is in the womb, is a scientific 'representation' and not a 'fact' or 'proof' that the child is 'alive'. Really? Yes, it is all in people's minds Stacy. A woman missing her period or it being spotty, after having had unprotected sex the month before, that is all in our minds. After missing the period, the presumed mother and possible father jump in their cars and go to the nearest gas station for a pregnancy test. According to Stacy all that is happening because they are experiencing something that is 'all in their minds'. Yes, some couples excited, and some panicking, were doing so because what they were experiencing was all in their minds. When the pregnancy test came back positive, it was still all in their minds according to Stacy. If you would have gotten a live rabbit, took it to the woman, told her to pee on it, and the rabbit up and died (certain proof of a pregnancy let us say), Stacy still would have said the pregnancy was all in our and the rabbit's mind. Thus, when Stacy showed up on the lectern to debate her rival for Governor of Georgia, she said with a straight face that when the parents go back to the OBGYN to get an ultrasound, the idea that the ultrasound represents the heartbeat of a developing fetus/child is all in everybody's minds. Stacy went to Spelman and Yale Law school mind you. Certainly, a woman as pro-science and pro-mandatory COVID vaccinations and punishments as Stacy, could not disagree that provided she or one of her loved ones had an irregular heartbeat as determined by ultrasound, she would believe it and accept whatever treatments the doctors provide. It can even be determined if a developing fetus has an irregular heartbeat or there is another problem but to Stacy it is all in our minds when it comes to the lives of children/fetuses. This type of liberal craziness is a direct result of the influence of the socialist-atheist-social justice-nihilist-LGBTQIA+ sexual algebra agenda, and its dominance in the academy, the government, and the denominational church in America.

Is an abortion clinic, notwithstanding whether abortion is legal, available etc., a safe space for children (fetuses)? Does delaying childbirth and child rearing until academic, professional and economic success are attained automatically create 'safe spaces' for women and children? Is it not the case that middle and late aged pregnancies (after professional/economic success) create health complications and risks in both the 40-plus year-old mothers and the babies? And yet we are told these are demands of feminism, culminating in the triumph of socialist-atheist LGBTQIA+ algebra social justice values we have today that so dominate the American University system, American politics, and the traditional denominational church. Do these 'high points' and 'high times' of that agenda automatically ensure 'safe spaces' for women and children? Whatever challenges are present in the world for Da Brat and Judy's 'love child', can having two 50-year-old mothers possibly help? I suppose it is better than nothing, to be sure. Are they going to do like Kim Kardashian and hire a 'Manny' (as in nanny) to do male things with the boy like throw the football around or rough house? Those are valid questions, but DEI and Ebony Bishops would never ask them.

Before I delve further into such matters, I'd like to tell you a brief critique of post-modern female superheroes. Lawd, feminists and womanists have given male superheroes a rough time. But I noticed something about female superheroes. All male superheroes have some imperfection, some kryptonite in their lives that completely debilitates them, and/or renders them unfit. Female superheroes, assassins, martial artists are not saddled with such limitation(s). Or so I thought, but upon further reflection, no matter how high the body count, or how many male warriors, zombies, aliens, demons, etc. she has killed, she indeed has a kryptonite! Do you know what a female superhero, supervillain, super spy's kryptonite is? It is over valuing some man and falling in love with him (that is to say willing to sacrifice for his love). Female superhero kryptonite is maternity and taking her place in the patriarchal system as mother, with household duties that hold her back from being her fantastical #Girlpower, #Girlmagic, freest most powerful version of herself. This powerful #Girlpower, #Girlmagic, etc., is her freest and most powerful version of herself (identity), which enables her to go out and compete with and even dominate men 'a la Woman King'. This 'self' thinks it has little or no need for men or domesticity. That is, until years of being a superhero/supervillain have taken their toll on her body and mind, and she wonders what she has missed when she sees her female peers perhaps without significant careers, but with children and men in their lives who love them. But menopause has put all doubts aside on whether true domesticity can be attained. Or she is a 40-year-old heroine, trying to find a man 'worthy' of her to challenge the forces of her biological clock, and possibly be her 'baby daddy'.

In this view of feminist/womanism, males, men and other patriarchal forms are props in women's lives that not only have no intrinsic value, but are simply stumbling blocks trying to hold women back from being their fantastical #girlpower, #girlmagic, freest most powerful version of themselves. For feminists and their LGBTQIA+ sexual algebra counterparts, loving a man (and presumably a man's love), children and household duties are kryptonite to the burgeoning career of any potential female superhero. They are a drain on her 'power'; thus she must refute, refuse, and demean them.

Think about it, in the name of seeing a man cut his penis off, take hormones, and act like a woman with all his heart, with all his mind, and all his soul, they will watch a former man, claim to now be a female start doing women's league MMA and pummel a born female like a rag doll (and call such a boxing ring a safe space for women and equality). Equally absurd is that if the same former man (before he transitioned female) as her boyfriend/husband beat her up, or because she wouldn't respond to his catcall approaches, it would be considered a sex crime, possibly a hate crime under those specific circumstances. But if a former man, transitions female, then joins a female MMA league, he can pummel and beat the brakes off women everyday legally in our current society and the post-General Conference UMC's mind. Former male, now transitioned female athletes, now smoke their born female counterparts in races, and we are told by our DEI Bishops that is a safe space for 'women'. Is a born woman MMA fighter in a fight with a man that transitioned female after puberty a safe space for born woman MMA fighters? Literally. Take every word of that sentence at face value. Look what happened to Muhammad Ali and other football players and athletes that have suffered from CTE. They were absorbing the blows of other men, a born female MMA fighter, fighting a post-puberty transwoman cannot get around the fact that women's bone density is less than men's (for what should be obvious reasons). How in the hell can that be a safe space for female MMA fighters? According to our UMC DEI Bishops it is.

Think how much you must hate a man, men, boys etc., to encourage them to cut their penises off as a means of self-expression or finding their 'true' sexual algebra selves? Can sane people, let alone bishops feel comfortable with themselves, telling a 10-year-old boy that he can express himself, by expressing hatred of himself, in the guise of 'hating' his sexual organ? How have we gotten here ladies and gentlemen? What type of pagan nonsense is this? This is precisely the levels of absurdity society is reduced to in the triumph of socialist-atheist LGBTQIA+ sexual algebra values in government, society and denominational Christian America.

Thus, the kryptonite for any female superhero, female CEO, female tech superstar, astronaut, CIA, KGB, Mossad, China and Iran equivalent, double or triple agent etc., is loving some man and domesticating herself in the patriarchy rather than fully embracing her #butch, #homoerotic, #girlpower, #metoomovement self which demands freedom from men and the patriarchy. To be free of them is to either not need men, or act like you don't need or want men. That has turned into 'Women's Lib'...freedom from men coopted and defined by the freedom to compete with and even be men if they so desire. So instead of submitting to what they think is the patriarchal system, they internalize the same exact values they are running from. If a woman thinks her freedom comes from running with men, competing with men, and dominating men the way men appear to dominate each other, that is not only a contemptible impression of what a man is, but a dangerous one too. If a woman thinks her freedom and success comes from sex transition surgery so that she is better able to imitate men's physical bodies and interact in male social circles without arousing suspicion how is this liberation! How is that a safe space for women and femineity? Is a clone ever liberated from the thing it is cloning? True freedom is in being one's authentic self, not acting like this or that social construct of what masculinity is.

I need not go into a Spenglerian rant in this context about how the decay and collapse of ALL major civilizations (with a grain of salt), necessitated a period of collapse in sexual order, sexual ardor, birthrates, fecundity, and childbirth. The 'collapse' bound society is so successful and so rich, that costly games and amusements become omnipresent and represent fun and freedom. Domesticity and family look like a drag for the 'freest' individuals. As the scale of the collapse bound economy grew, childrearing became more and more expensive with less and less obvious rewards. In the old days, farmers having a lot of children was helpful because at an appropriate age they can help you manage the farm. Also, the ever-growing expense of children in an atomized developed society and culture, burdened individual parents as opposed to extended families the way maternity and paternity in our evolutionary mammalian past was shared amongst extended families and related kin. In addition to economic and familial considerations, there is a growing sense of personal entitlement and personal freedoms, liberties, and entertainments in a thriving post-modern global economic consumer culture for which being saddled with a child, spouse, or multiple children are not congruent with exploring oneself. How can one be one's freest, best self, saddled with children who must be fed, housed, clothed, educated, and protected from hurt, harm or dangers, etc. Children require a lot of time. Maintaining the relationship between your children's father/mother and the extended family requires time, energy and sacrifice. How can one be one's best self with all these 'obligations' demanded in the patriarchal system? How can you run the streets, party and do drugs saddled with such patriarchal value systems? How can you travel the world and make decisions on a month-to-month basis stuck in the patriarchal system. Conservatives might be exaggerating, but they certainly aren't lying when they talk about wild eyed socialist atheist LGBTQIA liberalism as a literal war against civilization. All Civilization is based on the extrapolation of family values to national values. If there is unrest in the family, the unrest will eventually get to the wider economics, politics, and culture, and as Spengler warns, we will see the 'Decline of the West'.

A populace filled with wild eyed nihilist-hedonist youthful and naïve conceptions of freedom and living life like a burger slogan in expecting to always have life 'your way' and 'on your own terms', is civilization killing. Listen to Sinatra's rendition 'I did it my way'. It is not a triumphant song. It is the song of one going down in flames, with his only comfort being that 'he did it his way'. These wild nihilist-hedonist conceptions of freedom and the obligation to be free, begin to replace old obligations to God, family, community, tribe, and nation to reproduce physically (by the easiest and most historically and biologically effective means). And here the UMC goes running headlong into heedlessness with its pants on fire straight to the pits of hell behind DEI Bishops convinced they know the meaning of life, male and female, better than God. The heathen at least have the excuse that they don't believe in God anyway, our DEI Bishops use the same exact lingo and meanings the heathen do, and take the exact same positions, to argue and prove to God and the believers that they know best what a man and a woman are. Note, that not a single DEI Bishop has ever had the nerve to say that like Peter, an Angel came to him or her, in a dream on the rooftop who told them it was ok to consider any meat acceptable. Not a single DEI Bishop ever said, they were in fasting and meditation on the issue, and then they got a strange warm feeling and interpreted that as their support for the LGBTQIA agenda in the church. No, our DEI bishops are incapable of having an authentic religious experience, that is why all the justification they use for why the church needs to 'change' comes from the 'communications' wing of the LGBTQIA socialist-atheist agenda. That is why they use phrases like social-justice, transphobia, homophobia. If God has indeed accepted the LGBTQIA+ agenda after 2000 years, one of you should be creative enough, duly inspired enough, and close enough to this God that you claim you can correct, to have written your own NEW-New Testament. A 3rd Testament, comparable to the first two, where you outline this new outlook and your improvements to the

Christian faith. DEI Bishops ebony or not, can never, and will never do such a thing. They will simply parasitically infest the UMC like they have now infested what was formerly known as the Discipline, and eventually take over its host, their lives dependent like Kudzu/ivy on sucking the life out of healthy trees, weakening them in the process and eventually killing them in the end.

It was written by one far wiser than I that, "baby, your arms are too short to box with God." But here we have these DEI Bishops that consider it sport to box with God. They taunt him and mock him for not knowing what a man and woman are, or lying to the church about it for 2000 years. They dare him to get up off the boxing canvas (cross). Dare I say God played dead for Nietzsche, in his claiming God was dead, until Nietzsche, one of the foremost geniuses of our times died nearly broke, unhappy, friendless, and insane. Nietzsche was wrong. Nietzsche mistook the church and the death of the institution of the European church, for the death of God. The two are not equal or equivalent or the same unless that is, the European church would have stayed attached to the vine. But by gravity, it started pulling from the vine officially around the time of Constantine. By then, what Nietzsche saw and felt was the rotting purification of once ripe fruit, long severed from the vine, limb, stem and roots. It was not the stench of a dead God that Nietzsche smelled and felt compelled to document in his writings, it was the rotting flesh a once ripe European church, now completely detached from the vine, and rotting under the influences of science, materialism, industrialism, etc. i.e. post-modernity. And the American church, unless we repent is just as rotten as to be all but dead.

By claiming at General Conference 2024 the adoption of the LGBTQIA agenda by the church, darn near no questions asked, our DEI Bishops all but said God is dead, because the DEI Bishops must correct him with worldly wisdom, and make him palatable to the politically correct barons of the post-modern world, in order for God to limp on like some lame God and ghost of his former angry, jealous self. UMC don't bank on God being dead. As I stated earlier, he will quite often play dead, so that you go completely reprobate, such that when the punishment comes, you asked for every bit of the business end of the stick and cannot be said to have been treated unfairly.

Parable after parable Jesus gives about absentee landlords (landlords who play all but dead or busy). This absentee landlord has a problem. His tenants, self-appointed leaders, get too big for their britches and run the thing like it is theirs personally, and furthermore they gather unto themselves the fruits of the land and condemn the majority to near poverty and destitution. These rulers/tenants are oppressive in their reign. They manipulate discourse and thought to take advantage of others and make themselves right. Ah, but the true owner of the vineyard, the True and Living God will come back for His and assert the Rights he never gave up, but merely allowed to be usurped by these tenant/rulers (as it were to prove a point). He has watched in astonishment as you have accumulated powers, rights, and privileges, 'loosing and binding' in heaven and on earth, all yourselves like intoxicated drunken ninja masters. Drunk off your own rotting fruit, you are self-satisfied with MDivs, Doctorates in Theology, the books you write, the positions and titles you hold, and the theologies you espouse. So self-satisfied you redact God and the mammalian blueprint of human life itself, because it is not convenient to your world view. Proud of the vanity of your own imaginations, you continue until that moment God figures you have had enough rope to hang yourself. Sufficiently entangled in the things of this world, you hasten your own destruction and that is precisely what the UMC did at General Conference 2024.

Chapter 7 - Marxist Socialist Atheism

Chapter 7 - Marxist Socialist Atheism & The Post-Modern UMC
My heart breaks every morning I get up and see the crapstorm that is General Conference 2024. When will it end? When will it stop? As much as I hate hyperbole and do not want to offend people who have actually been tortured, watching the proceedings for a traditionalist is like getting waterboarded, toenails pulled out, and I am told that when the US military captured enemy Iraqi's and Afghans, they would keep their cells ruthlessly cold and blast heavy metal or rap music in their cells.

I have presented lots of arguments in this book, some I hope have educational value, others spiritual, and others humorous. For theological and philosophic purposes, I need the reader to ponder the question, is it possible to DEI one's way into heaven? Just asking the question, negates it, because being in heaven surrounded by people who got there because of DEI and not merit, defeats the whole purpose of a Christian life and avoiding sin if we presume one is rewarded for good behavior. Some theologians and even the deepest country rural Black traditions believe we wake up in heaven with our glorified bodies, all our physical sicknesses, emotional defects, transformed into perfection. But this is impossible in DEI heaven. In DEI heaven, you only got there because you belong to some marginalized group. If you go to heaven in a wheelchair, you're going to stay in heaven in a wheelchair because that is exactly why you got there in the first place. To be given your glorified and 'fixed' up body, you must leave because not only would you offend others, but once your weakness, handicap or point of marginalization is gone, your 'raison d'etre' for being there is gone.

Thus, in DEI heaven it would be lots of sick, handicapped, and mentally deficient people (by default). It would have to be something like bedlam and a lunatic asylum. If everybody in heaven is doing precisely what they want to do because of being handicapped and/or traumatized in their earthy physical, emotional and intellectual 'bodies', that is to say, the only reason they are in heaven is because of their emotional, physical and intellectual handicaps on earth, they are simply allowed to live with the same emotional, physical and intellectual handicaps in heaven. Why would God, as it were, 'fix' them in heaven, if he affirmed them 'just as they are' in their earthy bodies which were subject to all kinds of emotional, physical, and intellectual deficiencies. Do the liberals and their DEI Bishops even believe this God can 'fix' things? If we've accepted and tolerated every grievous sin and immorality, and then demanded at General Conference 2024 that 'God' simply tolerate it too, do you even believe in heaven, or that a God such as that will 'fix' anything in heaven, let alone on earth? Jesus preached, 'let thy will be done on earth, as it is in heaven,'...what heaven? If there is nothing wrong with all sorts of sins and the like on earth, why presume this liberal God will have fixed it in heaven, or that it would be any different in heaven than on earth? Who knows, it may be be, 'as it is on earth, let it be so in heaven', and in heaven you will find cripples, LGBTQIA pride marches, cheaters, liars, oppressors, worshippers of money, worshippers of all sorts of foreign gods. Seriously, if God doesn't think something is 'wrong' on earth, why would he 'fix' it in heaven.

These theological and ideological fallacies of our current crop of DEI Bishops, and their complete lack of understanding what their corruptions have done to the faith, the church, and spirituality will go down in infamy. As I said, this God they are selling now, cannot possibly have a heaven anybody would want to go to. Who would want to go to heaven, and it is just as miserable, corrupt and chaotic as everything that is going on down here on earth now? That is why evangelism is at an all-time low, and we are not gaining members. We of the UMC, and our current crop of DEI Bishops serve and sell a God who is confused, he doesn't know what a man and a woman are, he has no authority over couples that shack up. Lying and cheating on your taxes or misnaming things at the self-checkout to save .50 cents won't keep you out of the fellowship of the saints, the trustee board, or heaven! And yet what possibly could Jesus have meant when he said who would justify 'gaining the world, but losing your soul' in the process? This kind of God can't help anybody, doesn't want to help anybody and only our DEI Bishops and the socialist-atheist radicalism that has coopted them believe that people would seek out, let alone flock to an impotent God, who can't control his own house and has no idea what a man and a woman are unless He (via his DEI Bishops) resorts to LGBTQIA+ sexual algebra.

Presumably God would not correct somebody's behavior or reprimand them in heaven if he didn't attempt to reprimand them on earth. If the behavior were ok on earth, why would he limit it in heaven. That is, if the Liberal UMC DEI Bishops even believe in heaven. How can you believe in heaven, which you don't see, by believing the biblical testimony of people you don't think had enough sense to know what a man and a woman are? How can you be Wesleyan, but you don't think John Wesley knew what a man and woman are, and you believe that the Denomination he spurred would bring so much misery and pain in the world that instead of preaching the gospel, they go around apologizing for things in the church. The church is racist, patriarchal, went silent on women's abuse, is sexist, oppressed the LGBTQIA, and held back the working classes by not speaking out for economic and social justice. Well dang liberals, did anybody do anything right since Wesley...just Karl Marx huh? Furthermore, why would you want to lead such an organization you believe is responsible for all that misery. Go somewhere and do something that is as perfect as you act like your liberal socialist atheist LGBTQIA friends are.

The church fathers used 'Apologetics' to convince people unfamiliar with Judeo-Christian doctrine that enough of it bears 'similarities' to their tradition that one can 'become' Christian modifying only those elements of their existing faith traditions and institutions that go against fundamental Judeo-Christian doctrine. Now I'm afraid our DEI Black and proud #bodacious, #Blackgirlmagic Bishops just apologize. Like the Church Fathers, these 'apologies' are meant to draw people in and evangelize, but unlike the church fathers, our DEI bishops are evangelizing the church itself as an institution with socialist-atheist LGBTQIA values. Yes, they have been confused by the old seminary joke that 'Apologetics' and 'Apologizing' are not the same thing. But that is the version 2.20 beta version of Methodism they are running right now on degraded hardware and software that has been hacked to death by viruses and malevolent actors/actresses. That is their version of Evangelism, 'Apologize and people might like us'. The exact opposite is true, however.

The power of argument, theology, reason, tradition, mean nothing, we just find new marginalized groups to apologize to and that is the current UMC version of evangelism. You see how that is working (not good). We've let dang near everybody into the church without question on their behaviors and beliefs, only to keep losing members as fewer and fewer people are interested in what the UMC is offering. They'd rather be somewhere being spiritual, doing Yoga and Tai Chi, reading self-help books, reading diet books, and look at You Tube videos all day about how to be healthy and how to live your best life...**anything** but that idiotic drivel our DEI Bishops are selling. Literally, **ANYTHING BUT**.

Anything but the Church and the Bible, that eternal source of answers to all life's questions. DEI Bishops believe John Wesley, Moses, and Jesus either didn't know what a man and woman are, because they didn't know enough science and worldly wisdom, or they were confused, or did everything they did because they love patriarchy, and hate women, gays, and the LGBTQIA+ community. This is the God and Church the post-Modern UMC and its vaunted DEI Ebony Bishops are trying to sell; a God who apologizes to his creation and needs their help to stay 'hip' and 'relevant'. Insanity! The ever living one, needs the help temporal beings to stay relevant? Absolute insanity parading itself around as liberal theology, and to be honest there is a point at which it is sheer unmitigated blasphemy.

The question of whether God owes everybody or anybody an apology is something only a hyper philosophical, entitled, vain, arrogant, western oriented mind could dream up. I've met poor people and people from developing countries, and as rough as their lives are I have never heard them frame things like God owes them, because of their trials. Quite the opposite, the most religious of them are thankful for what little they have. But we don't teach that in post-modern America. The new UMC and its DEI Bishops want social and economic justice for you because God and man have treated you unfairly, and God's going to apologize to you via the UMC, and man is going to pay reparations because the new social justice UMC has adopted socialist-atheist sexualized Marxist redistribution schemes.

The current UMC views itself as though it were a redistribution machine from the 'haves' (men, Whites, etc.) to the 'have nots' (women, Black and brown). That ain't God, and certainly does not befit his church. As a matter of fact, it is diametrically opposed to what the church has taught regarding who needs to apologize! Repent! Repent! Repent! The Kingdom of God is at hand! The message of the church is that YOU need to apologize to God and live according to the basics of his word as best you can; praying for the Holy Spirit, knowledge and wisdom, and the communion and fellowship of the saints to do so. That is what the UMC used to teach, now we teach a God that will apologize to you for making you a girl/boy/black/white/poor/ugly/cute/ etc. In Jewish theology this repentance is called Teshuvah. One who repents is a Baali Teshuvah. In Islam the concept is called Tawba. Both concepts mean to turn, retreat, or repent from past sinful and/or evil behaviors and activities and to resolve to firmly do one's best to abstain from them in the future. Of course, this is easier said than done, but what we don't do is give up and say if you like whatever you like, that's just the way God made you.

Nearly all faith traditions are grounded in the idea that apologizing to God FIRST, with no assumption at all that he needs to apologize to you for something is the important thing. Our current DEI Bishops preach a God and agents of the church apologizing to you FIRST. Total submission lies at the root of this return by repentance. The prayer and hope is that God will not only strengthen you to (as it were) 'flee from sin' but that for doing so, God will reward you with greater consolations than your former sins could give. But one must attempt those things by faith.

That is what nearly all sane religions teach even if the religion itself is irrational and crazy. Even in the craziest religious system and construct, one must be obedient to some rules. That is the definition of a religion or religious exercise. But not for the post-modern UMC. We are now distinguishing ourselves by having as few rules as possible. Post-modern western Christianity has decided to retroactively forgive everybody's sin, even their own. As a matter of fact, most authentic conversions and religious experiences are rooted in and motivated by a profound regret for past sinful behaviors, or even thankfulness for one's troubles (because they drove one to seek God), as opposed to looking for God to apologize to you. Being thankful and teaching thankfulness, here again so important to authentic religious experiences and conversion, is the opposite of running around accusing God of owing you something because 'God' marginalized you or made you feel marginalized.

We don't teach that. Lawd if I hear another pseudo-Negro intellectual/theologian running around talking about intersectionality I'm gong to puke. I don't even know what it is and haven't bothered to look it up. It reminds me of a traffic intersection. Many accidents happen at intersections. Personally, I don't use the word because I dislike the flippant arrogancy and prideful disdain of self-satisfied social justice warrior/lawyer intellectuals that go around using the word. It is like my feelings on Michael Eric Dyson. Whether I agree with him or not I can't listen to him because of his pomposity and ridiculous self-satisfaction with his own vocabulary and artfulness.

All liberal DEI and Ebony Bishops are like this. They are long on sophistry and stringing together phrases that sound like they are saints. But under the soft velvet globe of sophistry, their fists are as hard as steel. One need only note the campus protests. Tearing up the school, that is to say 'occupying the school' is no more effective than mass demonstrations, but wild-eyed liberals will do it anyway because in their eyes the reactionaries (academic institution, laws, monied interests etc.) are hating on them and denying them their rights to presumably occupy and tear up the school buildings of their choice. Asking them to protest peacefully and stop threating the lives and safety of Jewish students and administrators is wrong, it is hating on them. Presumably this is because they come from or are representing a marginalized group. And in their marginalized little minds, in echoing socialist-atheist slogans and Marxist ideology, there is an implicit belief that the ends justify the means. So if they barricade themselves in classrooms, and knock the windows out to hang Palestinian flags, the ends justify the means.

For those of you interested in history, read the reflections and/or the memoirs of the old socialists like Lenin, Trotsky, Castro, and Guevara. They all thought the 'end justified the means' and they all had absolutely no idea, what they would replace the traditional bourgeois-aristocratic politics, religion, culture and family with. They knew they hated 'traditional bourgeois society', but they had nothing to replace it with and ended up imitating it (poorly), by default of having nothing sane to put in its place. This is the same exact way our wild-eyed socialist atheist LGBTQIA radicals love condemning patriarchy and bourgeois values, but they have nothing sane to replace them with. Unless you mean, idiocy like living in a culture where it is offensive to say to a co-worker 'I'm praying for you' because of an illness in the family, but quite ok to say to a grown man or woman, 'positive vibes to you, you're in my thoughts'. "I'm praying for you" is offensive, but "positive vibes to you," isn't. That I now know saying 'positive healing vibes to you' to a sick person is better and less offensive than saying 'I'm praying for you', that is when I knew my society had gone off the rocker. How is saying 'positive healing vibes' to somebody ill more rational and reasonable than saying 'God bless you, I'm praying for you'?

Of course the institutions radicals like Castro, Mao, Kim Il Sung, Trotsky, and Lenin set up failed because replacing all that bourgeois machinery that evolved over countless millennia of human social and political evolution was harder than they thought it would be. Unfortunately for the societies confronted by extreme radicalism, revolution in itself, is seen as the answer, but after the 'revolution', things are worse. Religious power and the power of religious texts in society is marginalized and minimized by leftist radicals as they seek to revolutionize society by undermining traditional values and standards. For instance, to Mao, the Chinese don't need Bibles, Qurans, or even ancient Chinese wisdom and philosophy, all the Chinese need is Mao's 'Little Red Book'. That will tell them all they need to know about how to look at the entirety of life. What a poor replacement indeed for thousands of years of religious texts! Marx's Das Kapital, Hitler's Mein Kampf, Mao's Little Red Book, all are virtually unreadable, and certainly unreadable by anyone that takes pleasure in reading. Not even the subject matter or their economic or social analysis lasted. That is how bad their books are purely as reading material. Similar books by Castro, Chavez, and many Third World radicals have not stood the test of time well.

Let us take Cuba for instance. To Castro, the people of Cuba didn't need Bibles, Priests, parishes, protestant evangelists, or Tai Chi and Yoga, all they needed is his books and huge outdoor events where they could hear a 'sermon' by Castro for 3 hours straight about the glorious Revolution. That is the same 'glorious revolution' that 50 years later would leave Cuba virtually bankrupt, and islanders desperate to get off their island paradise, because even an island paradise can be ruined by socialist atheism. The New post-modern left has replaced traditional gender pronouns. They have replaced God the father with whatever construct one deems less offensive. This is the world the socialist-atheist

LGBTQIA radicals and their DEI dummy Bishops in the UMC want to create. Nietzsche's 'Transvaluation of all values' in full effect. They want to replace the bourgeois traditional family with any old family construct. They said it would be helpful, but marriage and birth rates are plummeting among many communities. They said 'The Church' could be replaced and maybe needs to be replaced by a more general 'spirituality' but the sense of community cannot be duplicated by Yoga classes, book clubs, and You Tube preachers, philosophers and life coaches. All this is serving only to make people more and more unhappy as in the absence of true religion, we are making it up as we go along. Chaos masquerading as freedom, is not freedom at all. That is why we are more anxious, there is more unhappiness, more legal and illegal drug use, than ever. Again, I think 70% of the world legal and illegal drugs are consumed in America.

What we are realizing in America is that while bourgeois traditional Judeo-Christian values are not perfect, they cannot be easily replaced. That doesn't stop radicals from trying to undermine them, and doesn't stop the 'young and dumb' from being revolutionized by outside forces to willfully seek their replacement. Nothing replaces the stability derived from bourgeois values, the class system and religion. In their degradation and absence, chaos steps in and that is exactly what urban Black communities are experiencing all over America. The chaos of family instability, the chaos of violence and unpredictability, and the chaos of leadership with no clearly defined values other than complaining, protesting, and chanting burn it down...even though if you burn Walmart, Kroger, and CVS down women and children won't get anything to eat or their medicine. But for the nihilistic socialist-atheist liberals and campus protestors, and the UMC DEI Bishops that support and justify them, the end always justifies the means, no matter how stupid and self-defeating it is. This infestation and 'intersection' of socialist-atheist LGBTQIA 'ends justifies the means' nihilism, is how you get to a UMC and society that legitimizes the cutting off penises and breasts in the name of 'Sexual Freedom'.

I'm afraid America won the Cold War, only to 50 years later be dominated by Marxist values on our university campuses, Tik-Tok and other social media. Our American Post-Modern Empire, our Pax Romana has opened us up to socio-political-theological weapons more dangerous than nuclear weapons. Jesus counseled us to not 'fear that which kills the body, but to fear that which kills the soul'. American culture from movies to the internet is killing American souls every day, and if the church doesn't stand up against the forces of chaos in America, we will be in for domestic and foreign terrors, troubles, and trials even worse than those we are experiencing today.

8

Chapter 8 - Why I have Hope

Chapter 8 - Why I have Hope
It is not in fashion to use he/her pronouns. And yet his/her mentality is central to New Testament theology and the way the church understands itself. The Church is the mystical Bride of Christ and the Body of Christ at the same time. Twain have become one, united in a kind of theological marital/sexualized union (fruit producing), united in a kind of theological construct dependent upon the basic implications of the male/female duality. Mystical or not, it is impossible to have bride without a woman and it is impossible to have a groom without a man (at least for the sake of producing fruit). The metaphor doesn't work without men and women. The concept of the union (mystical or not) bearing fruit doesn't work without a man and a woman.

Spirit/flesh, male/female, become one. That is what it takes to make a baby the old-fashioned way that according to scientists, has been working for the past million or so years of mammalian evolution, and perhaps 500,000 years of human evolution from apes. There is a very important truism that says, 'if it ain't broke don't fix it'. This 'Brokeback Theology' that UMC DEI Bishops and Bishop's Councils practice is a clear case of them trying to fix things that aren't broken. If suddenly sex between men and women stopped working to produce babies, then we could presume to 'fix it'. But last time I checked, albeit infrequently, the old-fashioned way still works great, for poor people, rich people, Asians, Africans, Arabs, etc. So what in hell are we trying to fix it for. Really, this 'Brokeback Theology' presumes to correct God's errors and mistakes. And we pay these people $250,000 per year to correct God? The church is the bride, the future mother. The body which will be fruitful with good seed, sown by the Father/Son/husband masculine principle. Dear beloved brothers and sisters, we in the church in 2024 are the fruit of that union. Prayerfully there will be fruit in a functioning church in 3024. We (the Body of Christ/Corpus Christi) are in theological terms, the fruit of that union.

When children become criminals and go bad, I've noticed a very interesting phenomenon. Whoever the dad was, or if he ever was, he will not be there as his children suffer and are prosecuted by the law. The more hideous the crime, the less likely it is that the father will show up to court on behalf of his child. Of course, even if he wasn't present in his child's early life, but his child had Lebron James athletic ability, he'd figure out a way to show up after the fact and try to get some share of the spoils of his child's talent. But in a crime situation, you hardly ever see the fathers. But his mother will be in court every day. Her son/daughter did something hideous, but she will be there every day. The opposing side, the families upon which the crime was committed will sneer at that mother, insult her, threaten her, and even physically assault her because of what her child did. But she will be there every day...no man or father in sight on behalf of her child who did something hideous, and the law was forced to extract its punishment.

And tragedy notwithstanding, when the mother, the only person in the entire world that testifies on her son's behalf testifies, she will inevitably say at some point these words:

"He wasn't like this when he was younger. He was a shy sensitive child, and then he started running with the wrong crowd and got deeper and deeper, now he is accused of...."

The greatest philosophers, politicians, theologians, poets, and statesmen will never do an act so noble or tell a truth so absolute as a mother's lament over her child become criminal. Beloved, let us look in the mirror as children of the Church universal and children of Wesley. Have we children gone bad? Did we run with the wrong crowd and become destructive to ourselves and others? As children, do we preach what our parents preached 2000 years ago? Or are we now doing our own thing with our new friends? Are our priorities the priorities of the early church, perhaps the first 200 years or so, with the cap being the institutional developments during and after Constantine? What would the early church fathers and mothers, and perhaps Jesus himself say about us as mystical supernal great grandchildren? Is it that farfetched to think Wesley would look at General Conference 2024 and say "we didn't raise them like this, they liked church and said their prayers every night. But somewhere (a little leaven, leavens the whole loaf), along the way the wrong people got hold to them. They went sideways and I couldn't get my grandbabies back before they had run out and done these hideous crimes?"

Many of these women testifying about wayward children also freely admit in court that they needed help with the child. In key moments of the child's life and the values she was trying to give him, she needed help (external reinforcement/father etc.). But without the support and external reinforcement of the father, the child just spiraled even further downward, faster. All the current watchwords of liberalism failed her. Along the way she told the school counselors he needed counseling (secular therapy). Either it didn't help or was unaffordable. Along the way she told the police (government) that her child needed help and counseling, but of course juvenile rarely improves the qualities of its inhabitants. Along the way she told the preacher she needed help. But the church doesn't have a playground or youth ministry even though the preacher makes $120,000 a year. Is it really concerned about its own children, let alone the communities?

Oh, wayward UMC, there is our mother in court testifying that we weren't like this when we were younger. At one time we were on the right path, but now we children are criminals, corrupted by the streets and the world. Finally, the law has caught up with us children. Our DEI Bishops were wrong! Jesus never said he came to **abolish** the law, that is to say, ignore the evils Torah Law called evils. Jesus said he was the fulfillment of the law. That is an altogether different proposition than our DEI Bishops supposed as they go around un-calling sins, sins. With the stroke of a UMC Bishop's miter and pen, 2000 years of church tradition on sexuality is gone. Unfortunately, the law is catching up with us however. That is why our Denomination (Demonination) is broke, busted, disgusted, splitting and suffering drastic reductions in influence, membership, money, and power in American and global culture. Some kind of way we started running with the socialists, atheists, and libertines, and we adopted their lifestyle, their ethos, and their intellectual constructs, to the point that we are so unrecognizable to our grandparents (the church 2000 years ago) that we are criminal, and they must testify on our behalf strictly for DNA's sake, not because we actually bear resemblance to them.

No, listen to our mother in tears testifying on our behalf that there was a time we weren't like this. This very child (the post-modern UMC that you see today) that has committed serous crimes and sins, worth everything the law and the court is sentencing him with, used to love school, family, prayed every night, loved Sunday school. But he got to running around with the wrong crowd of nihilistic socialists and atheists, and now he is a criminal just like them. Don't take my word for it that they (nihilist socialist-atheists) are criminals, or think I am being mean. They will happily tell you themselves. Rappers are happy to pronounce that they are pimps, thugs, hustlers, strip club fanatics, and doped up nearly all the time. The LGBTQIA community is proud to go to schools, churches et al, and tell people about their rights to be themselves and to be free to the point of hacking your body to pieces and taking enough hormones to kill a small horse. They happily tell you this. Li'l Nas X releases videos with himself giving male devils and demons lap dances. Li'l Nas X could only be mocking Jesus when he filmed one of his videos of himself, a la Jesus up on the cross. Female rappers are happy to call themselves 'bad female dogs', 'boss female dogs'. Sam Smith is happy to go on the Grammys and do a Satanic ritual complete with devils, demons, flames, etc., mocking 2000 years of religion and theological constructs like it is a big joke. This is who the post-modern church started hanging out with, and acting like after it started running with the post-modern 'cool kids', instead of remembering the teachings of Mom (the mother church) and Dad (father). The UMC General Conference 2024 is what we get for all our running around with criminals and mockers of the Faith. Our DEI Bishops think it is hip to run with the 'cool kids'. They think they are with it. My Bishop in the N. GA Conference drives a Harley, I suppose to prove that she is a 'boss female dog' without having to say it. Perhaps the only way to know something is demonic, is the very fact that it is acting demonic, and says it is demonic. Saints of God if it looks like a duck and quacks like a duck...and says it is a duck, it is a duck.

And yet our 'grandma and them' want the court and the jury to see us as we were, not as the dreadlocked boy sitting angrily in front of them with tattoos all over his body and face, looking dangerous like some kind of wild demonic clown. Naw, 'grandma them' want the judge and jury to see him as the shy vulnerable boy he once was, before all that. Before he learned the lingo of the streets, and the complicated handshakes of the gang that take 20 seconds to do completely; and a lifetime in the gang to master the nuances of.

Brothers and sisters (sic), our mothers have been worried about us for a long time. They have had many sleepless nights as we have hung out with the wrong crowd, and allowed our thoughts, values, and ethics to be influenced by our 'new' friends from the streets. There 'grandma them were', wondering where we are and what we are doing, but knowing that whatever we are doing, it's with the wrong people; and late at night is the wrong time, and the only places open late at night are the wrong places. Grandma knows the consequences of being in the wrong places at the wrong times and how easily that leads to negative behaviors and activities you didn't want to happen. Like Jephthah in the land of Tob, running with vain and mean persons; pimps, thugs, hustlers, and gangsters, her child (potentially a great hero) becomes something else. But like the elders in the Book of Judges went to the land of Tob themselves, and recalled Jephthah and his merry band of hustlers, pimps, and thugs, it is time for the Church to reclaim its children!

I can imagine our grandmothers, the early church (first 200 years) testifying in court on our behalf. "Please don't go by what he appears to be now, what you see today. That is why I have hope for the UMC, the Black UMC and Black Methodism in general. The merits of our worried mothers is far greater than ours, even with our DEI Bishops, their miters, their PHDs and their newfangled friends.

Part II

Furthermore, I have hope based on other purely maternal instincts dormant in our Mother Church because her children have ignored her. Yes, that's right. A curious thing happened to me at the U-Haul rental place. When I returned the van, I was owed a refund because I used less time and mileage than the initial request. The young lady checking me out was very professional, courteous, and nice. Sensing my mother wasn't 'all there' (she has Alzheimer's), she said in an engaging cheerful friendly voice like we had won the lotto, "oh, wow you all have a refund of $50 coming, isn't that great?" And my mom, who I'm not sure could presently answer what planet she is on, said in all seriousness looking back and forth at me and the lady, "that sounds good, but could you recheck it because it seems like it should be more." My mama, without having the foggiest idea of the transaction, automatically acted like that's my baby, and you probably owe him more. I laughed uproariously and thought wow, there are some things at root in a mother that even Alzheimer's can't take away.

Ladies and gentlemen (sic), that is how powerful a mother's instinct is to protect and defend what she produces, and what she perceives as her child's interests. That is why I have hope today beloved believers. The supernal mother, the Bride of Christ, the Church, is jealous over her brood, just like her man but in a different way. And she will not suffer us to be lost if she can help, and/or isn't completely dead. No matter how powerful and strong the arms of the law, the world, commercialism, nihilism, Marxism, materialism, LGBTQIA+ sexual algebra, and vanity are she will not abandon her brood.

I have spoken much about the Bride of Christ, our mother. The supernal mother church. She will defend her own. Which of course gets us to the point why we are there in court, in jail, stultifying and suffering with only our mothers to support us. Where is our father? Why didn't he come and tell the same story to the court about how I wasn't like this always, and once I was a good kid?

Proverbs 10:1 A wise son makes a father glad, but a foolish son is a sorrow to his mother.

The first answer is, what do we say stereotypically as a culture, even liberals, when a child is going astray. We say he needs more discipline (not less), and more structure (family/education/religion), not less. Thus if you are a wayward child, or going wrong as an adolescent or adult, the first thing you need more of is discipline and structure. In the secular world and liberal worlds, they will happily admit that sports, regular music training, art training, martial arts, etc., provide discipline and structure in a child's life. But somehow the post-modern UMC thinks it's in its best interest to abandon its...wait for it...Discipline! Dang its structure, we nihilistically have something to prove and we will hack up the whole church in the interest of imposing our socialist-atheist LGBTQIA+ sexual alphabet soup agenda. Nearly every remedial act in the secular and sacred worlds requires discipline, but our DEI Bishops have concluded that abandoning ours (Discipline), in a haze of socialist-atheist LGBTQIA+ alphabet soup logic is better than the whole 2000-year-old history of the church that came before it. Believers that is insane, and nothing good can ever come from it.

Discipline, structure, and evangelizing and church building the old-fashioned way, family by family, community by community, not gimmicks and 24-page apologies to anybody in the entirety of existence that has ever felt marginalized. That is the business of the church, not coming up with social justice mumbo jumbo that makes some weird argument that the new 'woke' church respects all people's intersectionality.

You don't need people to figure out your learning style, or understand your uniqueness, you need disciplined study and structure. If you weigh 600 pounds you need discipline and structure in your diet and exercise. If you can't carry a note in a bucket, you need discipline and structure in your singing practice, not DEI bands and orchestras that will let you in because you are underrepresented, underserved, and/or marginalized. With discipline and structure, you can overcome all that without DEI, without reparations, and without fake 'Old Testament donkey' apologies that are 24 pages long for sins it is nearly impossible for the church to have possibly contributed to. But this is the God you serve that runs around apologizing for what he has done....an impotent, weak, confused, flagellating, flaccid God that is so bewildered by existence, He must be told by the very clay creatures He created, what a man and woman 'really' are.

Your mother in court testifying on your behalf about your horrible crimes, has excuses and valid rationalizations for your criminality. Your father, on the other hand, thinks you needed more discipline and structure. Furthermore, your father thinks either you'll learn the value of discipline and order the hard way, or it will kill you. Either way, he is done, and that is a choice you must make. Your mother will be there to the end, supporting you, watching you on the stand, on the cross and cry, bewailing the tragedy but the father will not. The choice is yours and the truth of the matter is that even if your father did intervene in your life to 'save' you out of love, you'd resent him for it and accuse him of purposely trying to control you and take control of your life. You will accuse him of not respecting your free will, your decisions, even though presently you are in a jail cell crying every day. But were he to get you out, you would resent him. As a matter of fact when you get out and get back to your old friends and ways, you will resent your mother and your father, and treat them like them saving you **again**, is just them colluding in some kind of sinister plan to rob you (the child) of your freedom of will, and your freedom to be and do what you want to do.

As hard and as cruel as that may sound of fathers, fathers walk away. Fathers run away. Father's get lost. Father 'figures' get found, but a father who adores his Bride, is angered by children that disrespect mothers. Back when we had fathers, there were men that scolded their, and any other male and female children by telling them things like 'don't talk to your mother that way'! Presumably you're darn sure not going to talk to your (The) father like that. But with all these absentee fathers, in absentee former patriarchies, now dominated by women, there is no one to say to unruly, disobedient, disrespectful kids, don't talk to your mother like that! That's why our children go around in public and on the internet thinking they can talk to anybody; in whatever way they want. Thinking your parents owe you something, and when they 'disappoint you', by quite precisely not letting or seeming to not let you do whatever in God's name you want to do, you resent the parents and talk to them any old kind of way. These children are so arrogant and coddled, that when the parents disappoint them, they rear up and react in anger and resentment at the parents. They demand their father and mother apologize to them for disappointing them. These entitled arrogant kids demand an apology from their parents because they were not as great as parents as they coulda/shoulda/woulda been in a perfect world, and thus condemning them to therapy and antidepressants for the rest of their lives. Or these ruthlessly ridiculous children demand an apology from their parents for not letting (or seeming to not let) them do precisely what they want to do (without criticism). That is also the whole notion behind most psychotherapy and generalized therapy. So called therapists with PHDs and Degrees in psychology try to unravel the influences of imperfect parents...because of course, every human child deserves perfect parents who invariably buy them anything they want and let them do anything they want. To a child, those are perfect parents. That a parent doesn't perform to that standard, now the psychologist/therapist must apologize on behalf of the parents about their imperfections, and let the child vent about their parent's imperfections, substituting the therapist for the parent. This is called therapy in post-modernity, and we live in a society of school systems, and government institutions that thinks everybody either needs or can use some (therapy). How is that? Was everybody crazy pre-Freud?

For years my mother hated paternity court and such fare. Now that she has Alzheimer's, I find paternity court, The Cutlers, Judge Judy, and Judge Mathis can sustain most afternoons in pure entertainment for a few hours. This got me to wondering what if there were some kind of heavenly supernal paternity court, and Jesus is looking at the church, the Torah, prophets and writings, the New Testament, The Discipline (pre-2024) and us (the modern UMC), and thinking these are not my children! This woman, my so-called bride, has been lusting after other dudes (gods), your honor (the Father). I don't know what she be doing. She disappears all times of the night and day, and sometimes doesn't come back for days. What's worse, she had other dudes (gods) raising my child acting like they were the Father. She was going to get remarried and give my children their stepdaddy last name. Of course, he was not as stupid as he looked or acted and didn't marry her, wouldn't marry her, and would never treat her better because he really doesn't want her, he wants to get at me. He darn sure doesn't want to waste his time taking care of other people's children; as I said he's not that stupid. Here Jesus is in Paternity Court looking at all these bad 'Old Testament donkey' grandkids (us), and thinking 'they don't even look like me'.

"When I married her your honor, honestly I was lonely. I had done got the brakes beat off me, she was there and aided ministry, tended and nurtured my wounds, and went through my trials and tribulations with me. That brought us together as one. Now I don't know. I'm questioning all these kids and I need a DNA test."

The reader may be wondering what the supernal DNA test is. What is your DNA, the Supernal DNA? The very word of God. To study it, read it, be concerned with its interpretation and implementation, theory and praxis, and to have that blueprint, imprinted upon one's existential life and to judge all matters regarding that existential life by the standards the Bible sets, to as great an extent as possible. You must (as it were), sequence the DNA of the Word in your life. That is how the Christian checks his DNA. Does that Christian have a lot of socialist-atheist LGBTQIA, materialist, nihilistic, willful pride, and arrogance splices of DNA in their theology and praxis? Our DEI Bishops might like God, and want him to be their 'Father', but you bear no resemblance to the biblical DNA sequenced in the 'word of God'; which is how we 'know' The Father. Once corrupted, a significant portion of their lives will be directed towards fulfilling that DNA mandate from the ingrafting of socialist-atheism. This is where Jesus gets the notion, 'you will know them by their fruit'. Bad DNA sequences produce bad fruit, fruit like division, discord, denominational splits, tumorous or cancerous growths etc.? Let them that have ears, hear.

The standard of the word of God, the 'sequenced' DNA outlined in the word of God tells you if you belong to Him or not. Let us get further testimony from Jesus at Supernal Paternity court. 'Your honor, I have conclusive evidence and proof that multiple times throughout our relationship, my bride, the church, has played the harlot and prostituted herself. Constantine and the Papacy (not the theoretical/theological idea) but what it became in the geo-political world of militarism, pomp, riches and circumstance. Like the ancient Hebrews during the time of the Judges and Samuel, God was not good enough for her and she wanted an army and king, land and dominions, machine technics (Spengler), like all the other nations of the world. And of course, prelates and wannabe church officials and ecclesiastics gorged themselves on the riches and privileges that accumulated, and presided over 'The Church' like their own private fiefdoms. Oh, UMC dearly beloved.

That wasn't the last time she sold herself for money either. Prosperity preaching and huge churches leverage millions of dollars in revenue, so here again prelates and ecclesiastics can circulate among the bigger more prosperous churches, passing them off amongst themselves and their friends with no regard for the needs of the local church. If the budget can't support the Bishops, let the bishops pay their own way! But they know that is futile because they are DEI Bishops that cannot preach and evangelize and thus pay their own way. So they'd rather cast lots for the positions as Bishops knowing that some will be eliminated. This happened at General Conference 2024. The Nakba. The Holocaust. The Pogrom. The church getting sold into slavery like West African Slaves during the European slave trade. I'm not comparing suffering; I'm highlighting particular types of tragedies. Perhaps General Conference 2024 might be better compared to Neville Chamberlain, Foreign Minister of Brittain coming back from negotiations with Hitler in 1939-1940 suggesting that he had 'secured peace in our time'. Yes. That is quite a more apt metaphor for General Conference 2024. They made a deal, thinking it would buy them more time to profit off the luxuries and stability of the old world, by capitulating to the new socialist-atheist nihilist notions that formed the critique against the old world. The DEI Bishops think they bought time for the old world, whether it survives and thrives or just survives; crippled. This is an illusion. It is not 'peace in our times' these DEI Bishops secured, nay, all they secured is the promise of a future war, a kind of 'total war'. The crisis in American families, the crisis in American cities, the crisis in American conservative vs liberal politics, the coming existential crisis in American geo-politics and the foundations of our political institutions, are all related. They all spring from one degenerative fact. The absence of true religion and piety in any civilization, is the definition of chaos and division. There are no stable belief systems or ideologies without stable religion. There are no stable families, communities, economies, without religion underlying them providing a basic bedrock of values. Capitalism is dependent not only upon the rule of law, but upon that 'good old protestant work ethic', saving and frugality. When you undermine the bedrock, whatever you have built on top of it will fall. This is precisely what Jesus meant when he referred to 'building your house on his words and teachings', that is to say a rock, as opposed to building it on sand, that can be easily washed away by the ebbs and flows of time, tides and new fads and fashions.

But let us continue with Jesus' testimony about his wayward bride/wife for the past 2000 years. "Next thing I know she is running with strange gods, yoga symbols, and rainbow flags tattooed all over her. The rainbow symbolized God's love and promise, not man's love, or feeble fleshly and materialistic sense of it. Strange gods who with strange fires and incantations attest to the power of God, without the anointing of God or proper respect for God. Remember what happened to Aaron's sons Nadab and Abihu. In Leviticus (such a rough book), they assume and presume some liberties they can take with God's instructions for His service, and offer 'strange fire' to God. God's response is to burn them up. Furthermore, in the immediate aftermath of this incident, the Torah records the commandment that Priests can't serve intoxicated. Some Jewish scholars believe the two incidences are related somehow, if not explicitly. Also instructive is what happened to Eli's sons Phinneas and Hophni. Quoted from Wikipedia, in the biblical narrative, Hophni and Phineas are criticized for engaging in illicit behavior, such as appropriating the best portion of sacrifices for themselves, and having sexual relations with unlawful women. They died a gruesome death in recompense, all for offering a 'strange fire' upon the altar of the Lord and using the Priesthood for one's own lusts and privileges. I do not wish bad on anybody. God is indeed a forgiving God, but the judgement must be made, and I told the Lord that portions of this book would be whooping 'Old Testament donkey' like my name was dad'. That is to say, Dad reserves the right, the right of final Judgement. Judgement day. It is coming saints. I didn't make it up. It is not made up and must be corrected like our DEI bishops think biblical sexual standards were made up and need to be corrected. This Torah prohibition against serving drunk or intoxicated would be well learned by todays DEI Bishops. I already told the reader about the rotting fruit that is the current UMC. It is rotting because it is detached from the vine, its life force, and it is intoxicating because it is putrefying and fermenting. All of our DEI Bishops and the new socialist-atheist pro-LGBTQIA UMC is drunk! They are drunk off the rotting proceeds (fruits) of the noble predecessors in

2000 years of faith including John Wesley, who we must now assume with all his religious and spiritual knowledge, did not know what a man and a woman are and needs DEI Bishops and LGBTQIA+ sexual algebra to wake him up and tell him. They are drunk. They are drunk off power, position, professional theological academic titles, and the vanities of their own imaginations. These 'vain imaginations' suggest to them that they can go around apologizing for God and forgiving sin like some kind of DEI Black Ebony Bishop fairy Godmothers. Whooping 'Old Testament donkey like my name was dad'!

But let Jesus continue his testimony and DNA test, and get the results. If all she did was sell her body for money, like Uncle Hosea (Auntie Gomer), I could forgive her for that and take her back, loving her wholly and raising whoever's kids these really are from these fly by night dudes that inevitably leave her in the lurch, no matter how much she proclaims her love for them or is willing to sacrifice for them. She had 'broke' lovers that couldn't reward her. She cavorted and consorted with, and had dalliances with them all, during the past 2000 years of our marriage.

Any old two-bit philosopher, philosophy, thug, pimp, hustler, and there she was running behind it apologizing and worshipping it. Gnosticism, antinomianism, Apollinarianism, the inquisition, religious wars, and now Marxist socialist atheism and the LGBTQIA, there she is running behind them, broke and bankrupt as they are, legs spread wide to please her new masters. That's why I'm here your honor (The Father). I am done. I'm not feeding or raising nobody else children. I ain't disciplining, nor providing structure for other folk children, when all they do is resent me for it, even though it is the best thing that could happen in their lives. These children, my stepchildren resent me, and are angry at me. I always keep a new toothbrush on me, because the one that is in the bathroom I know these crazy chillun have done something to. I'd rather die than go back to that whore and her bastard spawn.

Finally, our Gomer, the UMC 2024 Church speaks up and says "I object your Honor. Yes, all that is true but ever since the Garden of

Eden I get lonely sometimes. My attentions wander. I'm not excited like I was. I'm bored by the routine, the structure, the discipline, its deafening, numbing and limiting. I need some excitement; socialist-atheist LGBTQIA is different, exciting and new. I want to run free and fancy to experience life, not just live according to some Discipline, Order, and Structure. Give me that rotting putrid fermenting fruit laying on the ground, so I can get drunk, fantasize and lust like my descendant Noah after what I want to lust after, like big gigantic talking penises, excuse me snakes.

Jesus interjects, there you have it. She brings up a good point. I think she is gay. I can't compete with that. She loves herself like a female Narcissus, who upon seeing his own reflection in the mirror, fell in mad passionate love with himself. Every time I look around she's hollering #Churchgirlpower, #Churchgirlsrule, #Churchgirlmagic, and on and on to the point I get sick of it. Everything positive I do is either nefarious patriarchy and trying to control her, or what I'm supposed to do (as in what I owe her). Everything I do in terms of discipline is patriarchy and oppression. Yeah I'm supposed to open the door for princesses, but not princes built like Ving Rhames acting their best imitation of princesses. This is too much your Honor. I'm done. I'll be by myself. These bad 'Old Testament donkey kids', they don't want no daddy and I'm not going to take the punishment in disciplining and pruning them, and waste the time ordering their lives it would take to produce good fruit in their lives.

The Father, the Judge has let Jesus speak and let his wife, the Church, the Bride of Christ speak. At stake is a 2000-year-old marriage, consummated on the cross, morbid as that sounds. He is about to report the results of the DNA tests on the children and rule.

Section Front III

Matthew 21:38-46 38 But when the husbandmen saw the son, they said among themselves, This is the heir; come, let us kill him, and let us seize on his inheritance. 39 And they caught him, and cast him out of the vineyard, and slew him. 40 When the lord therefore of the vineyard cometh, what will he do unto those husbandmen? 41 They say unto him, He will miserably destroy those wicked men, and will let out his vineyard unto other husbandmen, which shall render him the fruits in their seasons. 42 Jesus saith unto them, Did ye never read in the scriptures, **The stone which the builders rejected, the same is become the head of the corner: this is the Lord's doing, and it is marvelous in our eyes?** 43 Therefore say I unto you, The kingdom of God shall be taken from you, and given to a nation bringing forth the fruits thereof. 44 And whosoever shall fall on this stone shall be broken: but on whomsoever it shall fall, it will grind him to powder. 45 And when the chief priests and Pharisees had heard his parables, they perceived that he spake of them. 46 But when they sought to lay hands on him, they feared the multitude, because they took him for a prophet.

9

Chapter 9 - Theological Nihilism

Chapter 9 - Theological Nihilism
I think the UMC General Conference 2024 is over as I write these words on May 4, 2024. I wondered sometimes what I would have done as an early Christian seeing Jesus upon the cross. Would I have denied Him. Would I have run? Or would I have been there with him in his miseries desperately praying like his mother and his few associates that he dies quickly to make the pain, agony, embarrassment, humiliation and suffering over as quickly as possible. In the meantime, watching him suffer and writhe in pain and discomfort must have been hard for his mother and close associates. Listening to the taunts and mockeries, "if you are God's son get down off the cross and save yourself? You can't save yourself; you don't even know what a man and a woman are."

That is how I felt when reading UMC Communications Office press releases about General Conference 2024. Just die quickly. Put the thing out of its misery. The hemorrhaging, the bloodletting, the loss in members, the loss in money, the loss in property, the second guessing, etc., just die you beast. The UMC is in hospice. While the old Mark Twain joke is always relevant, "rumors of my death are exaggerated", it is less relevant when a person is suicidal. If a person wants to kill themselves, the rumors might be mean spirited, but you can't blame others for thinking it.

One of my high school friends attempted to kill himself with pills and incredible amounts of alcohol, due to two failed marriages, crippling arthritis, getting his right leg amputated from the knee down, and a string of professional failures. Saints of God I am ashamed of my response, but first a few details. After ingesting the pills and alcohol, as he was about to lose consciousness and fall to the floor, he said he had second thoughts and dialed 911. They put him in the mental ward for 90 days. During that time, he had hopes is girlfriend and her children would provide a stable home and care environment. Around the time he was to get out, his girlfriend (and presumably her kids) stopped taking his calls. It was unusual but maybe she had been working, busy, or couldn't pay her phone bill without his income. On the day he got released, he excitedly called an uber to take him 'home', only to realize that his girlfriend and her kids had absconded with such contents of the apartment as contained any value.

Understandably upset, he went to her mother's house seeking answers, where he found his girlfriend and her kids had moved in, with the intent of leaving him and his mental health issues behind. It was at this time that some of our high school friends came back into his life, as he called around trying to get money to come home to Atlanta within days of eviction from the apartment. We sent him some money and he came home with one leg off below the knee, and missing other things we couldn't see. He had hopes that his older sister, who lived in a $400,000 home with only herself and her young adult child, would put him up for at least a few months until he could get back on his feet. She refused. I will not speculate on the reasons, but it is not unimaginable to think it for the same reasons his girlfriend and her children refused. Dealing with people's mental health 'issues' is virtually asking for a life filled with drama, much of it not your own. That is a lot to ask. All but trapped in a seedy and grimy extended stay motel in Gwinnett County, he got more depressed as our circle of friends willing to give him money and listen to his complaints about how unfair his sister was, were beginning to dwindle.

Finally, it was just me and a few others continuing to support him. This is the critical moment I not only felt like I let him down, but the critical moment I realized I need to stay far away from being a counselor on a suicide hotline. One day he called me complaining about life and needing money. I decided to get the most out of my $25 and started fussing at him. The reader knows from just the present work in your hands and E-readers, that when I go on attack and polemic mode, it gets pretty rugged.

I told him the first thing he needed to do was start going to church every Sunday and dang near every time they have a program. He told me he was Catholic. I had forgotten. Notwithstanding the vagaries of race, as he was surrounded by White mainstream and Hispanic Catholics, I noted the deficiencies in my argument but told him to go there any way or find a church to go to. Be seen, talk to people, and volunteer earnestly and in faith. Honestly, I gave him 'the drill' like that because nearly every time in my life I have gotten stuck, personal piety, the church and concerned members of the body of Christ helped to pull me out. Whether it was the criminal justice system and a felony, whether it was alcohol and reefer addiction, or whether I was stuck in personal and professional losses in South Carolina, rural Georgia, the projects, or wherever, I started going to church and that was how I got back on track. To the point that I have done my best to be resolved to stay on track, exceptional moments notwithstanding. Over the years of me figuring all that out, I have met great pastors, assistant and associate pastors, musicians, choir directors, and lay members that encouraged me and made a space for me. It was true for me, the stratagem never failed, and I gave him the same basic spiel as being what he needs to do.

A Biographic interlude

To be more specific, my self-esteem took a real blow after being treated like a criminal by, and rejected by the UMC for Ordained Ministry. My heart was broken yes, but a far worse thing was broken. The whole 'maybe I'm not good enough', 'maybe no one likes me', 'maybe there is something wrong with me' subroutine kicked in like I was in the 6th grade again. With everything that had happened to me, maybe the UMC psychologists and personality tests were right and I'm deficient or crazy. Maybe all I'm good for is the projects, the hood, pimps, players, thugs, hustlers, and other 'degenerates' and 'deplorables' and that is why I was rejected.

...so that's how I started living, like Jephthah in the land of Tob, drinking and smoking weed again, hanging with 'vain' persons. And yet I was always hyper religious, even in the Land of Tob, and would go to church regularly. Indeed, I went regularly but I was church hopping. I liked different services for different reasons. At Ben Hill, Cascade, Bethel, Hoosier, United Methodists Churches, there would be people I knew historically from childhood, and I took comfort in that. I'd go to one of those churches for the 8AM service. But at 11AM during those days, Craig Oliver and Elizabeth were in their prime. The Praise Team and Choir were numerous, and the musicians topflight. Congregational and liturgical songs were powerful, well-articulated, and well done. Choir selections and soloists were communal experiences like you were at a strange religious club. The selections and songs could last 15 minutes or more depending on 'how the spirit was running' in the musicians and the crowd. Then at 6PM on Sundays I'd go see the Holiness boys, like Bishop Bryant from the Church of the Lord Jesus Christ and Tony Smith; wild conservative stuff like that. That lasted about 2 years.

I was participating in the experiences, enjoying them and the experience of God, but I wasn't serving. Once your faith gets built up to a certain point, one realizes as good as experiencing is, serving is fulfilling in other deeper and perhaps more meaningful ways. There was a small non-denominational church near my home (5 minutes). Convenient at such times I had a rough Saturday night, I could roll out of bed at 10:45, take a 5-minute shower and get to the church by 11. So when I couldn't make it to any of the aforementioned places, that's what I would do.

It was so timely and easy, that I grew to do that more and more. They got to know me, I got to know them, even just in passing. But one day one of the mothers of the church, Mrs. Wiggs (now deceased) came up to me out of the blue and said, 'son I'm praying for you'. Somewhat taken aback, I was like 'ok thank you old lady' (in my mind), hee-hee, chuckle-chuckle. But the truth of the matter was that very day or so prior, the bottom had dropped out of my life, legally, professionally, financially, romantically, and my response was to feel that this 'lower level' of life was what God had in store for me, and I better just get used to an unfulfilled life...

"A Shadow of the man I should be,

like a garden in a forest that the world will never see; you've no thought of answers,

only questions to be filled,

and it feels like hell"

Lyrics courtesy of the 80's Rock band 'Big Country'

Beloved I kid you not, no lie, that was my rock bottom because nearly immediately after Mrs. Wiggs told me she was praying for me, my life began to improve, to the point I am today. When a tree hit our house, my church brought us furniture when we moved back in, and clothes for my mother. I didn't even know what size my mother was or how women's sizes worked. Far more importantly, the little aptitude I had in ministry, they appreciated, and encouraged me to take leadership roles. Keep in mind this is before I even joined. The Methodists had told me I was a zero, my ex-wives certainly believed it, and I believed it. That's why I was content like Jephthah to run around in the land of Tob, 'thuggin and hustlin'. But a mother of the church prayed for me. And they encouraged me and made a space for me to do things in ministry. And do I did. I thank God for the entire experience, feelings of shame, anger, resentment, inferiority and all.

I'd lie to the reader and say the only reason I included that story was to say, that's what I told my friend from high school when he came back to Atlanta depressed. I wanted that experience for him, and I thought that if he went to church often enough, regularly enough, and sincerely enough, establishing meaningful relationships along the way...like I did he'd eventually see improvements in his life. As a matter of fact, that is what I preach, that's why I preach. I preach that if you read your bible, undergo a life of personal piety (the desire for sanctification and holiness), and join a congregation you will be blessed whether you're suicidal, or you don't know whether you're a man or a woman; which not coincidentally, oftentimes manifest in persons at the same time.

In that sense, I'm like the old saints in the Jim Crow and Invisible church. We thought our grandparents, great grandparents, old aunts and uncles were oversimplifying when they said, 'whatever you're going through Jesus was the answer'. Not Jesus and secular therapy, not Jesus and Yoga, not Jesus and Tai Chi, efficacious as those other entities may be. Our ancestors were convinced, if even by ignorance, that Jesus was the answer. We thought that was the illiterate theology of old Black women tired of life and resigned to it. But it is the truth. Whatever your problems, the solution is in the church. Whatever the Black community's problems, the solution is in the church and religion! The solution is in the word of God and certainly not socialist-atheist LGBTQIA+ social justice tropes, sophistry, and theological masturbation. Furthermore, I preach a God that doesn't apologize. You need to first apologize to him.

We will end on this wise. The UMC today is like my friend...involved in suicidal socialist-atheist social justice nihilism. If I know I might die and be unable to do ministry effectively, but I cut my arm and leg off anyway because I am so into the LGBTQIA+ movement, that I will sacrifice the effectiveness of the church to feed, house, and clothe people, all because I want the church to be on 'the right side' of LGBTQIA+ sexual algebra and sexual alphabet soup history that is suicidal nihilist theology?

That is nihilist theology. Babies we know dang well are alive, should they be sacrificed so that the UMC is on the right side of history and women can pretend like they don't know how babies are made? Whose history? The revisionist history of socialist and atheist DEI bishops and academics who have infiltrated our universities and our seminaries and absent strong families and churches, they have infested (leavened) the whole loaf including the church with a spirit of nihilism, anarchy, and Marxist philosophy. What? At every conference session, must we have protests? Of all the things going wrong in the world, this is what the

UMC is worried about. And this protest is touted as good by DEI Bishops. Like Claudine Gay (DEI hire former President of Harvard), they pride themselves on reflecting 'diversity'. That is, if the 'so called' diversity revolves around pro socialist-atheist LGBTQIA+ social justice opinions, and not conservative ideas about the value of tradition. Conservatives are shut out and silenced, as representing reactionary old White men (who it is supposed cannot ever be right about anything, or who must by default be in their leadership positions through having held some woman or some minority back). Being a Black or brown man doesn't help either, as we are told we are eternally corrupted by internalized and institutionalized patriarchy.

I need not cite Edmund Burk with discussions of the vagueness of liberal radical speculations, prognostications, or their radical remedies for politics, religion, economics, and culture. These radical revolutions in this or that never work! They nearly always lead to chaos, and/or the totalitarian politics of China, Russia, Cuba, Venezuela, etc., hardly socialist utopias. Furthermore, if you look at the post-colonial African countries that tried socialism, including Ghana, Ethiopia, Egypt, etc., all look at those 'revolutionary' times as being a complete waste of time, having the dual effect stifling the economy, and creating an oppressive totalitarian state. Is the mere fact of a gay parade utopia? Sunny Hostin said if Jesus came back, before he solved world hunger, violence, poverty, sickness, or anything like that; he'd lead a gay parade.

Part II

For that matter why would the Methodists go full communion with the Episcopal church? Do not delude yourselves in thinking that this is being done in strength and that they are uniting in and doubling their resources in Christ; no they are united in, and doubling down on their commitment to the socialist-atheist LGBTQIA+ agenda and its values, and they have so weakened their representative churches, that they need each other to survive in their suicidal fantasy that the socialist-atheist LGBTQIA+ social justice agenda and its values are helping the church 'stay relevant' or 'modernize'. In addition, they are uniting against what they and their DEI Bishops perceives as pushback from reactionary, traditional, and 'foreign' (global) wings of their respective denominations. They are nihilistically, and suicidally obsessed with making sure their respective (but not respected) denominations are on the right side of history. This is an 'end justifies the means' attitude that suits Russian/Chinese anarchists far better than it suits the legacy of the UMC or the Episcopalian or Anglican Church.

The liberals will use every theological machination, every legal machination, like Paul didn't write what he wrote on Christians going to 'the world's judges' to solve disputes between Christians.

6:1 Dare any of you, having a matter against another, go to law before the unjust, and not before the saints?

2 Do ye not know that the saints shall judge the world? and if the world shall be judged by you, are ye unworthy to judge the smallest matters? (i.e. what a man and a woman are)

3 Know ye not that we shall judge angels? how much more things that pertain to this life?

4 If then ye have judgments of things pertaining to this life, set them to judge who are least esteemed in the church.

5 I speak to your shame. Is it so, that there is not a wise man among you? no, not one that shall be able to judge between his brethren?

6 But brother goeth to law with brother, and that before the unbelievers.

The current attitude of the UMC is a disgrace to Paul because the job of the church is to judge the world, darn sure not the other way around. The salt has truly lost its flavor if it is the other way around. The UMC church is using every social media and communications machination to make sure their churches are on the right side of history, to the point of being willing to sacrifice the integrity of the whole church. Beloved, you can't debate a person that says if I don't get my way, I'm going to maim and/or kill us both. And do it! There is no loyal opposition...very dangerous in a so-called organization with Democratic procedures and institutions. We witness this same type of polarization, the church imitating the world instead of the other way around, like Republicans refusing to even work on an immigration bill because it is an election year, and a worst-case scenario precipitates a better marketing position for victory in the 2024 presidential election.

How can you say you love the United Methodist Church and the Wesleyan tradition, and then be willing to maim and kill it in the name of socialist-atheist LGBTQIA+ agendas? We know what you are doing, you are sacrificing the UMC and God to your new idol...socialist-atheist LGBTQIA+ social justice theology. Look, there is the body of Christ! The church is on the cross, as UMC DEI Bishops, the Wesleyans, and the Global Methodist Church cast lots over her former glories and possessions; just to take whatever they can get legally in the courts of 'the world' and run.

Within months after I fussed at my high school friend, and simplistically told him he needed the Lord and a good church community, he was dead. His family did not list his cause of death, but I have not relinquished my initial assumptions based on his history. Of course I'm disappointed in myself. I wonder should I have been more sensitive? Worse, I wonder if my fussing and oversimplifying, telling him he needed Jesus, the word, a good church, and a wife, disrespected him, and showed disregard for his feelings, emotions, and needs? Did that contribute to pushing him over the edge...perhaps contributing to a later successful attempt on his life. Could be. Had I to do it all over again however, I would have behaved the same way (because I really believe in God and the Church to help people). The only difference would be that instead of just telling him what he needs, I should have gone to his seedy extended stay motel and picked him up on Sundays. I should have taken him to my church and introduced him around. My problem was abandoning him to what I assumed were his own internal spiritual resources. It is very possible however, to be so spiritually weak, with such little spiritual fuel in the tank, that you don't have enough for 'internal combustion' to take place.

I feel the UMC is in the same weakened state. I'm watching the UMC, my friend since birth attempt to hack itself up and commit suicide because it was all tripped out on socialist-atheist LGBTQIA experimental theology, a kind of nihilism that tells them being on the right side of history is not only worth more than the sanctity of the body, but even the existence of the body. That is the definition of the nihilism. The current UMC is like the woman in the Solomonic proverb. How did Solomon decide between the two mothers claiming the same child...the one that was willing to cut him in half or cut his penis off in the name of her own vain imaginations, not only was not the real mother, but a very, very dangerous psychotic person. Anyone willing to hack off body parts and encourage others to hack off their body parts based on a whim is a dangerous person. A whole church of people like that is a dangerous church. Let them that have ears, hear.

Part III

The weird part is that the rejection of the UMC was perhaps one of the best things that ever happened to me. First of all, the UMC I was willing to swear my life to, with all its psychological profiles, all its psychologists, all its District Superintendents, Bishops, and elites with post-graduate degrees is and was suicidal, the biggest psychological malady! Belonging to a suicidal organization that so desperately wants to be on the right side of history that it will hack itself up and kill itself, certainly doesn't make any sense. Can one make oneself more effective in ministry by cutting one's leg off? How does that logic work for the current UMC, which is slashing budgets for what 'good works' it still has left and can afford.

It makes no sense in 'the natural', that is to say, in the world either! Would you join a company if the company told you that for self-inflicted reasons, it was cutting its numbers, budget, and its strength, but you can content yourself with the fact that even though the business is barely viable and destined to go bankrupt, you can be proud that you are on the right side of 'woke history', as you die a decrepit death as a company. Who would join a corporation like that?

Would you accept a bike with one wheel, that the seller took off immediately before he gave it to you? Who buys one shoe, or buys a pair of shoes and then dashes one shoe away in the trashcan? Who buys ice cream without the cone or the cup...just put it in my hand? Church brothers and sisters, what would make a person buy one shoe, or throw one away is that is the fad and the fashion to go around with one shoe, like during the days of the hip-hop group Kris-Kross. Silly young and dumb teens, desperate to imitate their favorite 'stars' would wear their clothes backwards (in public). Of course, that 'fad' came and went. If it became a fashion and fad to eat ice cream in your hand, the young and the dumb and those who want to be hip would immediately begin ordering their ice cream in their hand, so they can slurp it out as it melts like their social media influencer heroes and heroines. You'd be 'old school' and 'unhip' if you wanted a cone or a cup, even though clearly the most effective way to eat ice cream is in some kind of container. But that is not hip enough for ice cream eating nihilists who need excitement and superficiality when they eat ice cream. They are desperate to eat ice cream their way, and if you prefer the old-fashioned way, you're old fashioned, sexist, homophobic, and transphobic. You don't have a right to eat ice cream your way, you must do it like the bishops tell us to eat ice cream, out of our hands like 'the world'! I don't want to belong to a religion that keeps up with the world, and I dang sure ain't going to follow a DEI Bishop that keeps up with the world's trends and history better than they keep up with God's.

Who would buy a bike with one wheel (presuming one wasn't in the market for a unicycle)? If it were in fashion and a fad to take selfies with a bike with one wheel, the young, the dumb, the hip, and the hipsters would be doing it, and encouraging you to as well. Remember the dumping ice water on your head challenge? Why is that necessary to just give to charity! But no, it is the fad, the hipness, being seen as being on the right side of 'fad' and 'hip' history that is important. To the point that, eventually some genius will start selling bikes with one wheel for the sole express purpose of dummies and zeroes talking selfies with them.

Is this how we now do theology after 2000 years, by worldly fads and trends? Is that how we do community, by rejecting the traditional family and the mammalian and biblical foundation of it? Is this how we preach a God who is the solution to all problems...by apologizing for Him, and his inadequacies and inefficiencies (as He surely wasted time making you a biological male or a female, when all you must do to control your own sexuality is practice LGBTQIA+ sexual algebra and alphabet soup sexuality). Must we apologize for a God of silences in the face of oppression; a God that makes mistakes in making some people poor and without any social justice or reparations, for all the trouble God and the oppressor put them through? That is a suicidal way to do ministry and that is why we are getting what we are getting in the current UMC.

The proof of my contentions is that rather than challenge themselves at the Bishop level to preach, to grow, and to stabilize churches and evangelize, they'd rather cut their own positions by lottery and casting lots, knowing full well they will still get their retirements and pension packages, and will still get paid for doing absolutely nothing. This is what happens when you get DEI bishops who would rather be hip and on the right side of history, than do effective soul saving ministry. Point being, thank God I did not attach myself to a suicidal nihilist UMC organization that would rather hack itself up to be on the right side of socialist-atheist LGBTQIA history than even exist.

The UMC is a suicidal nihilist organization, and it is the direct result of trying to be hip and on the right side of history, not God. Let me say that again. The UMC and our DEI bishops are more concerned with being on the right side of history (note God IS history as opposed to a secular history that begins with the big bang and leaves God out of it.) You know if grown UMC bishops and elders tell children its ok to cut their penises and breasts off if they want to, why wouldn't they cut up, mutilate and divide the Holy Mother Church, the Body of Christ. 'You'll know them by their fruit'! The best thing that ever happened to me was that the UMC rejected me even to be a Local Pastor. That is why

I feel so comfortable discussing these matters so freely, even though at one point I was extremely embarrassed and ashamed. No longer. Nearly all the people picked ahead of me, over me, under me, around me, by the authorities at the time for ministry, have either dropped out of the UMC for personal reasons or found they could make more money doing other things. All the psyche profiles, psychologists, etc., and they still managed to get worldly DEI elders, superintendents and bishops that would eventually hack up and destroy the church. No, keep trusting your psyche profiles, psychologists, credit scores, and criminal histories to pick prophets/preachers and see what you keep getting...the complete incompetence and irrelevance to the Black and White Methodist Church of our current crop of DEI Bishops. Thank God they didn't pick me.

Had they picked me, with my gifts and graces, I would have been defending the current crap they presented at General Conference 2024. I'd have to defend all that socialist-atheist LGBTQIA theology for a local pastor's appointment and salary of about $17,000 a year. I would have to defend socialist-atheist LGBTQIA theology even more if they had made me an elder in full connection, for $60,000 plus benefits. As the reader can tell, I would have been good defending that socialist-atheist crap theology, and debating its enemies because I am good at using anger and resentment to make quite often hyperbolic amusing arguments and be creatively argumentative.

God knows all things best. He knew the best thing for me was my rejection, even as I looked around and my wonderful good-hearted male and female (sic) seminarians were becoming local pastors and being promoted around me. As I stated earlier, many of those persons have washed out in mediocrity and/or gone on to do other vocations. Many of them and their promoters at the district level realized the hard way that preachers that look good on paper, with great credit scores, and a great career in the secular world, are not always effective in practical ministry. My rejection was the gift that kept on giving because I have far more power and impact criticizing our DEI Bishops and the current state of General and Black United Methodism than I ever would within the system. I know my readers are not naïve, and they can read between the lines at my anger, and my resentment at my UMC. But will the liberals address my pain as they have done to Hawaiians, women suffering abuse, and a litany of others the UMC is atoning for its treatment of? Will our hocus-pocus bishops be doing a 14-page letter of apology to me?

God forbid, I would have been at this General Conference, debating that crap for $250,000 a year, getting up preaching that God is so helpful and so good, but that he doesn't know what a man and a woman are, or has lied to us and deceived us for 2000 years, until socialist-atheist LGBTQIA+ sexual algebra had to tell him and our DEI bishops what a man and a woman are? That kind of a God cannot be omnipotent. If you really thought your God was 'all powerful', the only possible conclusion would be either that he doesn't need fixing, or if he did need fixing because of his mistakes, you'd be scared to tell him. Glory to God. In the same way, every employee is a little nervous about pointing out the presumed mistakes of his or her superiors. But the current UMC church serves a God it public corrects, publicly mocks, and public humiliates. Our current UMC doesn't even respect God as much as we would respect our earthly bosses...for shame UMC, for shame.

Chapter 10 - You just wait til' Moses gets back

Chapter 10 - You Just Wait until Moses gets back

It is a good thing the traditionalists split because they were not there to protest or (as it were), make a scene. Their mere presence would have been a resented thorn in the liberal DEI side. Their conservative values were silenced just as ruthlessly as Mao, Castro, Putin, etc. silenced discourse. That the liberals do not consider this compromising their own principles of democracy, fairness, and freedom is of no consequence to them (for the end justifies the means). The liberals used the democratic process at the current and previous General Conferences to pick a side and go with it. There could be no loyal opposition. To the liberals and our DEI Bishops, the conservative side was untenable in the extreme and made their new friends, the socialist-atheist LGBTQIA+ sexual algebra social justice warriors feel uncomfortable and unwelcome. Sounds mean spirited of the conservatives, doesn't it? But anybody with an agenda other than 'Jesus and Jesus alone' in a Church, is bound to feel uncomfortable. So the idea that just making people uncomfortable is some kind of sin is ridiculous. If you had members of your church that make homemade porn films and they wanted to put some of their films in the Church bookstore, you telling them no, would of course make them not feel their porn films are welcome. Ergo you are not inclusive. Furthermore, they will feel it is some kind of reprimand against them and their 'lifestyle' that you won't put their porn films in the church bookstore. Mother Jones ugly knitting is in the church bookstore. You will hasten to say that you are not judging them at all for what they do in private. You are merely saying that the church bookstore doesn't sell porn. But instead of doing that, in order not to offend anyone, the church starts selling homemade porn in the church bookstore. Many Christian authors will not want their books sold in a Christian bookstore that sells homemade porn. Considering that up until the moment we started selling porn, 99% of everything the bookstore sold was in some way about 'Jesus and Jesus alone', in considering who and what material would 'have to go', the authorities at your church decided to keep the porn and ditch the Jesus. And yet this is the 'throw the baby out with the bathwater' dimwitted move our DEI Ebony Bishops made (for $250,000 per year).

Somebody had to go, and it was not going to be their new socialist-atheist social justice warrior friends, so 33%, nearly the entire conservative White Southern, Southwestern and Midwestern UMC was amputated to be on the right side of history. 33% of the churches, up to 65% or so of the entire budget amputated, so our DEI Bishops could celebrate and dance in the aisles draped in the rainbow or Palestinian flags at General Conference 2024. Funny thing is, everyone told us the presence of Ebony and DEI bishops would help race relations. When 33% of the church, nearly all White, just ups and leaves, I do not consider that 'helping' the race situation or creating harmony between the races.

As I have said before it is a principle of Marxist and social justice atheism, that 'the end justifies the mean'. Thus, even if you must subvert the democratic process and silence people, that is ok because you are on the right side of socialist-atheist LGBTQIA+ propaganda history. The liberals will never admit that it was precisely their condescending behavior and subversion of democracy that drove the liberals into their corner paradox of having the unique 'pleasure' of being the ones to split the church into hundreds of pieces, all united, not in Methodism, but in dysfunction. How condescending, to in a debate amongst United Methodist Christians and theologians, to call one side homophobes, sexists, transphobes etc., in an ad hominem disparaging way, even though they swore to the same values to get ordained in the UMC they grew up in. They brought the rhetoric of socialist-atheist social justice propaganda into the church and in no way since, has the church been ennobled, blessed or grown. Why is this not being called a tragedy, a Nakba? The reason this is not being called precisely what it is, a tragedy for the UMC, a Nakba, is because of the power of propaganda wherever there is repression. The UMC Communications office released the play by play of the Nakba (General Conference 2024), and then propagandized the whole thing by showing the pictures of the gay couples and clergy kissing and dancing in the aisles at General Conference as they celebrated the dismantling of traditional sexual norms for preachers, pastors, and what was formerly known as the sanctity of the biblical family. To them, dismantling 2000 years of church tradition is something to celebrate, not rue. Clearly nothing is sacred anymore, is it?

Nietzsche was right, god (the god that submits to human science, reason and sexual whims) is dead. He doesn't know what a man and a woman are, and he is apparently powerless to make his original mammalian case or a new one. But there was a time when Christianity was more masculine, that if two gay people 'kissed' and 'french kissed' at a Holy Convocation they'd be summarily ejected. For that matter if two married heterosexuals jumped up and started kissing in a Holy Convocation or even local church bible study, somebody would yell out 'get a room' and/or told them to 'sit their Old Testament donkeys down'! Not at genial General Conference 2024. Everybody was letting it all hang out. As rainbow flags flew and waved, they danced around like the Children of Israel dancing naked and beating drums and tambourines around the golden calf. Rainbow flags were waved around like some kind of bizarre new form of patriotism at General Conference! For Christ's sake, I'm glad there are hardly any 'real' representatives from the 'United Brotherhood' left to have been at General Conference because I'm sure a motion would have been made by our DEI Bishops to force them to change their name 'The United Brotherhood' to something more inclusive. If these united brothers would have said anything our DEI bishops didn't like, they would be summarily shouted down and/or ejected as representing the reactionary patriarchal forces of the old church. According to the liberals, the 'old church' is on the wrong side of socialist-atheist LGBTQIA+ social justice history. Ironically (because they are so into freedom), our DEI ebony bishops like to 'get people told' and 'stand up' for the marginalized...quite precisely by marginalizing other people.

I could imagine fights breaking out. Yes goodness. Thank goodness the traditionalists, like Elvis, who DEI liberals don't like either, have left the building. Elvis represented the forces of White appropriation of Negro culture, etc., I am told by liberals and DEI bishops. And yet, he and Johnny Cash for instance, were committed Christians (for all their ups and downs), and are well documented doing traditional Christian hymns, songs, and even early Black gospel songs. As a matter of fact, the story is told of how Elvis loved to walk past the Black churches on Sunday and listen to emphatic singing and preaching along the way. Segregated though the times were, poor Black people and poor White people never really lived far from each other in the south. But to our DEI Bishops, they are the wrong color (as in not Black or brown), the wrong sex, and cis gender, and thus represent the forces of patriarchy, sexism, transphobia, and homophobia, and must be neutralized, silenced, and made irrelevant, as are the White men of the post-2018 I think General Conference. Church, do you see how the liberals propagandize us?

The advent of DEI Bishops was supposed to prove that race issues and race relations were getting better, and that DEI Bishops would even make things better. But in the end White mainstream United Methodist churches in mostly the south and Midwest upped and left and the liberals gave them the out to do it after what to them was the disastrous vote in General Conference 2018 to uphold traditional notions of family. Imagine the irony, they couldn't stand traditionalists, they were determined to be on the right side of socialist-atheist LGBTQIA social justice history, so they created a way for liberal churches to leave with their property. And that my friends opened the floodgates to the Nakba, the demise, the complete dissolution into irrelevancy of the post-modern, post-General Conference 2024 UMC today as liberal and conservative churches, provided they were powerful enough, took the chance to exit (with dignity, what a joke).

Put 'holiness' before the 'herd' brothers and sisters. Theology and praxis, as well as Holy Convocation gets reduced to a question of sex? How old is sex? Yet in 2024 a church of well-paid and educated lay and ecclesiastic grown men and women celebrate the triumph of the social-ist-atheist LGBTQIA social justice agenda on ancient church policy, by dancing around the golden calf naked, cloaked only in their rainbow flags? This they say was in the best interest of the church and helps the church (supposedly putting it on the aforementioned right side of history at any cost). Do you not see the UMC propaganda machine preaching the exact opposite of reality! What in the world has happened church? No matter how you feel sexually, Holy Convocation should not be about prancing around, same sex or hetero-sex kissing in a romantic sense. What is that to celebrate?

Church is about God, not sex other than the basic mammalian and biblical construct we have clearly outlined and delineated by over 13 million years of earths existence and evolution. Either you trust it (God)...or you trust socialist-atheist LGBTQIA+ sexual algebra social justice propaganda. We know clearly from General Conference 2024 who is the trust of our DEI bishops and the new UMC; a church that is weakened from extreme bloodletting, but that can console itself because though it is dying and near dead, it is on the right side of history.

This 'Brokeback Mountain Methodism' is suicidal. It is like taking a small sword after the loss of a battle, and disemboweling yourself to do Hari Kari because you wanted to be on the 'died with honor' side of proverbial Japanese history and are willing to inflict potentially mortal wounds on yourself to prove how loyal you are to the 'died with honor' side of Japanese proverbial history. That is a dangerous mindset. It is dangerous for people like this to be in control of the church. Schisms are fine but when one side stands triumphant and victorious, for the sole fact that it drove the other side away isn't Christian or rational. You won, but not by praying, piety and your so-called holy conferencing, but by driving the other side away. You won by legal machinations and lawyers, not the Holy Ghost. You won by your own version of the exclusion you proclaim to hate and be so actively against.

Part II

They make it sound so good. Holy Conferencing, Prayer rooms and moments of reflection and discernment. Really? Our DEI bishops and lay folk went into 'Holy Conferencing', 'Prayer Rooms', and moments and meetings of discernment and discussion, and then y'all come out of all that holy discerning and cannot tell anybody except others as foolish and confused as you pretend to be what a man and a woman are...without resorting to LGBTQIA+ sexual algebra/alphabet soup propaganda!

Christian Holy Conference about the future of our UMC church, draped in Palestinian flags, and with Yoga placards? Dancing in the aisles to celebrate that your God is so ignorant, that he doesn't know what a man and a woman are, without our DEI Bishops explaining it to him, and using socialist-atheist LGBTQIA social justice rhetoric. Dancing in the aisles, stark naked except your rainbow flag covering, around a new 'golden calf' fake god that doesn't know what a man and woman are without you the clay, explaining it to him. You celebrate your new pagan god that you have cleverly substituted while Moses was away. You celebrate, dancing around your fake god that is so powerless he'll not only let you (the clay) insult him and fuss at him for not knowing what a man and a woman are good enough for you and your comfort, but he appears equally powerless to punish you for your crimes as you dance naked around the golden calf draped only in your rainbow flag. Clearly this god is silent either because he knows our DEI bishops are right, or he is powerless to defend what he has been defending for 6000 years. They celebrate by dancing in the aisles around their fake god, substituted for the one Charles, John, and Susannah Wesley and countless others bore witness too. This new god, this golden calf, this ersatz god, is on the right side of history. The liberals dragged him kicking and screaming to the 'right side of socialist-atheist LGBTQIA propaganda history'. You can't be afraid of a god, let alone reverence him, when you are at a so-called holy conference dancing up and down the aisles in celebratory fashion about a matter completely antithetical to his established word and church tradition. All this in complete defiance of the ordinances and oracles of God. Do the liberals do this because they do not fear him, or is their faith in something else...

If Khrushchev wasn't in a dead cold vodka driven society, with a dead Marxist philosophy, and doomed political culture, his saying that the way to defeat the capitalist is to sell him enough cheap rope to hang himself would have been pure genius. The Chinese turned it into a global economic and political artform in the post-Nixon era and it has undermined the position of American workers, and undermined American and European technological superiority. I can imagine the concept must be a truism in other ways too. Guy gets a Porsche and it's the best day of his life. Within weeks he's wrapped the car around a tree dang near killing himself because he 'felt the need for speed'. How many times has one last hit of cocaine, crack, etc., resulted in overdoes, hospitals and Narcon. One last fling, one last potato chip, one last chocolate Sunday, and next thing you know, you've got diabetes and high blood pressure. In philosophical terms I learned in systematic theology, this can be likened to Occam's razor or the golden mean. Surprisingly enough considering modern Islam's reputation in the west, the prophet Muhammad said his religion, was one of the center, not the extremes, in family life, practice and piety.

Watching the events of the UMC 2024 General Conference as it committed suicide has been extremely unpleasant to me. Our DEI bishops have been right there at the center of the action, acting the role of Dr. Kevorkian in assisting the suicide. It is the same kind of cultural narcissism and nihilism that make some elderly or sick people think that because of the pain of existence, they (or society) have the right to kill themselves. Because they feel they have outlived their usefulness, they have the right to kill themselves? We live in a world where the elderly, the children, penises and breasts, and even children we know darn well are alive in their mother's wombs are expendable if deemed by the individual or society. This is not good. Ladies and gentlemen that is further proof how post-modern nihilism and narcissism has infected the church and driven it to its knees in madness.

We are left with a church with no power and witness. How can you witness to a once omnipotent but now impotent God that needs you to explain to him what a man and woman are. Thus, its only strategy of evangelism is making itself appealing in a worldly sense, and apologizing for some sins it cannot possibly be responsible for or be held responsible. But these DEI bishops like getting ahead of the curve of history and apologizing for the church, apologizing for God making people male or female, and putting them in poverty, even before anyone has asked for an apology. This is the new evangelism.

Yes, our mother has played the harlot, making herself appealing to the world with lipstick, rouge, fake eyelashes, jewelry, cymbals around her feet, and dropping it like it was hotter than the sun itself. There she stands on the corner seeking to entice male and female passersby with her delicacies. The man of the house is not home she says, he will be gone for weeks. Come, turn in and come into me. This she says to every two-bit decadent and thief. Come unto me, my master is not at home. Every two-bit hustler with a philosophy she runs to admiringly, not understanding that the price of admission to the counsels of the ungodly is to either attack and humiliate your traditional God and yourself, or let them do it.

I know and am familiar because that was the price of admission to hang around some of my more militant Afrocentric and harder core Muslim friends. They all blame Black Christianity for either being the White man's religion, or retarding the Black revolutionary mind/movement or both. This they do because they are ignorant of the true state of the Black church. Ethiopian Judaism and Christianity precede the European church and the first European Christian states. In lieu of educating them and informing them of the value of Black Christianity, in my old days, I imitated them and their critique, to hang out with my new friends and not offend them accidentally.

Being afraid to offend others is a good thing. Being so afraid of offending others that you are afraid of offending them accidentally is a sign of low self-esteem. Many of us know or have known grandparents for whom the throttle has come off their mouths. I remember at a family event Uncle Eddie greeted my female cousin whom he had not seen in years with; 'oh wow, you must be living good, you've gotten so fat'. Believe it or not, he thought the living good part, and fat part were independently and together compliments. We were all horrified and hoped she didn't really notice. But she cussed him out and went to the bathroom and cried. Till he died I don't think their relationship ever healed. She never forgave him for that, and for his part, being in his mid to late 80's and slowing down mentally himself, there was no way to explain to him how he may have been wrong, or what he said inappropriate. When we tried to explain, he understood that she was mad, but he didn't understand what he said that offended her.

I knew, however. Uncle Eddie and many of my parents, grandparents, and great grandparents' generation were sharecroppers and relatively poor. Let Uncle Eddie tell it, he didn't get his own pair of shoes until he was in his twenties, and he didn't see anybody fat until the 1950's. According to him, nobody was fat. People were bigger or smaller, chubby or thick, but nobody was morbidly obese because it was too much walking and working to do. You ate what you ate, at mealtimes. There was no snacking in between meals, because there were no at hand snacks unless it was fruits, pickled or preserved vegetables, and the like. There were no high calorie mass produced sugary and salty snacks. There was no 'fast food' either. I kinda believe Uncle Eddie because even when I was growing up in the 1970's, childhood diabetes was virtually unheard of. Most working-class families either didn't live sedentary lifestyles, or were too poor to spend a lot of money on rich high calorie meals.

Overeating was hardly possible because a family might consist of 4 to 6 children and others. Because everybody ate at the same time, sneaking food was more difficult. Plus, there was the social constraint of everybody knowing their place. Little children at the children's table, and no matter how hungry you thought you were or wanted to be, little children got one chicken leg, a scoop of rice, and a scoop of green beans. Older adolescents got two legs and heaping scoops. Daddy got heaping scoops and whatever pieces of chicken he wanted, which if he had any sense, he deferred. He didn't defer because there were narcissistic self-righteous nihilistic post-moderners upset at the inherent patriarchy waiting to criticize him, he deferred because he knew the harder the times got, the more sacrifices he would have to make for his family. He got the big piece of chicken because there would be times he didn't eat; he must work hard to make sure everybody else ate first. Girls got less than boys, mama got less than daddy. Oh, how unfair that is. Oh, how wrong that is. Oh, someone must either protest or abandon the traditional family completely because it cannot even eat together fairly. Away with the patriarchy! Even adolescent girls in some families didn't get two pieces of chicken but their brothers did. What a patriarchal crime against adolescent girls, who in today's time can eat all they want, only to spend their teenage years bulimic and with eating disorders, desperate for liposuction at 17 because somehow grandmas 'Old Testament donkey' and thighs manifested on her at 16, instead of 36. Because of the dispensation of the chicken, this proves to the liberals and DEI bishops that not only is the whole traditional family system corrupt and designed to hold girls and women back, but that the church that promoted and tolerated such an arrangement for 2000 years must be just as corrupt, just as guilty as the patriarchal traditional family, and must be done away with. This is what I mean by the current UMC being suicidal in its thinking.

This is how we got to the theological and philosophical moment in the history of denominational Christianity in America, that we have suicidal denominations that make void 'The Word' they should be standing on, in the name of adopting the trends and fashions of political correctness, and socialist-atheist LGBTQIA+ sexual algebra and sexual alphabet soup values. Not only are our denominations committing suicide, but they are proud of it and want everybody to watch on the UMC global communications technology platforms. This is just like crazy people killing themselves and/or others on Facebook live. Our UMC DEI Bishops and the Communications office want the world to see our implosion into utter irrelevancy. This is how you get a suicidal church that is 'proud' to be suicidal. That is what General Conference 2024 was.

General Conference 2024 was the product of a church that is like angst filled teens, so filled with self-loathing and low self-esteem, that it has an inordinate desire to copycat worldly and trendy fads to be 'hip' and 'cool' for the 'cool kids' (socialist-atheist social justice warriors). Teens living in $300,000 homes, proud of wall-to-wall wi-fi, but on the inside their self-esteem is so low they cannot see the blessing, only the crimes of their parents, and thus they must self-destruct in feigned apologies, and tearing up elite universities and denominations to prove how remorseful they are for their parents (and their parent's church) supposed sins. And it's their right according to nihilist socialist atheist pro-abortion logic. If you can kill your baby because your baby will make you unhappy or hold you back, what do you do when you are now holding you back because you're too ugly, too fat, too short, too tall, too smart, too stupid, born a biological male, born a biological female, and the bullies have worked you over sensing your weakness, and now you want to commit suicide (or cut your penis and breasts off).

Part III

Recently I watched a documentary on the bird of prey called the Osprey. Osprey and some other bird species, as it were, mate for life and while the mother is sitting on the eggs, 24 hours straight for 30 or so days, the father brings her at least one meal a day. This set up continues as the mother, homebound, watches over the nest to protect the vulnerable eggs and newly hatched chicks. The father brings more fish back, and the mother rips tiny pieces of flesh to give to her brood.

Hooray, thank God we have DEI Ebony bishops who will need to apologize for God because he put female Ospreys in that restricted position, simply based on the presence of their wombs. Having a womb is unfair to female birds? God was unfair to them. By whose standard...the males you resent? Even more, our DEI ebony bishops feel that ideologically, they must liberate Osprey females. Who knows what kind of independent life a female Osprey could lead were she not tied down by patriarchy and children. She could be soaring the skies, hunting and fighting for territory just like the males, or just like female Jedi and female superheroes. Being a mother is not enough. No, our DEI bishops must liberate female Ospreys because that is the only way a female Osprey could possibly be happy and content, out there competing and fighting with male Osprey and winning.

With no children and no male, according to socialist-atheist LGBTQIA+ sexual algebra, she can somehow be her best self, defining her life, and the purpose of it for herself. For if God does not know what a male and a female are, he certainly doesn't know their purpose either, by default. Their socialist-atheist LGBTQIA+ defined purposes are bigger than the narrow roles and purposes, mammalian and biblical life seem to dictatorially restrict our sexuality to. The 'natural' set up God has seemingly built into creatures is not good enough for man. We must thank our DEI Bishops for knowing better, what the purposes and value of life is, and what makes a good life. Not the 10 Commandments, but socialist-atheist LGBTQIA+ social justice propaganda. Imagine the clay telling the potter, not only is he wrong for making me a boy, I'm going to cut my penis off to prove how wrong God is. Surgeons' and doctors' participation is perhaps understandable due to monetary, medical, and professional considerations, but the participation of the church in such a thing is blasphemous!

As amusing as this is, there are terrible consequences. Let us assume our DEI bishops have liberated female Ospreys. Females no longer must have males or kids. She can fly the skies as freely as she wants, and do precisely what she wants to do. Surely that makes female Ospreys and female humans necessarily happy and fulfilled…wrong. Osprey birthrates plummet. Male osprey hunt and fight all the time, because they don't have homes with responsibilities to go back to minus a female. In the old days male Osprey rarely fought to the death because each adult male knew he had to go home and feed his wife and his brood. Now he has nothing to lose in fights and becomes much more willing to resort to lethal violence against his brothers. Female Ospreys, liberated from the domesticity of their nests, flying the world, fighting the males for dominance, etc., get injured more from being smaller (MMA with transwomen), and what is worse, the Osprey birth rate collapses at all the 'freedom' everyone has. But of course, it is better for Osprey society that the entire Osprey civilization dies out, rather than go one minute further continuing to repress its womenfolk. That is despite the fact that dead things cannot be fixed, but broken things, as long as they have life can. Then the Osprey civilization will be on the right side of socialist-atheist LGBTQIA+ social and economic justice history. Dead, but on the right side of history. Being on the right side of history is better than existing. That idea is a classic theme of nihilist revolutionary anarchical sentiments. That is the summit of nihilist narcissistic socialist-atheist theology and philosophy. Being 'right' (on the right side of history) is more important than being alive, and that is what the post General Conference 2024 UMC is teaching today.

The tragedy of liberated Osprey females goes further. For liberated females, their priority is not their children and certainly not some male (supposed she loved him). Thus, the family structure that fed and defended her and her children is gone. Osprey fathers find their roles unnecessary. Either female Ospreys can afford to appear to raise their offspring by themselves, or the 'Osprey State' will take responsibility for feeding, babysitting, and educating the Osprey children that don't have fathers and two incomes. In such a situation Osprey mothers and fathers can spend large amounts of personal time going off trying to find themselves and live their best selves, and look at countless hours of YouTube videos and social media from 'influencers' trying to do so. Ensconced within this new brave world of pure freedom, and surrounded by technologies and trinkets, one's sex is not something God/the Creator designed for you, but that you design yourself through the practice of LGBTQIA+ sexual algebra and sexual alphabet soup where you can redefine your sexuality based on your own personal redefinition. Again, Nietzsche's transvaluation of values, transvaluating something so basic as one's born physical sexuality, as though the physical differences between penises and vaginas are something to ignore like the direction of the wind.

Vulnerable Osprey babies find themselves more and more in the position of having to fend for themselves in ways they never had to before with two parents in the household contributing. Inattentive parents, desperately spending all their energies trying to find themselves and live their best lives; expending all their energies in a relentless search to get to the bottom of their own well of lust and deviance. The inattention to their children, they justify as being good for children because they are free. Osprey children now eat what they want or can get for themselves from fast food joints and convenience stores. No longer are meals communal. They call uber to go places. They are not made or forced to go to church or religious services regularly, whether the parents go or not and usually they don't in such circumstances. They dress how they want to dress, which is merely an imitation of what they see on tv and in the media. To ask them to dress in culturally or religiously appropriate ways is seen as anathema in post-modernity, and a means of holding youth back from expressing themselves (as though expressing oneself is a supreme value and justifies itself simply by the fact that it exists publicly expressed). The idea that 'expression' (the more extreme/the more radical) is the supreme value, and justifies itself, or anything is the danger that will ruin western civilization. American and European Christians, patted themselves on the back at how free their art and politics were 30 years ago, when so called artists started getting publicity for their art by urinating or defecating on crosses, pictures of Jesus, Mary and/or other specifically Christian religious symbols. Now everybody had to look at the fruit of what the rejection of traditional values looks like in the form of the 2024 Paris Olympics where threesomes were insinuated, as if the French had to show the world that they invented the phrase (if not the act), 'menage-a-trois'. Really?

A resetting of the last supper, complete with a child, transvestites, transmen and women, and a performance by a dude with a beard doing a highly sexualized dance. Yes indeed world, behold the fruit of the past 1200 years of the rise of Europe and European Civilization. Indeed, what do you think Spengler (Author of The Decline of the West) would have said watching the opening ceremonies of the Paris Olympics? Paris made a mockery of the supposed value and culture superiority that made Europeans traipse the world 600 years ago stealing native lands and natural resources, ridiculing and demeaning native politics and religion converting them to the European version of Christianity, and enslaving them. Those same supposedly superior European Christian cultural values, White people themselves now mock at the Paris Olympics...with their own 'Pale White Rider' and horse and other esoteric mockeries one really must know about Christianity to recognize.

And yet these wild Osprey kids, that now fend for themselves, were once used to respecting their parents, adults, and the enforcement of respecting their peers. Now Osprey gangs of youth slide in the vacuum created by the lack of stable parents, extended families, elders and religion. Whether the gangs are in inner cities, or they are on elite college campuses threatening Jewish students and faculty with insult and physical violence; this is the result of blindly going around thinking 'expression' is the supreme value. Thus, nearly deaf, dumb, and blind, our youth go around 'expressing themselves' by trying to free everybody their parents, the patriarchy, and tradition has been holding back (foreign and domestic). Like drug addled addicts, narcotically addicted to 'expressing themselves', no matter how ridiculous and illogical the issue over which they are expressing themselves is, our youth are destroying their own society, community and institutions. But of course, the anarchists, socialists-atheists, etc., are only too happy to stand around hollering 'burn baby burn' as they enable the destruction. The problem for our young and dumb, but highly expressive children becomes that their benefactors have absolutely nothing sane, worthwhile or effective to replace the traditions and institutions that burned down with, which leads to further instability and chaos.

It's perfectly apparent, even to DEI bishops that in liberating female and male Osprey, from traditional bio-physical roles, utter chaos and the collapse of the natural Osprey world would occur without technology and AI coming to the rescue. Birth rates decline inevitably in post-modern free societies (per Spengler). But for some reason liberals think they are doing society a favor...killing it in the name of freeing it. You could not tell them, and they would never believe that liberal DEI Ebony female bishops are not doing some kind of favor to all women and human society automatically simply by existing. And yet ask women, 40, 45, and 50, or Vivica Fox at 60 suggesting now she's ready for a man, to jump start their biological clocks and ovaries after a period from 18-40 trying to make themselves happy in the worlds of academia and professional life. Now they will spend all the money they earned during that time of freedom, being successful in those worlds, trying to have a baby by invitro, freezing eggs, surrogacy, and all sorts of other expensive machinations like Brittany Griner and her wife, and Da Brat and her wife. And the current post-General Conference 2024 UMC and its DEI bishops will pat them on the back and say not only what great trailblazers they are, but what great role models they are for other women. Really? I rather suggest Deborah and Jael from the Book of Judges in the Bible. Deborah inspired a nation to resist oppression, Jael (Kenite descendant of Moses Ethiopian father-in-law) stabbed an enemy of Israel (Sisera) in the forehead so hard it pinned him to the ground. But now I am to believe Da Brat and Judy, and Brittany Griner and her wife are heroines and feminine role models?

Ask any subgroup or marginalized subgroup in America are they happy, and not only are they not happy, but they also blame traditional patriarchy and the church for their unhappiness...grown men and women...in 2024? That is why they are on a permanent revolution, always having to be 'woke' and vigilant against the forces of microinsults involving sexism, racism, homophobia, and transphobia. Anyone in a permanent revolution is by default unhappy. Not only did Mao's Cultural Revolution against 'the remnants of bourgeois values' bring unhappiness, it cannot be said to have fixed anything in the way Mao wanted it to because not long after Mao's death, China opened to the west and got more and more capitalist to the point of where China is today with the 2nd largest market/economy in the world, scheduled to be the largest in the next few decades or so.

But facts such as that, never stops liberals and lefties from always protesting and viewing tradition as a disappointment. Let me go hard, even too hard for a second. Whenever I look at the average Black Republicans and DEI Bishops, they nearly always look like they were the type of kid to get bullied when they were children. On the surface you might be tempted to think Candace Owens is somewhat photogenic but combine it with her attitude and no matter what she looked like in high school she was unpleasant to be around. I get the same feeling around our DEI bishops. I could be wrong.

Take our Bishop in North Ga for instance. She rides a Harley and is proud of it. According to her it helps her define and project herself in a certain type of way. She's out there riding on the highway in her leather outfit, looking cool. What type of person does that? People who grew up not only broke and without enough material things to make them feel as complete as their peers appeared to be, but also the type of kid who felt powerless growing up and thus time she gets some money she gets a superficial symbol of strength and power. It even has an aura of 'danger' to it (in lieu of an all-powerful omnipotent, omnipresent, omniscient God that one fears to contradict). She bought a Harley. The

Harley, that 'hog' she is straddling between her legs follows orders at least, if the 'people called Methodists' no longer want to or not.

I'm not a therapist or psychologist except in the sense Nietzsche, Kierkegaard, Schopenhauer, or Spengler were, but there is a truth in my sentiments what type of person gets a Harley, or plastic surgery. Growing up with poor self-esteem is not a crime. Many of us do, including myself. But does God fill the hole created by low self-esteem or do things like Harleys, titles, and position? The holes in the lives of people with a history of poor self-esteem are deep, because they viewed some aspect of themselves or their bodies as not being competitive with their peers. So time they get some money, there they are trying to 'fix' God's mistakes in their lives (as though that were even possible). They are upset with God because he didn't make them cool or hip enough or the right sex...because of course in post-modern UMC God doesn't know what a man or a woman are and makes mistakes with birthing people males and females. So one must take one's life, body, and soul into one's own hands and fix oneself because the post-modern God is not capable. He has already crippled you according to your logic by making you Black poor, gay, a woman, whatever. So you get a Harley, Porsche, fancy designer purses, or some other symbols of 'power', to help you feel 'powerful'. In a world where everybody is fixing themselves with legal and illegal drugs, sex reassignment, and pansexual explorations, the Post-Modern UMC is incapable of making the argument to people that God's way, God's standard, 4000 years old or so, is the best one people have and certainly nothing post-modern socialist atheist LGBTQIA social justice warriors have come up is good enough or stable enough to replace it. But unfortunately, our DEI bishops came to the opposite conclusion and have replaced practical biblical theology and praxis with the wholesale adoption of socialist-atheist values.

Furthermore, many 'ugly' people resent tradition and authority because either its values seem to negate them, or tradition and authority did not protect them from bullying as children. So they subconsciously and inherently resent tradition and authority and cannot wait to get a little power so they can take it down a few notches. God forbid they get in power and they will sabotage the whole heap trying to make up for wounds, anger, and resentment they received at the hands of traditional authority. Time their side (of angry resentful people) gets some power in the traditional church administration, they will turn their back on the discipline they swore to uphold and weaken it to the point of ultimately tearing it down into irrelevancy. If the new adapted revised discipline can say something completely against scripture, it is cutting out the legs upon which the church stands. In essence they are getting the church and patriarchy back for what it did to them...aka their politics of grievance.

That is why every time you turn around our DEI Bishops are apologizing for something. Apologies in themselves are not bad, but as politics, theology and evangelism, they will not work. They resent tradition and authority any way it is constructed, and that is why the liberal world of our church, our colleges, our wider society and our children take on the appearance of being chaotic, simple minded, and self-destructive. Why tear up the church? Why did the liberals think it was necessary. Why tear up Harvard, Columbia, Emory, etc., in student protests? Seething anger and resentment at tradition, and the politics of grievance against authority is why, and the solution is not coddling them like our DEI Bishops and letting the young and dumb tear down something they won't know the importance of until they are older.

Part IV

I think I mentioned before my ex-father in law's excellent advice when I told him I didn't intend to disrespect his daughter and bring dishonor to the family by my public economic and professional insecurities, my smoking reefa, and dranking ways. He told me it didn't matter what my intentions were, only the effects are relevant at this point. With that in mind I want to bring another argument to bear in the discussion of the damage DEI Bishops have done to not only the Universal (as it were) United Methodist Church, but the Black United Methodist Church, and Black community as well.

With the rise of DEI bishops, this was seen like Obama, proof of a post-racial UMC church. DEI Bishops would protect the interests of Black churches and ease our way into full communion (post-1968) with our White mainstream counterparts. We would supervise and pastor each other's churches and have cross racial appointments and a new fantasy land of harmony would be brought about. But what actually happened? With the rise, ascension to power, and coronation during General Conference 2024 of liberal agenda DEI Bishops, 33% of the UMC, largely White, largely southern and midwestern, and not coincidentally African and global Methodists, up and left the post-1968 communion. The liberal DEI Bishops reaction was worse than 'let em go, or we're better off without them'...which they also said. Their reaction was to label the largely White, largely southern, largely midwestern, traditionalists, as racists, homophobes, transphobes, and defenders of big money and corporate forces against the poor and working class. These 'deplorables' who refuse to get on the 'right side of history', don't even deserve the right hand of fellowship or even common communion anymore! They were dismissed as Trump loving...as an epithet. The sexual conservatism of the African and global church was discussed as though those communities were backwards and ignorant, and must be led strongly, if not forced to adopt western sexual trends. Any slur they could get their hands on they hurled at their fellow Christians in the name and rhetoric of their socialist-atheist LGBTQIA friend's agendas. At these liberal bishop's ordination ceremonies when they became Elders, they swore to defend and uphold the Discipline (as previously written) and the traditional values it represented. Now, they call everybody who still believes in the values **they** swore to (for ordination purposes) racist, homophobic, and transphobic. Ladies and gentlemen this is not a healthy church. It is a suicidal church that will hack off its body parts to try to stay hip and relevant to contemporary post-modern worldly values.

There are some schools of Rabbinic thought that suggest the problem with Sodom and Gomorrah weren't that they were gay. To be frank,

Sodomy went on in the book of Judges amongst the tribe of Benjamin in a weird parallel to the Sodom and Gomorrah narrative. In both narratives there is this idea that they were forcing people (men specifically) to either allow themselves to be sodomized or participate in sodomy. That activities happen in people's private lives in a town or city, at least in this context is not a problem that requires retribution by God. It is when men go around demanding sodomistic rights and privileges from strangers, travelers, angels, priests, married men with their wives, and we might suppose young men too, etc., in these two examples, that is when the retribution and punishment is fierce and there is wide scale of destruction. The idea is that what singled them out for destruction is not the existence of homosexuality (however its manifested) in the populace. What singled them out for destruction is that they would force it upon people of the township, random passersby, victims of slavery, war, etc., which of course the stories of the orgies in Genesis and Judges represent. The issue with Benjamin revolves around a group of men forcing sex and sexuality upon people, like a group of men seeking to force themselves upon Lot's guests.

Were I to slide in my argument through the back door (no pun intended), they went from merely being gay and doing it gay, to demanding it in every context and situation. Demanding it without opposition or critique is for all intents and purposes, the same thing as teaching it. The Bible does not tell us to teach that. To do so is to teach something else. Thus I'm afraid the UMC has partly brought its current miseries upon itself. The crap storm that was General Conference was the equivalent of fire and brimstone (without fire and brimstone). And I fear a fate much worse than in the crap storm that will demand its due from American society and culture in the future if we don't repent. I fear a real fire and brimstone from a God who like David said, is long suffering but terrible in his wrath.

You swore to teach the Discipline and God's way. Now you say they need fixing by Marxist socialist atheism and LGBTQIA sexual algebra agendas. This included Yoga placards at General Conference that were

ONLY an outrage to the Asians, not Christian theology (at a Holy Conference). The Asians were offended because the Yoga symbols were used by Modi, who they accuse of Hindu Nationalism. Our DEI bishops didn't see any problem with the Yoga placards, at a Holy Conference where the fate of the UMC Church in many regards was decided. What a crap storm. What a terrible end for a once powerful denomination in American culture, and the rise of the White and Black bourgeois middle classes in America. Nietzsche has Zarathustra exclaim 'god is dead, for you yourselves have killed him'. How dispiriting: a god who dies at the hand of science, technology, secular philosophy, and the socialist-atheist LGBTQIA agenda. A god who dies before the might of Greece, Rome, Europe, and America as man, humans and the natural environment get trampled underfoot by the same Greco-Roman-American power and might...even to alter nature and natural means.

But on the 3rd day He got up. He didn't know what a man and woman were according to our DEI Bishops but they will at least pay lip service to Easter and him getting up. Everybody thought he was dead. Jesus played dead, while they mocked him and told him he doesn't even know what a man and a woman are, how is he to get himself down off the cross? They mocked him, the King of the Jews? He's not my King, he's responsible for crimes against humanity, crimes against homosexuals, crimes against transgenders, crimes against women, he deserves to be on the cross. This god is a criminal and must be crucified.

But he got up. He was just faking to be dead while you mocked him, pierced him and sliced him up like a sacrificial lamb, considering parts of him 'nonessential'. Our DEI Bishops told us they'd be good for racial harmony and reconciliation. #EbonyBishops, #Blackgirlmagic, #Blackgirlpower was going to save the day (like Star Wars Acolyte and life creating lesbian space witches was supposed to save the franchise). But all it got us was a ruined and dilapidated church universal, and a Black UMC so devoid of witness it is completely irrelevant to the post-modern Black experience in America and its real needs. Our DEI Bishops think our children don't need fathers and families, Sunday school, playgrounds, camping trips, etc., they need the language and freedom to contemplate their sexuality at 8, start taking hormones to retard puberty at 10, and cut their penises and breasts off at 17. That is what they need according to our DEI Bishops, not Jesus and/or scripture.

Our DEI Bishops told us they'd be good for racial harmony and reconciliation. But the only way men, and White men in particular, can get a seat at the table is to come into the room apologizing for countless millennia of patriarchal crimes, and with a humility so profound they hardly look up from the floor around the presence of the 'strong Black women' leading them. At a time when the Southern UMC, Black and White, should be coming together as a bulwark and strong tower against a powerful rising tide of nihilism, socialist-atheism and LGBTQIA agenda, we have allowed the same forces to split us. Living in the Bible Belt, Southern culture, southern Christianity, Southern Methodism must mean something for Southern Methodists of all races. It should be something specific and be a conservative force in the Methodist movement in America. Can it be said any more eloquently than Jesus said it? A House divided cannot stand.

As my father-in-law said, intentions notwithstanding, 25-30 years of DEI Ebony Elders and Bishops, and our relationship with the White mainstream UMC Church is worse! If 33% of them up and split off, and most of the others would too if they could afford it, or had the strength of internal leadership, that is not bringing #Backgirl magic in a positive way to the UMC. To add insult to injury 25 or 30 years of DEI Bishops and the Black UMC is weaker, has less relevance to Black America, and is less appealing to Black America than it ever was! And for $250,000 a year! And there is not a thing our current DEI Ebony Bishops are doing that can even possibly make our denomination appealing or edifying.

How we cherish, adore, and celebrate our DEI Ebony Bishops. But they are no good to anybody's church, not the Black UMC, or the White mainstream UMC. There they are with fat salaries, fancy robes and miters, with fancy symbolism on them. 'There she is', 'Miss DEI UMC America Bishop' with 14-page mumbo jumbo apologies to accepted historical disgruntled minorities and groups. There she is preaching a theology that ignores the fact that the church, which never advocated any crime, is held responsible for crimes committed by members, and which is held responsible for crimes committed by others because members and leaders stood by and watched those crimes being committed. One day, you will be held accountable for encouraging people to cut their penises and breasts off, a cruel, cruel, sacrifice indeed.

You encouraged, not just stood by and watched, but encouraged 12-year boys to resent their penises and hack their manhood into oblivion and take enough hormones to kill a small horse; in the name of the socialist atheist LBTQIA+ sexual algebra agenda. Not just stood by and watched silently, as you accuse the traditional church of being silent on racism, sexism, etc., but the UMC has taken the position of encouraging and advocating crimes against the human body in the name of LGBTQIA+ sexual algebra and alphabet soup theology. These are Bishop's duties these days, not just to stand by and watch crimes silently, but instead to encourage the mutilation of children in the name of sexual freedom. Patriarchy and tradition 'controlling' sexuality...bad! Socialist-atheists LGBTQIA social justice warriors 'controlling' people's sexuality and forcing down their throats a new 'normal', to our DEI Bishops is good? Their words. "The church was silent" as racism, women's oppression, transphobia and homophobia hurt people. Thus the church must apologize and be condemned for its 2000 year old silence against racism, sexism, transphobia and homophobia? But the current Post-Modern Post-General Conference 2024 is just as silent, if not more silent as kids are encouraged to hack themselves up in sacrifice to the god of the 'right side of history' as determined by the socialist-atheist LGBTQIA social justice agendas. Our DEI Bishops made no critique of Sam Smith's performance of a live satanic ritual at the Grammys. When will our DEI Bishops apologize for themselves and quit forcing the UMC church and God himself to apologize.

Jesus counseled us extremely effectively that by whatever means ye judge, you will be judge. He taught beware of 'motes' in the eyes of others, while there are logs of firewood coming out of your eyes. This is the whole principle behind forgiveness. Forgiveness is never served in an environment where you make people feel like they must apologize and acknowledge their crimes all the time, whether they are men, White men, or even children. That is not 'forgiving' someone, if every time they come around you or say your name, they must apologize for their historical crimes and take a 2nd class seat behind those they are told they oppressed. That, socialist-atheist LGBTQIA social justice warriors call 'justice'. It is certainly not the spirit of Christianity and Christ.

Ladies and gentlemen, it is a measure of cruelty to make somebody feel like they have to apologize and defer to others all the time. Jesus said 'my yoke is easy'. Our current Bishops want the UMC to wear the yoke of going around apologizing all the time like Catholics of a certain era used to do penance by wearing spiked undergarments, and every so often affecting movements that purposely cause the spikes to dig into their flesh and create pain. All the UMC apologies at General Conference 2024 had the effect of a Medieval Catholic, sitting there self-flagellating himself with a whip only long enough to slap his back as he whips it repeatedly over his shoulders. If you've ever seen any of those 'Da Vinci Code' movies there is always some crazy priest doing something like that, presumably because he feels so terrible about his sins or the sins of his church, just like our DEI Bishops. Except our DEI bishops wouldn't have the courage to whip themselves in apologies for 2000 years of the church's crimes, and content themselves to metaphorically whip southern, White, male, and conservative wings of the UMC for not coming along fast enough as they sacrifice themselves to the new god, that according to socialist-atheist LGBTQIA social justice warrior class, is on the right side of 'history'.

It's just self-flagellation, surely self-flagellation and apologies don't hurt anybody if it is done by consenting adults? But there are problems in this in 'the natural' as well as theologically. It happens that quite often like Patty Hearst and her relationship with the SLA, the psychological condition commonly known as Stockholm Syndrome can occur. Thus, the very people that kidnapped and threatened her, she began sympa-thizing with to the point that within months or so of her kidnapping, she was helping them rob banks. Does this not sound like our DEI bishops who began their careers swearing to conservative values at or-dination. But once they began interacting with, identifying with, and emulating socialist-atheist LGBTQIA social justice warriors, they nearly completely left the old UMC behind and now consider themselves 'rev-olutionaries shaking up the system' simply because of their new friends. Not coincidentally, their new friends developed their movement and lingo hating the same conservative values and institutions you swore to, but your faith is not such that you can resist the worldly temptations of new friends with new ideas, and acceptance.

Similarly, a person that is abused sexually, can oftentimes begin to take a kind of pleasure in it like S&M. I'll never forget reading some autobiographical material on Vanessa Williams (Former Miss America) where she linked her willingness to pose nude prior to the Miss America events, with the fact that during her early teen years she was sexually abused by an older cousin. Initially she was repulsed by the whole thing, but as it happened repeatedly and was not under her control, what could be enjoyable became somewhat enjoyable to her and made her more comfortable acting sexually than she ordinarily would be. A very good friend of mine in seminary I knew was somewhat effeminate, but the details of things or people's personal sexuality don't make much dif-ference to me because I am not interested what they do in their bed-rooms. I am interested in what we teach, and the only reason I am publicly opposing the new UMC Church is not because gay people ex-ist, or have interests, but because I don't think we should change the basics of church teachings. Often in our conversations I'd tell him the same thing I tell all my male friends...you need a good woman in your life. I only realized how much me saying that so often offended him, when he pulled me to the side in the hallway at seminary one day, and said George, there is nothing a woman can do for me (emphasis on the word NOTHING). Stunned, I replied 'I dig man, my fault', and never repeated that to him again. I respected him and his wishes. That incident probably helped our friendship. Later we were talking before a service at the chapel at Gammon Seminary, and as the organizers we were early, waiting on others to get there. We were talking and in a candid moment, he told me that when he was 12 years old, he was raped (his words) by his maternal aunt and his uncle, and that this transpired over some years. Here again, people's emotional and behavioral reaction to past traumas or what has happened in their past I am not judging. What people do in their own bedrooms and how they feel about what's in their pants (or not), I am not judging. My problem is that when we conform church teachings to people's suffering and traumas, that is a problem. Even the most liberal DEI Bishop wouldn't have the nerve to say to an alcoholic and drug addict that because all their ancestors and extended family were/are alcoholics, the individual should just give into alcoholism and drugs because that is how the Lord made them, a family and family line of alcoholics and drug addicts. Give in to the spirit of alcohol and drugs young man or woman, it is your destiny, it is how God made you. Even a DEI Bishop wouldn't have the nerve to say to a person that became an alcoholic or drug addict because of intense suffering, that they should now just give into it because of the strength of the compulsion, which was derived from the profound impact of their previous experiences of suffering, and the little relief alcohol and drugs provide. Yet somehow with sexuality and sexual issues, the brakes are off the UMC, and we are heading down hill unable to stop.

Did you see how the liberals danced in the aisles to celebrate the repeal of bans on gay marriage, ordination, and teaching. It was the religious equivalent of a denominational theological orgy, or a Dionysian outpouring of the triumph of sensuality over spirituality like the opening ceremony of the Paris Olympics when a man representing Dionysius laid out on the table half naked as if to be eaten, as one of the meal delicacies. Yes dear ones, dear tender ones, it was an XXX rated collective orgasm as the proponents of the socialist-atheist LGBTQIA+ sexual algebra social justice theological agenda jumped in the aisles, hugging and kissing as sexual prohibitions were repealed. It was an orgasmic reaction, an explosion of 'joy' on the floor as the self-flagellation took on record proportions the way some people can't achieve an orgasm unless they are being beaten, looking at porn, etc. or have other highly specific requirements. The dude that played in the television series Kung Fu, David Carradine, died in Thailand in a closet in his hotel room where it appeared as if he had hung himself. However the authorities in Bangkok (you can't make this stuff up), didn't think it was suicide because the belt around his neck was attached to some kind of rope around his genitals, and working the ropes harmoniously, the stricture pressure around his neck and genitals enabled him to achieve an intense orgasm...excepting that particular night, he didn't get the rope proportions correct.

Part V

There is only one theological construct that I could possibly see as justifying the liberal position. As I have stated early and often in this work, the liberals/DEI Bishops are doing a kind of suicide. They are sacrificing the health of the church for the church to be on what they presume to be the right side of history (as defined by socialist-atheist LGBTQIA social justice liberalism). Them being leaders, there is I suppose a world view that would consider liberalizing, and literal and figurative Post-Modern Christian evangelism, Christian apologetics, apologizing for crimes the church is supposed to have committed and allowed to be done in its 2000-year history. This unfortunately has the effect of making the church manipulatable by any old two-bit trauma hustler (ethnic, sexual, etc.) philosophy, and worldly doctrine, and putting 'the Church' completely in harmony with any definition of sexuality (except the biblical one).

DEI bishops call their obligation as leaders to put the church 'on par' with and in harmony with, what they perceive are unalterable trends and truths in human culture. The body of Christ, the Church they represent, must now conform to the world, a world which is now saying that it is a right and freedom to mutilate one's body in the name of sexual identity, and furthermore that those who mutilate their bodies and take all sorts of drugs and hormones in imitation of their desired sex, must be congratulated and celebrated because of the courage it took to mutilate one's body and take enough hormones and drugs to kill a small horse. DEI Bishops argue the church needs to 'get with it'. The 2000-year-old church needs to adapt its teachings, even fundamental teachings about the nature of 'reality', to the world and what is 'trending' and 'popular' opinion in the world. This deficiency in logic comes from the supposition that what is trending is automatically on the 'right side' of history. Yet how often is it, that what is popular today, isn't tomorrow, and what is unpopular today, is popular tomorrow. Music, literature, arts, and yes, religion find themselves coming and going in the popular 'what's hot' and 'what's not' contemptible mass public mind. But the church should be above such considerations. What's hot and what's not, might be allowed to bear an impact on practice, but we should never allow it to impact the Word of God, or standard fundamental traditional doctrine. The people we inherited (Wesleyan Christianity) from did it that way, and to as great an extent as possible in terms of doctrine and the Word itself we should respect that. Variations can be made in individual praxis, but not basic doctrine.

This notion our DEI bishops have, that they are saving the church by supervising the mutilating of it, dismembering of it, and killing of it, is almost like when chemotherapy or amputation is necessary, or required to save a person's life. But is it? Sometimes it is indeed medically necessary to save the person's life. These arguments I might have gone for. I still might go for them in my 'tacit relationship' with the UMC...especially for $80,000 a year and health benefits.

But the streams and spring have dried up. American society is different than it was during the rising of the early American Methodist, Baptist, Presbyterian, Episcopalian, and denominational churches. Church was the only entertainment, no tv, social media, cable, or travel. The church was the center of community. Anything and any preacher that called itself a church and had the cache to put up a building was darn near guaranteed a captive audience of dozens and hundreds of families that could walk there. Many times, communities grew up around churches. For any poor person, the keys to meeting a good woman or man from a good family, middle class life and coming up in the community were helped and furthered by joining a good church. Long before post-modern Americans paid money to 'network' we did it in our churches. Whether this networking was for jobs, business opportunities, or marriage opportunities, the Church was the fount and center for any community. These days are different, and the church must compete. The well has run dry amidst demographic and socio-economic shifts in family and religious temperaments. In the meantime, the UMC went out and hired DEI Bishops who can no more compete with the internet and entertainment worlds about what it really means to be responsible for American civilization, our communities, the crime, the poverty and other social problems, than the men on the moon. There are real negative trends in the American identity, society, and civilization that the church should be addressing, but the only qualification for Bishop is that they are the right sex and the right race! This is why the Israelites had to go back and get Jephthah from the land of Tob. In our post-modern times, the continual loss in membership in the UMC happens and will continue to happen no matter how much sin our DEI Bishops wipe away with the stroke of the pen and rulings by Judicial councils. There is a decline in the prestige and the power of the UMC in America as endless squabbles make us look petty and self-absorbed. As Rome burns, we are celebrating Gay rights. As American civilization collapses into violence in our inner cities, and complete self-degradation on television, the UMC is celebrating gay marriage and gay ordination, knowing full well none of those things are drawing people to the denomination. Quite the contrary, people are running away from it. The well is running dry. 33% of the UMC's most effective and prosperous churches in the south and Midwest 'hauled Old Testament donkey' away from the church taking their apportionments with them. The well is running dry.

The liberals are screaming bloody poverty, quite precisely because our genius DEI bishops, who never built their own 'hustles', were willing to sacrifice the discipline and money of the UMC, to be 'one the right side of socialist-atheist LGBTQIA+ history'. I get it. But there is one philosophical and theological problem with being 'on the right side', the 'woke side' of history. An omnipotent, omniscient, omnipresent God is ALL history. For Him there is no right side or left side, front side or back side, top or bottom of history. It is all one history, His History. What is on the humanly defined right side of history today, will be on the scrap heap of history and derided the next. What was in the past considered the right side of human history gets mocked. The right and wrong sides of human history and their spokespersons, hurling polemic arguments and ad hominem attacks against one another in fighting for control of human religious and political institutions is a human construct. That's why they (right sides and wrong sides) have no pertinence and switch around 180 degrees every ten or 15 years of a culture's life. The rise of modern and post-modern communications and social media technologies has sped up the process of cultural values becoming obsolete.

In this kind of gyroscope of values, our DEI church leaders follow 'the world' from trend to trend, cause to cause, one set of ideals to another. Or do we stay focused and fixed like the old Black church had its mind 'staid' (stayed) on Jesus. The old Black church had its mind 'fixed on Jesus'. Does the current Black UMC under our beloved DEI Ebony Bishops? The old church was used to singing about how 'I woke up this morning with my mind on Jesus, went through my day and went to sleep with my mind staid on Jesus. Fixated on Him, His word, and His (biblical) values. That is how I (we) maintained our sanity during what our ancestors went through in the Antebellum south, Jim Crow, and Civil Rights era struggles. And you DEI bishops mean to tell me that therapy is better than a mind staid on Jesus and serving the Lord? That is the Jesus you are selling, the one that doesn't know what a man and a woman are, let alone what sanity is. How can He know what sanity is, he doesn't know what a man and a woman are (apparently with a penis staring him in the face without resorting to DEI bishops 'to explain it to Him using LGBTQIA+ sexual algebra and alphabet soup rhetoric)! How can he fix my insanity, he was wrong about what a man and a woman are (for 2000 years of church history). Apparently, the fact he created and evolved mammals with the same exact male/female sexual distinctions as humans, must be a mistake on his part of some sort to according to our DEI bishops. Apparently, God was unfair to mammals to have created them with penises and vaginas, as necessary to reproduction.

The Jesus and Christology of our slave ancestors and their so-called masters knew what a man and woman were; that is to say, what his word and being mammal demanded a man and woman were. The very same way his Father in Heaven knew what a mammalian male and a mammalian female were when he created them out of the clay of our ape ancestors DNA. We would do well to cite Job here for our DEI Ebony bishops.

> 4 *"Where were you when I laid the foundation of the earth?*
>   *Tell me, if you have understanding.*
> 5 *Who determined its measurements—surely you know!*
>   *Or who stretched the line upon it?*
> 6 *On what were its bases sunk,*
>   *or who laid its cornerstone,*
> 7 *when the morning stars sang together*
>   *and all the sons of God shouted for joy?*
> 8 *"Or who shut in the sea with doors*
>   *when it burst out from the womb,*
> 9 *when I made clouds its garment*
>   *and thick darkness its swaddling band,*
> 10 *and prescribed limits for it*
>   *and set bars and doors,*
> 11 *and said, 'Thus far shall you come, and no farther,*
>   *and here shall your proud waves be stayed'?*
> 12 *"Have you commanded the morning since your days began,*
>   *and caused the dawn to know its place,*

13 that it might take hold of the skirts of the earth?

16 "Have you entered into the springs of the sea,
or walked in the recesses of the deep?

17 Have the gates of death been revealed to you,
or have you seen the gates of deep darkness?

18 Have you comprehended the expanse of the earth?
Declare, if you know all this.

19 "Where is the way to the dwelling of light,
and where is the place of darkness,

20 that you may take it to its territory
and that you may discern the paths to its home?

21 You know, for you were born then,
and the number of your days is great!

22 "Have you entered the storehouses of the snow,
or have you seen the storehouses of the hail,

23 which I have reserved for the time of trouble,
for the day of battle and war?

24 What is the way to the place where the light is distributed,
or where the east wind is scattered upon the earth?

25 "Who has cleft a channel for the torrents of rain
and a way for the thunderbolt,

26 to bring rain on a land where no man is,
on the desert in which there is no man,

27 to satisfy the waste and desolate land,
and to make the ground sprout with grass?

28 "Has the rain a father,
or who has begotten the drops of dew?

29 From whose womb did the ice come forth,
and who has given birth to the frost of heaven?

Lawd, Lawd our ancestors knew the genius of His word. Just based on a slave's exegesis of Job and Exodus, an ignorant slave could legitimately question where the slave master got the authority to tell Africans they deserved to be slaves? What 'forces' in European Christianity derived the right to tell the pre-slave trade European church that brutalizing Africans was okay because it was all Africans as subhuman were good for. Could it be the same 'forces' now promoting DEI Bishops to tell us God doesn't know what a man and woman are? This world told us, we were born to be slaves, his word didn't because the ancient Hebrews were slaves, and they were His people! His chosen heritage. Former slaves under hard bondage. Glory to God. Even during slavery no matter what 'the world' told you, you had a place in God if you lived His word. God's word. God's meanings in life. Not mine. Not yours. Not socialists, not atheists, not radicals of any sort focused on some one aspect of human existence like sexuality, but Gods word in total, and as a wholistic model for defining the 'good' life that is pleasing to God. God is a mind regulator, not me doing my own thing. I submit to his word, the 10 commandments, the meanings and warnings of the traditions and the prophets, the wisdom literature. That is how I regulate my identity, my sanity, my purpose(s) in life, what I owe my family, my peers, my professional associates, etc., not what I think or who I think offended me or has been holding me back. My behavior doesn't have anything to do with others, it's according to the **word**, not **'the world'**. The church can teach nothing else without committing suicide, which is precisely what our DEI bishops are intent on doing. One stays sane by being fixated on God, keeping a mind staid on Jesus not socialist atheist LGBTQIA social justice rallying cries! As a matter of fact, that is a precise reason to do insane things like mutilate, cut up, and hack up the Wesleyan Church in America, and tell children and adolescents its ok to mutilate, cut up and hack up their bodies in the name of affirming a sexual identity different from that of their apparent mammalian birth. Then you have a celebration at General Conference 2024, running up and down the aisles, dancing around the golden calf made of the heaped up cut off penises and breasts of your adolescents...a proper blood sacrifice to you new god fashioned from the works of your own socialist-atheist LGBTQIA social justice worshipping hands. **But you just wait til' Moses gets back.**

I must keep fixated on Jesus/the Mind Regulator/His Word/His Father/The Holy Spirit etc. But why would I fixate on, or trust a God, that instead of correcting and helping me, apologizes to me for what he has done to me in my past, and rewards me by letting me do whatever I want to do no matter how destructive it is. This is an illusion of a loving God, an ersatz god, a golden calf, that lets you do whatever you want to do around it (whatever), even men and women dancing and prancing down the aisles in rainbow flags same-sex kissing. What a convenient God that you take seriously only as you want to, or as your human socialist atheist LGBTQIA+ social justice logic dictates. It is written that the ancient Hebrews danced around the golden calf in celebration of their ersatz god, the people getting their will while Moses was gone. Aaron the ersatz priest/prophet, while Moses was away, wasn't enough; Moses oral instructions to the elders and the practices Moses instituted weren't enough; whether they could do any of them without him or not. This is the same way I would imagine the pro-gay lobby belittled it's Aaron substitute priests, ersatz priests, and bishops in the absence of a real man of Moses stature. Thus, they bullied Aaron into helping them build the golden calf. And they celebrated, dancing around the golden calf, dancing in the aisles like the UMC General Conference 2024 in celebration of the triumph of the exact opposite of God's word, and values via Moses, via Jesus, via Paul, via Augustine, via Luther, via Wesley when the repeals on homosexuality were announced.

Worship the new golden calf the liberals have constructed out of human theology mixed with socialist-atheist LGBTQIA+ social justice philosophy. The remaining weakened institution of the UMC, is left with its ersatz Bishops and elders, and their rise through DEI instead of talent or a call. Think I'm being rough and unfair? As much as Bishop Dease loves to ride motorcycles, so much so that it is plastered all over her bio, whereas her husband, children and/or her books are not. Also not on her bio are the famous Methodist and Non-Methodist churches and preachers she has preached for, raising the roof with her dynamic worship and preaching. Perhaps she and the Methodist church would have been better served if we paid her $300,000 per year to be a social media influencer on sites devoted to Black female United Methodists that ride Harleys...I can see it now...the one...the two...the many.... (Star Wars Acolyte reference)

Let them dance around the golden calf, Moses is coming back. Moses is coming back soon and humble as he is, he is rabid in the interest of his God. There he is along the horizon, gathering the Levites around him, the Storm of God's wrath darkening the skies around them. Dancing wildly around this golden calf; men, women, and fake men and fake women prancing in the aisles draped in their rainbow flags kissing each other at a Holy Convocation, General Conference 2024. Oh how they danced and pranced and waved their rainbow flags, a colorful tapestry to drape around your golden calf. This is a golden calf that represents a monument to sexual idolatry. It wouldn't have surprised me if they had stripped naked in celebration as they danced.

Judges 11:1-3 KJG Judges 11:1 Now Jephthah the Gileadite was a mighty man of valour, and he was the son of an harlot: and Gilead begat Jephthah. 2 And Gilead's wife bare him sons; and his wife's sons grew up, and they thrust out Jephthah, and said unto him, Thou shalt not inherit in our father's house; for thou art the son of a strange woman. 3 Then Jephthah fled from his brethren, and dwelt in the land of Tob: and there were gathered vain men to Jephthah, and went out with him.

Chapter 11 - Biographical Adventure I

Chapter 11 - Biographical Adventure I: Why I have Hope - when I realized Mrs. Dudley was a real Ninja, not like Mbaba Hakeem

I was born into the AME church, but I grew up from aged 12+ at Ben Hill, UMC in Atlanta, GA. One of my childhood friends and neighbors were the Dudley's, who were long attendees of Laster Chapel UMC, our sister church. So, when Trinity AME, Laster Chapel, and of course Ben Hill had youth programs, I'd go. It never failed that I went to two or three vacation bible schools a summer, which I didn't mind because as an only child, there was food, sports and girls, and that was enough for me, much like men today I suppose. Of note was Mrs. Dudley's and Laster Chapel's annual Daytona trip during the summers. I was 15 or 16, hormones raging, 80's hip-hop & R&B the soundtrack to our little teenaged lives; stimulating our understanding of the possibilities in 'love'. We always looked forward to the trips. We'd bring our boom boxes and as many cassettes as we could carry.

I remember taking about 3 or 4 Coach buses down to Daytona. There was an adult bus. There was a bus for families with small and smaller children, and there was the teen pre-teen bus. The fourth bus may have been a young adult bus. I was on the teen bus and as an older 'cool kid' I duly took my position in the back of the bus as did my friends, all the other 'cool kids'. We immediately started doing what young and dumb kids do. Talking loud, 'joaning', and trying to impress each other with our boom boxes or the most subversive music. Half the competition was volume. So the music talking, and 'joaning' got louder and louder. We thought we were having a good time. It turns out the bus driver did not, and about an hour into the trip he began 'feeling some type of way' and complained about these teens back here making too much noise and tumult.

Perhaps by walkie-talkie (as it was pre-cell phone), some kind of way he told the other bus drivers, and Mrs. Dudley and the adults found out about our shenanigans. So at a rest stop, they put a nervous young adult lady on the bus to function as chaperone. This poor woman I am sure they drafted by casting lots, or she picked the shortest straw, or she was the paschal lamb, scape goat, all rolled into one. She came on the bus, and nothing changed and perhaps our 80's teen angst behavior got worse. We knew from how nervous and little she was, that she was not going to discipline us verbally, and while I never talked back, we had some kids there who weren't afraid to buck on nervous teachers and adults that lacked presence and authority. The only disciplinary tool she had that worked a little, was to threaten to tell Mrs. Dudley on us. The problem with that was that it made her authority even less respectable, and furthermore made her a target of our ridicule and our contempt. It further emphasized her powerlessness in our teen and pre-teen minds. All we must do is keep her from telling Mrs. Dudley. This poor woman was not the authority, she was the symbol of authority, and that was compromised by her nervous apologetic weakness in our teen minds. We humiliated her by ignoring her, and then there were a few of us that would even insult her with audible insults just seeming under one's breath.

Finaly she and the bus driver brought out the big gun, Mrs. Dudley, mother of the church. There is an old picture of Mrs. Dudley and another mother from the church, Mrs. Chamblee, in the early to mid-1940's as little girls in the Laster Chapel Sunday School Youth Program! Laster Chapel United Methodist Church history includes such gems as the church congregation being about 120 years old, and was started in a literal brush arbor by newly freed Black Christian families from the area meeting under a Methodist banner.

When this Daytona Youth trip occurred, Mrs. Dudley was perhaps in her 60s. She was in her prime then, as she still is now, believe it or not. I'll never forget. The bus driver and chaperone being sufficiently convinced that they could not make the 12-hour ride to Daytona Beach, Florida, with this kind of chaos going on, something would have to be done. All the buses pulled over into a rest stop. And we saw one solitary figure coming towards our bus. It wasn't the pastor; it wasn't somebody's daddy. It was Mrs. Dudley, and we all watched horrified like it was happening in slow motion, her dress trailing behind her like some kind of Jedi, Sith, or ninja outfit in the wind, like Dearth Vader or Emperor Palpatine coming to check out an installation reputed to be dysfunctional.

Suddenly it became all too apparent where she was headed, the teen bus. And we could tell by her stride and her demeanor that she meant business. Beloved, a criminal silence drifted over the entire bus as someone announced, "Mrs. Dudley is coming, Mrs. Dudley is coming, 'oh holy Old Testament burying material'. The door to the bus flew open like Mrs. Dudley used the Force to open it, by just raising her hand towards it. She marched up the steps, did a hard left like a true soldier from the old empire, and marched straight to the back of the bus where I, and all the cool kids were gathered nervously.

She gave us a 60 second lecture on how we were setting a bad example for the pre-teens and younger teens on the bus. Her eyes darted across the back section of the bus, perhaps the last 3 or 4 rows, in each of our eyes as she lectured another 30 seconds on how if she 'has to get back on this damn bus about some disciplinary issue', we were going to know something...and then the incident happened that made me realize Mrs. Dudley was indeed a Ninja/Jedi/Sith Lord. She repeatedly said that if she had to get back on this bus, we were going to know something, with her piercing eyes darting to and fro. She looked at each of us individually and said "some of y'all are looking at me like I'm joking, like there is something funny, like I'm a comedian." And of course, to be honest, we were teens and pre-teens, you know we were smirking and looking like we wanted to laugh when we thought she wasn't looking. But her eyes were darting back and forth so fast (like the teacher was used to bad kids she knew were up to something), it was inevitable she caught one or more of us looking crazy, or looking like we want to laugh. And that just got her wound up. So wound up indeed that she put her ninja move on us; just enough to show us she was that realness. Looking into each of our eyes she continued, "y'all think I'm joking, I said something funny, y'all think I'm funny," and I promise the reader that while looking one way, she slapped a young lady in a completely different direction, concluding her speech and demonstration of Ninja/Jedi techniques with one more repetition of "If I have to get back on this bus, because of some disciplinary issue, y'all go'n know something." Then, like hurricanes and storms, she came and went, marching off the bus the same royal dignified way she came in. And the young adult who was our chaperone immediately jumped up after Mrs. Dudley left the bus and said "See, I told y'all to be quiet."

Me and the 'cool kids' were stunned. And yet we all silently agreed on one thing, one tactical and strategic understanding; if Mrs. Dudley, whom everybody called Aunt Emma, has to get back on this bus for a disciplinary problem, somebody is going to get slapped again, and it wasn't going to be me. I need not say, we behaved much, much better during the rest of the trip. The story I told is not politically correct. It would not be recounted in official UMC Communications and Publications because it is not in line with current 'Safe Sanctuaries policies'. Perhaps the statute of limitations in a legal and theological sense have run out. In Mrs. Dudley's defense, it was not a full-on slap to the face. It was more a consequence of the young lady looking at her with a smirk, and Aunt Emma deciding to 'fix her mouth' for her. It was a quick grabbing twisting motion more than a slap. Also Mrs. Dudley, Aunt Emma, because of age and physical diminishing, has slowed down on her willingness to use light corporal punishment. All I know is that kids have gotten worse. They got all these rights and privileges, even to change their sexuality, but their behavior isn't any better than previous generations and they accomplish less with more than previous generations of post-Civil Rights era Blacks.

Did Aunt Emma fail the official 'United Methodist Safe Sanctuaries Test'? The sad fact is that after familial and social forces like her in the church, the only corrective forces left are the police and juvenile for many of our children because their nuclear families are so dysfunctional. I want to emphasize another result of Aunt Emma's use of 'soft power'. We teens began to 'police' ourselves. We 'the cool kids' told each other to chill when we or some of the other kids got too loud. When the younger teens and pre-teens did little dumb stuff, we'd take responsibility for fixing and solving the problem because God forbid Aunt Emma has to get back on this bus and handle a disciplinary problem. We didn't want her to hear about any problem on our bus that might tempt her to come back and do something as drastic as physically discipline us, or split us up in the adult buses. No other 'disciplinary' incidents occurred on the way down to Daytona or the way back to Atlanta....because we knew, if Aunt Emma has to get back on this bus, we were 90% sure that somebody was going to get slapped, and there was a 90% chance it would be one of the 'cool kids' because she was looking at each of us when she slapped the girl.

As teens it's publicly humiliating to get slapped, male or female, by an adult or peer (ask Chris Rock who I suspect is still traumatized by the Will Smith incident). Thus, Aunt Emma had the remedy for teen intransigence that day. We were cornered in the back of the bus as she stood over us glaring from the aisle. She knew right where to come, the back of the bus. We were trapped. The reader might wonder if the girl she slapped was traumatized. The answer is NO. She's a grown, relatively healthy, professionally productive woman today with a husband and family (at least at the time of writing). After the slap, as Aunt Emma walked away, tears began welling up in her eyes, but we 'cool kids' were like 'sista don't worry about it, it could have been any of us, so you don't have to feel embarrassed'. Privately each of us was thinking, 'thank God it was her and not me'! So we didn't want her to feel bad and didn't 'joan' the girl or treat her like anything less than she was before, or act towards her like she should feel traumatized. For that matter we were all traumatized. She shouldn't be any more traumatized than we were simply for having been unlucky enough to be the recipient of the punishment for the crime of looking at Aunt Emma wrong, and thinking Aunt Emma was a comedian when she wasn't trying to be funny. Funny enough, the rest of the trip we were treating her like we treat Military Veterans by saying and implying, 'thank you for your service'. She dang sure took one for the 'cool kid' team that day. We honored her for her service and sacrifice. She took one for the team. She was an honorary member of the 'cool kids' from that point on. She was our sacrificial lamb, our paschal lamb as teens, to keep the wrath of Aunt Emma up off us. But that's still better than the Maya ripping your heart out and throwing you off a cliff, or into a volcano trying to appease the gods.

But of course, the current UMC apologizes for the collapse of Incan society too, by the hands of the Catholic Pizarro, even though in the year 1533, Methodism wasn't even a glimmer in Luther's eyes or theological cojones. This is something else our DEI bishops must apologize for, because 'the church', even the Catholic Church, sat by as natives were murdered and their lands plundered. DEI bishops in 2024 must apologize for the White man, who like that Jedi in the Acolyte, is happily in a coma, just waiting to commit suicide in atonement for his past sins against a coven of lesbian witches, the beautiful world they created while they were living in a flammable mountain shaped like a vagina, and doing bizarre mumbo-jumbo rituals, typified the hand motions they made when repeating the phrase...."the one...the two...the many" as they cleaved the sky with their hands in upward thrusts, and moaned in ecstasy.

Part II

These early experiences in loving local churches, filled with my friends and family influenced my idea of 'United Methodism' writ large.

Later in Seminary and seeing the Annual Conference operations level for the first times, I was thoroughly impressed, and thoroughly convinced of the United Methodist system. Equally strong was my desire to work for and in it. But the root of that was these early experiences with my church family being an extension of the families in my community, families I knew, and the churches they attended. Seminary and seeing how Conference works from the floor, etc., was ok, but I especially enjoyed seeing people from churches I had attended or served in varying capacities over the years I was in United Methodist ministry.

People in my community I greatly respected and who did much to further my development and the quality of my experiential existential life, gave me positive feelings that I took to Seminary and 'Annual Conferencing'. I assumed that if they love this 'system', then on their behalf I will love it and do my best for it. This I had no problems with, certainly not in an Afrocentric sense. By then I had done 'real' Afrocentric theology with the Black Interfaith Community in the West End and Southwest Atlanta for years. I did not need some sort of engagement with White Methodists, or the White mainstream in general to 'feel' as though I was practicing 'Afrocentric theology' or that they had to accept it and make a seat for me at 'their' table. Thus, my attitude as I encountered my White mainstream UMC friends and associates was one of genuine interest and appreciation for the differences I encountered. I was not resentful of the differences or the painful history of race relations in America. I did not need White folks for that. I did not need 'reparations', or 'for them to repair me', or 'help me'. I appreciated the cultural differences and wanted to appropriate both traditions at the highest levels of articulation and performance.

For instance, I grew up in the theology and praxis of the Black Christian experience, that communal prayer is generally extemporaneous. Except where it is liturgical or something the individual praying has rehearsed, there usually is the appearance of improvisation and spontaneity. But I noticed at North Georgia Annual Conference and other events involving my White mainstream UMC brothers and sisters, that prayers were oftentimes written out and read. Honestly, my initial reaction was to see a liability in that predicament, the classical argument being that it 'takes the spirit out'. But in truth, there is a value in it, that is not explicit or implicit in 'spontaneous' improvised prayers. Both have a value. Written prayers can capture pregnant and poignant moments just as well or better than improvised prayers. The Holy Spirit is the antecedent, not the form, in spiritual works and matters.

Another thing I loved about White mainstream UMC events and Conferencing, was that nearly everywhere you turned there were groups, break out groups, subgroups, and a host of lunches, dinners, etc. In some sense it would be impossible to do them all. In the old days, this tendency for all this grouping and conferencing was a sign of vibrance and life. As the socialist-atheist LGBTQIA social justice wings of the church began to control the debate, all this grouping (in the absence of practical unity on basic matters of doctrine) became a liability. You can spend your entire day in session(s) that reaffirm your position, and not 'conferencing' at all (with other sides). Thus a whole lotta talking and voting goes on, but the pronouncements the sub-groups come up with mean nothing because they are purposely divisive and polemic.

The net effect of this 'division' and 'discord', is that the Post-General Conference UMC is continuing to invite and welcome people to some place increasingly fewer and fewer people want to go. Welcoming and continuing to invite people some place increasingly fewer and fewer people want to go is not evangelism. Oh yes, one last story about real evangelism. I'll give you an example of real evangelism amongst the youth.

There was a young lady I was particularly attached to in High School in the youth choir at Ben Hill UMC. (Cue my Yoda impersonation voice) 'Enthralled I was by her beauty, sophistication, charm, and seductive nonchalance'. I would wait and figure out ways to be accidentally near her instead of going straight home after choir rehearsal. I would only leave after she did. Finally, we began casually talking. She had a boyfriend at the time, I knew from middle school. That limited our interactions somewhat, but in many ways, she was the protype of nearly every woman I'd consider attractive from then on out. Whether she was on my level or not, too. The question I'm answering is, how do we evangelize teenage boys. It ain't rocket science.

Chapter 12 - Biographical Adventure II

Chapter 12 Biographical Adventure II

Oh, how proud we the Black UMC are of our Ebony DEI Bishops. But what will our current crop be known for; presiding over the suicidal dismantling of the UMC, and the 50-year decline of the Black UMC in terms of numbers, influence, and respectability in the Black community of faith and without it. Rather fondly do I remember being in Seminary at ITC, the Interdenominational Theological Center along the campuses of the Atlanta University Center. Every so often we'd get a princely/princessly visit from one or more of our Ebony Bishops. During the question-and-answer sessions, half of us would be worried about the vagaries and mysteries of the ordination process, and the other half worried about how you get a better appointment.

Many of us were in our own little fantasy land about how professional ministry worked. Because of the demands of the UMC at the Deacon and Elder levels, we were far more worried about navigating the system than we were about serving the people and doing good ministry. Some kind of way many of us had convinced ourselves that by our presence in ministry, we were doing the UMC, the Body of Christ, and Black people a favor. Much of that was because like colleges and universities today are facing the effects of liberal anti-institution students and professors, the Seminary has long been a haven for liberal and even atheist academics and researchers. These anti-institutional liberals have had the effect of destroying American seminaries and the university system from the inside.

I remember my first paper in one of my first classes. I was extremely proud of it and gung-ho about doing well because it took a felony and 2 divorces for me to be traumatized enough to get to seminary in the first place. That was hardly a direct or admirable path in denominational or academic terms. I wasn't motivated by theology in general, or a strong sense of Christology, but over a lifetime I had seen how effective the church could be in my personal life, and the lives of the families in my community. Thus, I was not motivated to go to seminary trying to be on the right side of theological or denominational history. I was there because the church cleaned me up and I had seen it clean others. I had seen it create families and communities in the wilderness.

I turned my paper in and eagerly awaited its return and grade. Even then I thought I could write, but I was eager to see what a Seminary level academic professor thought of my work. I received it, flipped through to the end and saw my 95. When I saw what my professor docked me 5 points for, I was amazed. I referenced in positive terms the traditional family, and the idea of the importance of creating healthy bible based Black families. In red, were 3 big question marks written on the page with my grade. Dr. Aymer wrote "who told you what a healthy family looked like or was supposed to be like?" and she objected to my referencing God as a 'He'. Thus, I was docked 5 points. It didn't matter. I didn't care enough to lie or act differently for the sake of fitting in.

Sufficiently humbled however, it now dawned on me that seminary would have a much greater secular feel to it than I had imagined. These days, had I been in the same circumstances I would have bucked back, strode right up to the professor and said in response to her question posed in red on the back of my paper, "the same person/entity that told you what a healthy family should like, when you called yourself a Christian or a variation of a Christian. And what are you doing here teaching a God you don't believe has any authority over humans that we don't 'give' him". But back in those days I was just happy to be there, and equally convinced there was a place for me in the UMC. So, I learned the preferred gender pronouns and resolved to use them in academic terms, the same way I was quickly disavowed of my King James Version in favor of the NRSV. I took the phrase 'Father God' out of my seminary public and academic discourse, if not my personal discourse.

For those and many other reasons, ITC and its United Methodist constituent Gammon, the United Methodist arm in the Black academic theological tradition is a dead man walking. The Black church is failing, shrinking and losing what relevance it had in Post-Modern Black culture and families. If ITC is depending on Black churches to survive it is dead in the water, and if Gammon is depending solely on the viability of the White Mainstream UMC and its benevolence to survive, I'm afraid they will soon be dead in the water as well. The current post General Conference 2024 UMC church does not have the resources to support its commitments to African American education, even seminary education. Sooner or later if it hasn't already, ITC and Gammon Seminary will be the Morris Brown of the Atlanta University Center, destined to experience further funding and accreditation problems. And there is nothing our Ebony DEI Bishops can do to save it, even with the Ebony Bishops that went to ITC/Gammon. Because of their theological and ideological commitment to the socialist-atheist LGBTQIA+ agenda, this led to them hacking up the traditional pre-2018 UMC. Because of that disastrous policy spearheaded by our DEI liberal Ebony Bishops, the net effect of this self-immolation in the name of the new god, was to reduce the amount of funds available to already struggling Black churches, Black HBCUs, and Black seminaries like Gammon/ITC. This has been the effect of the disastrous reign of our DEI Ebony Bishops.

I do not want the reader to think I am joaning Gammon/ITC. I got in enough debt to purchase a starter home, but it was worth it academically, emotionally, and spiritually. Until I got to Seminary, because of the bitter fruit of my 4th grade experience, I had this idea that it was better to keep your light under a bucket. My idea was that if people see it, it attracts negative attention. In that way a kind of mediocrity crept into my life that I embraced because it kept me safe psychologically. Believe it or not, two female professors, both UMC and Dr. Ed Smith were the first to treat me like I was smart and that they had expectations. Dr. Anna Crawford, and Dr. Carol Helton of the UMC, both professors at ITC, were a real blessing in my life. They always made great comments on my papers, that let me know they were really reading them and half-respected my opinions. In class discussions they would encourage me to participate if I had been quiet.

This maternal attention had a restorative effect on me. I grew more confident in my abilities. I grew more confident in what I was thinking and what was coming out of my mouth. That is not to say they agreed with me then or would agree with me now. But that confidence carries over into how one does and says things, and it is that confidence that inspires other people to follow you, or allows you to lead them in a tacit or official way. Dr. Helton's classes taught me some interesting things about myself too. As I said, I was a 'hide your lamp under a bucket' guy. I think some professors and pastors have the gift of the Holy Ghost working sometimes, and they can see through and under buckets. Dr. Helton saw through the bucket. For a significant portion of my adult life, my motto was 'it takes genius to be this mediocre'. By that I meant that it takes a lot of work to put yourself squarely in the middle of the pack on purpose. You don't attract attention in the middle of the pack. Said differently, while it's of course 'hard' to get a 90 on a test, you must be capable of getting a 90 or 100 in order to purposely get a 75.

That was how I 'glided' through undergrad and the beginning of Seminary, trying my darndest to be mediocre, not attract attention, etc. That was until I heard the screeching brakes to my 'gliding' in Dr. Helton's class. The class was UMC History, and you had to get a B in it to fulfill the requirement for Gammon Seminary, the UMC constituent of the Interdenominational Theological Center. I'm good with history and books, I'm ready to glide through another class, prepared to do minimum required to get a B. I was able to get 'B's and A's' on most assignments and the only thing left was an end of term paper. I would love to see what I wrote then now, except that I know I'd be humiliated and embarrassed by it (though that hasn't stopped me from writing yet). It was not well researched (probably like this book), and I had some conclusions she neither appreciated nor thought warranted. In hindsight, the only difference between my past 'anger and resentment' towards the UMC for seeming to me to make my 'journey' hard, and my current 'anger and resentment' for the same feelings today, is that back then I cared. Today, the clownish, muddled and confused policies of the current UMC and their DEI Bishops is proof enough that when I submitted myself for ordination back from 2003-2013, they were just as incompetent as they are today. They could not have recognized my talents, gifts, and graces, and the bigger tragedy for United Methodism is that they had a great overestimation of their skills and capacities to recognize and make good leadership decisions over the White mainstream and Black UMC.

Meanwhile Dr. Helton stuck a 'D' on my paper, and because of the way she averaged and tallied her grades, I would have to 'smoke' (no pun intended) the final exam. Surely then I'd leverage a 'B' out of the class. I knew I could do well enough on the final and my reasoning wasn't all out of self-confidence. There was a developmentally disabled guy in the class, and I knew his grades. Thus in my ignorance of Dr. Helton, I believed there was no way 'in hell' she would possibly flunk him with a good conscious or give him a C and make him take the class again, knowing full well he had no pretensions to the ordination track and was more or less in seminary because he loved the Lord, and after the legal confirmation of his disability he had more free time and may as well go to seminary. I was confident some of Dr. Helton's mercy would rub off on me.

After the final (which I doubt I smoked unless I meant the pun), she told me she had to speak to me after class. Indeed, I had done well enough on the final, but she told me that she was still going to give me a C and make me take the class over. She reiterated that my paper stunk up the place, the putrid aroma still in her nostrils, causing her to recoil and wince in pain, just at the mere memory of the fetid, hideous, intellectual stench wafting off my paper. "I know you can do better". Wow! It is so rare in life that you meet people who act like they believe in you or care enough to act like they believe in you. Sufficiently humbled, I did my best in her and my other classes after that because, to use a phrase, if Dr. Helton and Dr. Crawford thought I had some talent...maybe I do. Thus my concern was not to disappoint their confidence.

I noticed something similar with a dog I had when I was in college. Great dog, but I thought he was weak because if I fed him outside, the neighbor's dog would run over and eat his food in front him, as he snorts, gruffs, and puffs but does nothing until his food is all gone. Initially I tried to discipline him by fussing and figuring that if he let the neighbor's dog eat his food, he wasn't hungry. But the idea of my dog being hungry I could not stand, even if I was trying discipline him. I didn't have the heart to not feed him a meal or two, hoping he got angry enough to fight for his food. So one day after the other dog ate his food, I waited an hour or two and then went out to feed him again. As I started, the neighbor's dog immediately ran over and started eating the food again. My dog stood there and did nothing. Properly insulted by the nerve of this dog, I started fussing at the neighbor's dog and shooing him, which of course he paid no attention to as he greedily ate all the food. I began gently pushing him away with my foot, which he took offense to, and he growled and bit my foot. Why did the neighbor's dog go and do that! My dog boo-boo jumped on him so quickly, I was startled at his aggression. I ended up having to pull Boo-boo off the neighbor's dog because he had gone in so hard in defense of me. Boo-boo wouldn't fight for his own food, or in defense of his own interests, but he would act completely out of character if necessary to defend his perception of my interests. That is how I came out of the gates of Dr.'s Helton and Crawford classes. If they thought I was somebody, whether I thought I was or not, I would defend the best of their expectations.

I was determined that in the confidence and encouragement they showed in me, in front of other students, I not only needed to perform well in their classes, but my other classes as well. I imagined the horror of them talking to other of my professors and them saying 'that Negro ain't crap'. I made a 'set my face towards Jerusalem' decision, and from then on out if I didn't do well, it would not because I either didn't try my best or that I was aiming for mediocrity, or just had my light under a bushel.

As that process was playing out, another psychodrama from my childhood played itself out and stopped cycling in my mind. Believe it not, most of my life I thought most of the people around me were 'smart' and certainly the people everybody and elites say are smart, are actually smart, whether I thought so or not. I never included myself in that group and no one seemed to include me in that group, so I just assumed people were smarter than I. But in my determination not to let Dr. Crawford and Dr. Helton down, I started doing my best nearly all the time, and a very unusual thing happened. Whether I was smarter than my peers or not, I did not know, and would never pretend to such hubris as to say such a thing, or believe it in my spirit. The strange thing was that 'others' seemed to think so, which was a very unusual feeling for me.

I certainly wasn't proud, and it reminded me of the fourth grade when I won the talent show and then felt a lot of pressure to perform for the 2nd talent show later that year. Strangely enough I felt little or no anxiety because I wasn't just going off me and my smarts. Dr. Helton and Crawford told me I was smart, and so my confidence was that preparation. Knowing your schtick can get you through a lot of situations. But at the highest levels, listening, adapting, and reacting are the hard parts in an argument, speech or discourse. As you start developing a reputation for being smart and effective, others treat you like you are that way, and you develop a kind of stability in your hustle. It is that stability that blessed my interior and exterior lives. Just in the natural (not a clinical diagnosis), I wasn't stable. My sense of limitations kept me halting and hesitating. The unkind words or sneers of peers and elites could throw me off track and for a loop. But I got stable in my own head at ITC/Gammon Seminary, and I will forever be indebted to it (and apparently the Student Loan Corporation). I hope and pray that we can reverse the trends in Black churches, Gammon Seminary, and the Interdenominational Theological Center.

Part II

Who has overseen and presided over this great catastrophe in the Black UMC and wider UMC...our beloved, right honorable, and right reverend DEI Ebony Bishops. They are artificial creations, like artificial plants or Christmas trees. From a distance they look hardly indistinguishable from real trees and plants. But get closer, and you see the defects. Get close enough to smell, and note the antiseptic plastic smell. Get close enough to touch and feel the plasticity. Yes our DEI Bishops are artificial. Like a good set of artificial teeth, the liberal White UMC has gone out and bought them some teeth, a wig, and new set of worldly fashionable clothes, and thinks it is a new church.

The UMC has gone out and gotten plastic surgery trying to make itself look like the world, but in the end all we have done is mutilate ourselves and make ourselves look alien like the late Michael Jackson, Joan Rivers, Donatella Versace, and it seems we must add Serena Williams to the list. Like the false penises and fake breasts, our church now promotes fake men, and fake women. A church that recognizes and justifies the artificial is probably artificial itself! Is our church authentic post-General Conference 2024.

Bishops that can't preach themselves 'happy', let alone anyone else inhabit high places and positions of power. Bishops more concerned with being on the right side of history, than God's side of history run the Church. That is why no one is interested in joining. They can see how fake it is. During General Conference 2024, the UMC Global Communications Agency (I bet their budget wasn't slashed), perfectly produced packaged soundbites, podcasts, and video feeds, but is that evangelism? One need always beware of persons who spend way more time promoting themselves, than they do 'being' themselves. That is the position our UMC church is in. We no more know what we 'are', than the God we claim to serve, that presumably either didn't know what a man/male or a woman/female are, or purposely lied to us for 4000 or so years.

Some 2000 years out from Christ our Church no longer knows its identity. It doesn't know what it is or understand the heritage it was born with. Black women for generations have felt so apologetic over their 'medusa' hair, their natural legacy, that they have spent billions on hair straightener to point of using dangerous chemicals, and/or bought the hair of other races of women trying to 'make' themselves attractive, instead of 'being' attractive.

Our church is like a 700-pound person who dang sure had no short-cuts to getting that big and fat. The person put in all the eating, all the calories from fat, all the work and all the overeating and indiscipline it took to get that big, but then he wants a short cut to losing weight like gastric bypass surgery. We live in a society of cheap and easy dieting, and it has gotten to the point where folk diagnosed with diabetes and high blood pressure can't buy enough Ozempic because overeaters, celebrities, and body worshippers have bought it all up, and glamourized its effectiveness and use. Similarly, our church wants an easy way out. The easy way to look hip for their mediocre minds, was in endorsing the Socialist-Atheist LGBTQIA social justice warrior mentality redistribution and reparation schemes. The easy way to make a Bishop is to find one that is politically correct to socialist-atheist LGBTQIA social justice warriors and stick him or her there; not go through the spiritual hard work of call, prayer, discernment and aptitude...and uh...preaching ability. Those are the demands of being on the right side of history.

The Discipline is a foundation laid and built upon the biblical rock. That is why it has lasted. Once we tore down the Discipline, it has the net effect of uprooting the Bible. To go digging through it looking for stuff to change or say was wrong, is the behavior of a suicidal church that cannot stand because it is divided against itself and perhaps does not deserve to exist. Can an otherwise sane man, have a reason to kick one leg out from under himself; to take one leg and start kicking the other with it, and vice versa? This is the current body of Christ under the Post-General Conference 2024 UMC. This monumental shell of a denomination, a house made from sticks, built upon sand cannot stand. The whole heap is going to collapse upon itself. Its foundations are weak, and if what we witnessed at General Conference is not the final collapse, it is the sound and feeling of roof tiles failing, walls shaking, unstable floors cracking, and causing people to stumble because they are running so fast to get out! Let them that have ears, hear. A building in such a shape can stand in perfect weather. But let the storms come or the earth shake, and that building is a deathtrap. Dear church. What have we become?

Part III

Let me tell one last story from seminary that I think the liberals and/ or our DEI Bishops might get a kick out of if they picked up this book accidentally. I've already noted the liberal spirit at the ITC/Gammon. All our Pastoral Care and Counseling teachers were thoroughly in the pro-LGBTQIA socialist-atheist social justice camp. I was in one professor's class who if not gay, was certainly effeminate, a fact that didn't and doesn't bother me in the least. But I was a conservative when I got to seminary, I stayed a conservative, and I talked a kind of conservatism; sorta well thought out, but admittedly heedless.... In his class I would make comments about the need to support the Black family, stabilizing families, marriage, and things like that to stabilize and increase the quality of life in Black communities. Liberal theology doesn't think that is necessary or important for improving the quality of life for Black people in America. In their minds, more than we need stable families and fathers in homes, we need socialist atheist, social justice redistribution schemes, we need abortion, and we need to eliminate homophobia, transphobia and sexism. Oh, and imposing the new religion, which oddly enough is an inversion of the old 5% (5 percenter) religious architecture. For those who don't remember, the 5% Nation were a splinter group of the Nation of Islam or Black Moors, or a combination of streams, and their central philosophy was encapsulated in the idea that 'the Black man was god, and they called black women 'earths'. Well in the new feminism and womanism, the inversion of that is that the Black woman is 'god' and black men are immaterial, and all must worship her in her feminist womanist coven of witches with #Blackgirlmagic superpowers (the one, the two, the many). For those who think I'm exaggerating, have you ever noticed the way the LGBTQIA+ community worship and idolize Black women. Donna Summer and disco, Diana Ross, Patti Labelle these are the heroines of femineity who Ru Paul and the White transvestites and transgenders grew up imitating. They made a caricature of the usually big, boisterous over-the-top strong Black woman, make up, fake hair and all, and decided that was the static image of Black women they wanted to frame in order to emulate (it is hard emulating a moving target). If that is not enough, from Drew Barrymore needing a hug from 'Mamala' to the White female movie character archetype that needs to get her groove back with help from her fast-talking Black female friend, who is irreverent, earthy, and ignorant, but a good and loyal friend, with a good heart, who always magically makes the right decisions in the end. Those ideas have triumphed in the public square and the mainstream UMC church and the Black community is worse for the wear.

Like a dummy, I speak up in class about such issues. I thought in a respectful way...but I was wrong.

Apparently, I had the misfortune of mocking a grown man, making $40,000 or $50,000 a year teaching, in addition to pastoring his own church, feel like he was not in a 'safe space' in his own classroom. As I've matured, I've learned to sorta watch myself because I have been told that sometimes I come off like a bully. Growing up in the rough and tumble of the 'hood', you have to be somewhat forceful in your opinions and sorta have to understand your physicality and how it might be used. If you don't, quite often you will get taken advantage of, or peers and people will have you believing and doing anything.

Thus understood, in the hood you have to effect security in your position intellectually, and you must have a type of physicality behind it, that lets people know that if they think they are going to threaten to 'kick my old testament donkey' and/or make me believe what they believe or do, you've got a tough battle ahead, for which it may be best to leave it alone and let me go my way, and thee thine.

But I wasn't as conscious of how I might be coming off then, even though it is not my intention to hurt people's feelings, intimidate them accidentally, or on purpose. Finally, the professor, a bright wise man who taught me great and useful things about pastoral care and counseling felt like he had to take me down a notch or two, somewhat publicly humiliate me, a la my 4th grade teacher.

In hindsight I sorta understand that my comments regarding traditional values itched him the wrong way. He was effeminate and probably gay, and all this talk about family and the responsibility of Black people to strengthen their nuclear and extended families and have children, I probably should have left alone. But one day I hit a nerve, so he took about 5 minutes to attempt to psycho-analyze me in class-in public. He said the reason for my espousal of conservative values and views is because I was anal retentive. Bright as he was, I have no doubt he understood sticking the word 'anal' would cause me to react in a way that he would further humiliate me. But I sorta knew what 'anal retentive' meant and didn't really have a problem with being told I was overly orderly, unnecessarily meticulous, suspicious, and reserved even if it was a defense mechanism for prior trauma. And if that meant stubborn, rigid, and overly passionate about organizing, classifying and collecting objects that was fine with me.

So I did not act offended and I knew damn well that these characteristics, while certainly not without shortcomings, also had their benefits. I certainly was not overly neat or stingy. Though I was offended, I had enough sense to know he was putting me in my place and expressing a distaste for my opinions. But to his credit, he didn't attack me and my positions unfairly or aggressively. I sincerely believe he attacked my positions because he validly wanted to create a safe space in Seminary for Socialist-atheist LGBTQIA liberalism. Allowing my conservative statements about the family to go unchecked and unqualified, was not consistent with that.

But for a person to claim they want to be in a 'safe space' and then teach in seminary, which is known for teaching a 4000-year-old religious tradition that since day 1, has never presented itself as a 'safe space' for homosexuals and transgenders is problematic. It is like a pacifist paying to go to a boxing match and then complaining that the boxing ring should be a 'safe space'. It is like going to the zoo or the aquarium, and thinking it is a 'safe space' for animals because they are caged. It is like signing up and paying for the Playboy Channel and then complaining that there is too much sexual content. It is like going to a bookstore and asking for televisions because otherwise that store is discriminating against TVs, and it is not a 'safe space' for TVs...in a bookstore.

This is the lunacy, much of it self-inflicted, of the current post-General Conference 2024 UMC, and our ineffective and incompetent DEI Ebony Bishops that are artificial and inorganic; gene spliced with the biblical tradition and the leaven of socialist-atheist LGBTQIA social justice philosophy.

Chapter 13 - The bully you love to hate

Chapter 13 - Biographical Adventure III – The Bully You Love to Hate

Lastly (in preacher's terminology), I want to close on that bullying, tangential line of thought. The classic biblical example is Joseph. His brothers, the other sons of Jacob, wanted to bully Joseph and put him in his place. That is why the brothers needed to get him away from Jacob. Away from Jacob the pecking order was clear among the brothers. When Jacob was around, Jacob preferred Joseph, like a first-born son, completely ignoring seniority. That's a bit much for a group of teenage and young adult brothers to take. They started out just wanting to bully him and put him in his place but as their anger and resentment grew, so did their idea of tactics to take their brother Joseph down a notch or two. It is interesting to note that surely a gifted kid like Joseph should have seen the looks on his brothers' faces when he was being preferred over them. Surely, he should have noticed the discomfort he caused in his brothers when they were told of his 'dreams' and saw his 'rainbow' coat. Colors were expensive and to the ancient world represented a specific technology, workmanship, and craftsmanship to produce. It is not a coincidence that most things in the world are brown and green; to have yellow, purple, olive, and red was special. If that wasn't enough, Jacob told Joseph not to be talking that way around his brothers. That is evidence of the purity of Joseph's love and admiration for his older brothers. He loved and admired them so much he didn't think it possible that his brothers would have as much jealousy and malice towards him as they did. The brothers wanted it to be like the old days, before Joseph, when Jacob respected the pecking order. In their mind all they had to do was get Joseph out of the picture, 'by any means necessary'. Suffice it to say here that as smart as Joseph was, sensitive as he was, and spiritually adept as he was, he still loved and admired his brothers and wanted to spend time with them. Even Jacob was suspicious when Josephs older brothers showed up actually wanting to take him out and let him have fun. "He's always here up under you dad," according to the sages, learning the principles of Torah from Jacob, even though the written Torah would be 400 years and a period of slavery in Egypt away. "Let Joseph hang out with us and have some fun, for a change pops!" Jacob must have been suspicious, no older brothers or sisters really want to spend time watching their little siblings, it slows them down, and puts a cramp in their style. I'm sure Joseph had begged them for months to let him hang out with them, and they refused. Then suddenly, they ask Jacob to let him come with them? Such was the strength of little kid's admiration for their older siblings and the bigger boys and kids in their neighborhood. It is very powerful and can have the horrible consequences that we see every day in urban neighborhoods as gang and gun culture become the norm.

I was a sensitive, thoughtful child that liked to read a lot. Prime meat for bullies. The advantage I had was being somewhat athletic. But as a kid in a new neighborhood or school, you're gonna get the business end of the bullying. Weirdly enough, like most children, in some way I viewed bullying as normative. Older brothers, sisters, and cousins, apart from adult supervision, let us be frank, are not always the kindest to their younger, smaller siblings. Do not get me wrong, this should never be cruel and sadistic, but it is an important means of social organization and structure that has implications throughout life. I was watching a documentary on Japanese society, and it featured a middle school baseball team. The older players had younger players that carried their bags and did what we called growing up 'do boy' type of stuff. It turns out that this pattern is repeated at many levels of Japanese organizational life, and quite often there is a social obligation to the people under you and those over you have a social obligation to you. This kind of cohesion can be abused, but in looking at Japanese culture, its survival and its accomplishments, much of it is due to the uniquely reinforced social obligations built upon age and seniority.

Thus, to some extent, 'bullying' (which is not the best connotative or denotative word for what I'm trying to describe but shall suffice for the purposes of this essay) is considered 'normative'. That is why many kids don't tell, and don't snitch when others or they themselves get bullied. It seems no adult can stop it and if they tell and the adult tries, usually that only succeeds in making it worse. Furthermore, it is not uncommon that a kid tells an adult he's being bullied, and not only does the adult scold him or her, and tell them they need to toughen up, in some cases the adult might tell the bully the kid 'told on' him and make the bully even more angry. I'm surprised the liberal Bishops in the UMC haven't attacked children for 'standing by' while their peers are bullied. No liberal is dumb enough to believe only LGBTQIA+ kids get bullied, even that is precisely the way they make it seem. Payless shoes can get a kid bullied, nose to big (too little), feet to big (too little), 'flicted', 'too dark', 'too light', too tall, too short, an outsider, etc. But let the liberal agitators in the UMC tell it, only girls and LGBTQIA+ kids are getting bullied. I'd like to record here my reaction and recollection to bullying. There are bully individuals in every crowd, and what is worse they usually have a clique of kids around, hangers on too weak to desire to intervene or intervene on anybody's behalf, even their own. Typically, bullies do not attack each other, preferring to concentrate on the low hanging fruit; kids with no friends or that have apparent deficiencies. Thus, new kids are always at risk. Early on in my life, because I was nearly always 'new' to situations, when I went into new situations, I learned the hard way to find out who the bullies were. After you find out who the bullies are, you need to pick one and get on his team (amongst boys they are boys, amongst girls they are girls). The better you pick, the better your immediate future life as a child. He might bully you, but all the others won't, which cuts down on your bullying. You're not as isolated.

When I say pick your bully, you had to be careful and discerning with your pick. You wouldn't get many picks, and one bad pick could be disastrous. At the low end of the spectrum there are bullies that are cruel and sadistic. "That ain't what you looking for kid." You want a bully whose 'yoke is easy, and his burden is light'. At the top end of the spectrum are bullies who are smart, competitive, well-liked by adults and peers, and they really care about those in their clique and don't treat them like 'tools' (literally and figuratively). They are better bullies, but they are still bullies and are quite capable of giving the business end of the stick to discipline their tribe, or others if necessary. But for the most part, they are benevolent bullies.

Most of us children were caught between these two extremes growing up and I certainly was. As one gets older, you learn to pick bullies better to avoid cruelty and sadism. But another curious thing happens after a while (if you are lucky). You not only get big enough to compete and defend yourself and your interests credibly (you don't have to win, just make your opponent pay as high a price as possible), one day you look around and you are big enough to bully others. That was an exciting time in my life. I had some examples of good bullies, so I was determined to be a good one, not a cruel or sadistic one.

I'm sure you liberals and liberal theologians are screaming bloody murder and desperate to make me apologize and speak out against bullying. But let me at least finish the story of why bullying is an important function in childhood (and the life and organizational paradigm). Kids, the shy ones, the quiet ones, the disabled ones, need protection...desperately. A cruel and sadistic bully in your life makes a hard life worse; telling an adult quite often makes it all the more horrible. So what is a kid to do (in the short term at least). Pick the best bully you can and hope he lets you get on the team. That strategy reduces bullying greatly, and provided the bully is not cruel or sadistic, is a better option than telling a teacher...at least in the short term. Find you a bully you like or can deal with first, before you become the target.

Thusly educated, once I was big enough and competitively advantaged enough to be a bully, I couldn't wait to be a bully because I felt I'd be such a better one than the ones I had previously been exposed to by experience. Once you are big enough to compete and defend yourself, you have the potential to be big enough and competitive enough to defend others you may have under your suzerainty for any reason (family loyalty, neighborhood loyalty, church loyalty, etc.). Instead of being cruel and sadistic, I was encouraging and always made the people under me feel like I was in their corner and would help with anything (from harassment to schoolwork). Not only that I'd promote and support them for things I appreciated they were good at.

Inevitably your team gets stronger because in the natural, people react to and reciprocate people being kind to them and protecting them, and others want to be on your team, because everyone on your team thrives and accomplishes things no one, certainly not the other cruel and sadistic bullies would have expected from such a motley collection of weaklings, the disabled and the vulnerable. As your team swells and excels, girls find you much, much more attractive. In such circumstances, you become a 'power' in elementary school, middle school, high school, college and in the professional world. Yes. By being the best bully you can be. Of course ideally, you became such a great bully/leader because you were mentored by some great bullies coming up. And of course presumably, your great bullying, had the effect of mentoring young men that came up under you.

And yet what a strange quid pro quo. In exchange for allowing myself to be disciplined by you, your obligation is to protect me from the other bullies, the world in general and the full consequences of individual failure. Collective success is insurance. It protects me from individual failure. But what happens if increasingly, your bully of choice either can't defend you from outside forces or refuses to? What happens when your bully keeps getting his 'Old Testament donkey' kicked and every time you turn around some 'worldly bully' is pinning him to ground, making him say 'uncle', and making him apologize for being alive? Do you have confidence anymore in your bully, or do you understand intrinsically, that after your bully gets his 'Old Testament donkey' kicked, you're next.

You better go back and get Jephthah from the land of Tob with the pimps, players, thugs and hustlers, and make him 'bully in chief' of all the armies of Israel. You submit to organized leadership, discipline, training, and tactics, and prayerfully he will lead you against the Philistines, and the '-ites' and '-isms' that are currently terrorizing and torturing you, and making the UMC apologize all the time for its very existence. Jephthah would not be in the bible if he were a DEI leader. DEI leaders apologize to their enemies and capitulate to their versions of history and 'right'. When Jephthah fights the Ammonites, one of the first things the bible cites him doing is refuting the Ammonite King's territorial claims, that is to say, refuting the Ammonite version of history, political geography, and what the right side of 'history' is for the Israelites.

Judges 11:11 Then Jephthah went with the elders of Gilead, and the people made him head and captain over them: and Jephthah uttered all his words before the LORD in Mizpeh.

Judges 11:12 ¶ And Jephthah sent messengers unto the king of the children of Ammon, saying, What hast thou to do with me, that thou art come against me to fight in my land?

Judges 11:13 And the king of the children of Ammon answered unto the messengers of Jephthah, Because Israel took away my land, when they came up out of Egypt, from Arnon even unto Jabbok, and unto Jordan: now therefore restore those lands again peaceably.

Judges 11:14 And Jephthah sent messengers again unto the king of the children of Ammon:

Judges 11:15 And said unto him, Thus saith Jephthah, Israel took not away the land of Moab, nor the land of the children of Ammon:

Once you accept the enemy's version of history, you accept the validity of their arguments. When your leadership starts speaking in the enemy's terms, that organization is really in trouble, and that is what is happening with the post-General Conference 2024 UMC. One of the reasons I love the book of Judges is because it is not about a perfect world where there are no bullies. It is a book about the fact that absent men of the stature of Moses, Aaron, and Joshua, all sorts of men of quite often gross imperfections, may be called upon like Jephthah and Samson, and yes, even a woman, like Deborah, may be called upon to Judge Israel. What was their job? Their job was to discipline the children of Israel, and to unite them against the forces of external and internal oppression. Their job was to recognize and act against the forces of chaos and tumult, that result when a people is without discipline. Acting without discipline makes one vulnerable because it makes it easier for one's enemies to take advantage. Were Jephthah, Samson, Deborah, Ehud, Othniel, Gideon etc., bullies. Yep, but they were benevolent bullies, not cruel and sadistic bullies I'd like to think. Whatever cruelty and sadistic behavior they had, it was certainly better than how Israel's enemies would bully them, and they for dang sure were better than the Philistines, the Ammonites, the Canaanites, et al. In addition a benevolent bully can always be judged by his benevolence. You are at the whim of tyrants when they are forced upon you and we know from history that when a tribe loses a battle, they can lose land, women, children, and may even go into slavery. That is why since time immemorable nearly all forms of government in the end look like benevolent dictatorships.

Our church is facing an existential threat for which its current DEI leaders are woefully underprepared. DEI bishops or bullies that can no longer defend us, and we the 'Body of Christ' are on our knees before 'the world' apologizing and capitulating under the ridiculous notion that if we apologize enough and capitulate enough to our new masters, the new socialist-atheist LGBTQIA social justice warrior agenda bullies, will take their feet off of our necks. But don't worry. According to our

DEI Bishops, our church might wither and die, but it will be on the 'right side of history'.

Chapter 14 - DEI Bishops Contradict themselves

Chapter 14 - DEI Ebony Bishops Contradict Themselves again in a hailstorm of Oxymoronic Idiocy

Ladies and gentlemen (sic), only a few people complained after the passing of the Pro-socialist-atheist LGBTQIA agenda at General Conference 2024. 1) the few White and even fewer outspoken Black conservatives left after the mass exodus; and 2) the African/Global (largely conservative) UMC. Let us note that the liberals go on and on hollering about Black and brown people, and then when they get a perfect opportunity to help some Black and brown global people in their virtually suicidal attempt to stand up against the Goliath like forces for the new 'woke' UMC Church, they don't side with or even respect their so called 'Black and brown' friends on such an ideologically simplistic matter as whether or not the definition of a man and a woman are the mammalian and biblical definitions of what a male and female are. Thus, they ignore the opinions and beliefs of the global Black and brown church in favor of being on the right side of White liberal socialist atheist LGBTQIA history. For all intents and purposes, it is a new White liberal socialist atheist LGBTQIA+ western Imperialism against the largely Black and brown United Methodist churches outside the United States. Those indigenous cultures' conservative sexual understandings were present in those societies long before Christianity ever got there. That White western liberals and their DEI Bishops are trying to eradicate basic traditional sexual understandings in those developing societies is disrespectful. The idea of bringing the global (Black and brown) churches up to the 'standard' of White European and American sexual 'understandings' is not only hypocritical but criminal.

When the European White man forced fed the natives Christianity, that, the current UMC and its DEI Bishops must condemn and apologize for. But when they force feed LGBTQIA+ sexual algebra down the developing world's throat, the developing world's Methodist churches must 'get with the program' or else! This is the precise opposite of respect. The lies of the liberals, and the hypocrisy of the liberals and their DEI Ebony bishop spokespeople did a great harm to the American United Methodist Church, and the UMC as it has presented itself in the developing world. DEI ebony bishops got used as a tool by White liberals in the post-1968 UMC, which was sexually conflicted by the sexual and racial revolution, and the labor/social justice movements, all at their height during the 60's. It was disastrous for the American UMC and European Church, and it is proving disastrous for the UMC in other countries which are splitting off left and right citing the current post-General Conference 2024 UMC liberal pro-socialist atheist LGBTQIA social justice agenda. Thank God the church in the developing world had the nerve to protest at General Conference 2024, and I can only applaud them for using the obvious incompetence of the post-modern American UMC to chart their own course. They know full well if we don't, that you can't sell a God who saves, if he doesn't know what a man/male or a woman/female are. What is He saving if he doesn't know what a man and a woman are? What can he save if he doesn't know what a man and woman are? How can he be a healer, if he doesn't know what a man and woman are? How can he be omnipotent, if he doesn't know what a man and woman are? How can he be all powerful if he tolerates human beings (the clay) challenging Him on what a male and a female are, i.e. what mammals are?

What is altogether worse for Black America, our DEI Ebony bishops have bigger fish to fry than violence in the Black community, de-church-ing in the Black community, underperforming schools, and the current nihilist Black culture that glorifies guns, drugs, and the objectification of women (largely Black women). The bigger fish our DEI Ebony Bishops are frying, is to be worried about making sure your children and children all over the world apparently, can hack their penises and breasts off if they want to, and take enough hormones and steroids to stunt the growth of an elephant. Wait a minute, I thought drugs were bad, and the church should say NO. Well, there is a liberal DEI Bishop caveat. Recreational drugs can get a candidate for ordained ministry questioned to the 'nth degree', let alone for being convicted of selling them at a felony level (ah-em). But taking gender changing drugs is, ok? Having 'random' sexual encounters with women of the opposite sex will get a candidate questioned, but having random sexual encounters with people of the same sex is ok. In that case it is assumed to be a contingency that the sex had to be random because of discrimination against gays, and the lack of sexual and marriage equality for homosexuals. A talentless, giftless, uninspiring man is just that. But a talentless, giftless, uninspiring woman or gay person, and regardless of how talentless and uninspiring they are, they must be elevated and given the chance to be publicly mediocre and untalented just because being publicly mediocre and untalented has been monopolized by men for all this time.

Dead weight DEI bishops that are no good to anybody, their White mainstream liberal UMC masters, or the Black UMC, are killing the UMC and its witness. They are no good to their White master because they are no longer capable of rallying, representing or delivering the 'Black UMC'. There are no more big Black UMC churches that 'deliver' the numbers (financial and evangelical) to their White mainstream Annual Conferences and Jurisdictions that make them relevant. Here in the North Georgia Conference, the number of Black United Methodist Churches strong enough to support an Elder in Full Connection, that is to say, a 'Full-Time' pastor, at full minimum salary has gotten steadily fewer over time. Note that the rise of DEI Bishops 'coincidentally' and 'magically' happened as the strength of Black United Methodist churches has gone down.

Worse but interrelated, the Black church in general has lost relevance and power in the post-modern Black community discourse, and the Black UMC has lost even more power in the past 50 years. This shrinkage is clearly deleterious to the Black UMC and the White Mainstream UMC; and our current crop of DEI Ebony Bishops is complicit in, aiding and abetting, this crime against the body of Christ. They are literally dead weight, causing death, death dealing.

And while I'm on this subject I'd like to say something about why female political leadership traditionally was rare. It was rare because hitherto human beings have been violent. Intertribal war, internecine war is the rule, not the exception in human history and even with the rise of modern technology, education, and more diverse entertainments than ever before, our aptitude for violence has not weakened. In the old days, let us use the book of Judges as an example, the theological and political component always necessitated a military component. I don't care how many other talents a leader, male or female had, if he or she was not battlefield capable, there was absolutely no reason to follow that person unless you wanted an 'Old Testament donkey' kicking. If you wanted to lose all your land, and you wanted to run the risk of your wife, daughters, mothers, aunts and grandma being lucky to get sold off as domestics and sex slaves, pick an incompetent leader without military skill, no matter what his or her other attributes.

Thus, even women had an interest in the military and martial qualities of whoever became their leaders. Their lives depended on it. And life wasn't like the movies, so women heroes were kicking men's 'Old Testament donkeys' endlessly, and relentlessly like Furiosa. There is a reason Amazon Women and even the Women Kings celebrated Viola Davis, are blips in history. For that matter, you see how good the Agojie (female warriors) were against the White man. I supposed enslaving other Negroes, even men, is infinitely easier than defending yourself against the White man and his superior military tactics, organization, and weaponry. For most of history, women couldn't afford to indulge in independence even as a fantasy for the same exact reason men couldn't indulge independence from women even as a fantasy; the genetic biological impetus to birth genetically relevant children. Even if babies can be replicated technologically, the easiest and most efficient way is still the old-fashioned mammalian way. That is the case whether you are Britney Griner, Da Brat, or Elton John. Prior to post-modernity, no one thought the fact that men have more upper body strength than women, was because of an accidental oversight of God or nature, or that it automatically means God hates women...that is until recent history. I can't imagine a group of feminist apes, running around lamenting their plight and trying to liberate other female apes to create a gay super troop of free Warrior Queen female apes and celebrate such a thing...until now (Star Wars Acolyte). Most mammal females would lament the fact their males became so useless and incapable. What's the use of free help, if it's the only help you'll get...until now.

Even with superior tactical, organizational, and religious skills, Deborah still needed Barak. And they both needed Jael (the Black Kenite woman and descendant of Moses' father-in-law) to kill Sisera. Jael drove a tent peg into Sisera's forehead hard enough to pin him to the ground. How is the bible a patriarchal fantasy land where women have absolutely no agency! Deborah and Jael were clearly exceptional women, with strong personalities, but not because they were doing the same thing on the battlefield men are. Deborah and Jael would have been 'dead weight' on the battlefield at best, and a distraction to their own side at worst. Instead of carrying out the strategy, some men would have felt overly protective over them, and concerned themselves with saving Jael and Deborah rather than carrying out their specific mission.

But according to DEI Ebony female bishops there is something wrong with saying men and women need each other and developed a historical type of relationship over countless generations of mammalian and even pre-mammalian evolutionary history. I'm extremely fascinated by research into evolutionary biology/physiology, evolutionary psychology, evolutionary sociology and what I like to call evolutionary theology. This love of science however, does not change the strength of my affections for and fascinations with God at all. This is because while I am fascinated by man's scientific attempts to come up with and have a discussion on 'How' something(s) happened using the scientific method, I am far more fascinated by man's religious attempts to come up with and have a discussion on 'Why' the things that we know as creation and the universe have happened. As appreciative as I am of other faith traditions (because 'why' can only be a matter of faith), my faith tradition is Judeo-Christian and to as large an extent as possible, since I've been saved, I have been answering the question of 'Why' with the biblical tradition as best I can. Science can tell me the 'How' as best it can, and I truly feel indebted and marvel at all the technological products of man's wisdom. But I'll leave it to religion to tell me 'Why' that which is (including me), is. Glory to God. Sure, I'll 'rock with you' on the 'Big Bang', but as far as I'm concerned, when the 'Big Bang' did occur, it was God up there wherever doing the banging.

A woman 'needing' a man is not anathema, and of course the opposite isn't either. What is anathema, that is to say a curse on a person, is the precise opposite of not 'needing'. It is a curse on a woman to rear children all by herself, meanwhile everybody is acting like they are perfectly capable of such a feat because women can do anything, except educated women don't typically 'do it by themselves'. A man is cursed if he has baby mamas, no clear relationship to his children, or positive role in his children's life. Better for him if he submits to the demands of a woman and the requirements of familial life. It will prolong his life and be better for him. It will help him restrain himself in many areas of his life that frankly, without female 'oversight' would spin out of control. What happened to the idea that God made us, men and women quite precisely to need one another. It is not a good idea that man be alone, and when Eve is alone too long, she starts seeing things and talking to big Black snakes (lol phallic symbol sex toys) that are vaguely, and enticingly familiar and that Adam thinks might 'replace' him. What is the problem with a church that teaches men and women to need one another, to love one another, to procreate and raises families in nuclear and extended families, in community, etc., and how that is natural in an evolutionary (biological/physiological, psychological, sociological, and theological) context, ordained by an omnipotent creator God, documented in print in the biblical context. What is wrong with teaching that? Why cannot the UMC teach that? Because it and its DEI Bishops have been corrupted by the socialist-atheist LGBTQIA social justice agenda.

But of course, if you have ideologically rejected the idea of a God that would and could ordain a 'natural order', that is, you go around preaching a God that doesn't know what a man and woman are, the end result will be the current dysfunctional post-General Conference UMC. In complete contrast to the idea of 'natural order' (no matter how evident and obvious it is), our UMC's current policy is that men and women don't need each other at all, it being a mere cis gender convenience, and everybody can be perfectly happy and fulfilled chasing some idea of their sexuality to point of practicing sexual algebra and sexual alphabet soup trying to figure out what they are. No wonder our children are bat crap crazy, and they all need therapy. These 'familial delusions', oh my how a little leaven, leaveneth the whole loaf. The idea that a bishop in the UMC can stand up and say a pansexual lifestyle is consistent with doctrinal progress, and the flowering of the implications of 2000 years of church tradition is ridiculous. Katt Williams recently joked that if one claims to be a pansexual, that means he or she can have sex with anything, whatever they see that they want to have sex with. Who would claim such thing with a straight face, and what kind of church would claim this is consistent with biblical teachings? How can Katt Williams recognize the lunacy in this, but our DEI Ebony Bishops do not! How did we get here? When did we allow socialist atheist LGBTQIA social justice ideology to shape the theology of the church.

I must qualify my position on abortion here, because I understand how easily it can be misconstrued. I am for legal, safe, available, abortions on demand. That being said, there is a difference between that and our church actually promoting abortion as a tool for women's social or economic liberation. Like Ozempic made it 'easy' to lose weight, women are going around acting like they don't know how babies are made! And when the 'unfortunate' happens, and a woman is faced with academic and professional choices, something has to give, and it's not going to be her, or some dead beat dad (she picked). The child must give its life for relatively grown women and men unsatisfied with the 'potential effects' of a one-night stand. Adults running around acting like they don't how babies are made, or how diseases are contracted, but who is made to suffer for their ignorance but a 'dead fetus'. Post-modern women, opt to make choices for an easier, or more pleasant life, sans child, like it's simply a matter of no one has the right to inconvenience a woman when it comes to a decision about her body, not even an innocent baby. This innocent baby we know doesn't know how babies are made but his parents damn sure did, and still took it out on him when it was inconvenient.

God forbid women are inconvenienced by their own stupidity, as though they don't know how babies are made, and do not know the consequences and challenges of sex, maternity, and paternity. When a woman ends up on paternity court with 2 or 3 possible fathers; during the same time she is surrounded by feminist/womanist liberal propaganda and rhetoric about what she can do with her body, and who she can have sex with, is this (post-modernity) a 'safe space' for women? Is this, paternity court, a benevolent and beneficent byproduct of feminism/womanism and women's sexual right(s) to have sex with who they want, when they want, and why they want to have sex, the baby being the least of concerns with regard to her freedom?

No, the baby isn't the least of her regards, the least of her regards is a patriarchal interpretation of her father's responsibility to her to have protected her womanhood until she was woman enough to have enough sense to protect her womanhood (her mind and her womb) herself. She met a dude not going anywhere, had sex with him, because of course she was 'free' to do so, with no patriarchy, no religion. Now her deadbeat dad baby daddy is no good to her or his child. Does patience not have to be enforced sometimes on children? A good parent tells his child that just because I put the ice cream sandwiches in the buggy does not mean you could/should eat one now, we haven't paid for it. A good parent tells his child that just because we went through the line and paid for the ice cream sandwiches does not mean we should rip the paper off and eat one while walking or in the car where it might spill as it melts. A good parent, mama or daddy, protects their child's (male and female) baby making capacities until hopefully the child has enough sense to protect their own so they don't end up with a disease or a child by the human equivalent of a rabid wolf. Whatever happened to 'shotgun weddings'? Ain't nobody got no daddy no more. The negative extreme of this is the type of abuses to women that happen in Afghanistan in the name of family honor. However, being too far on the other extreme where men are preached to constantly that they shouldn't feel any type of 'binding' way about women and women's bodies, let alone have an opinion as regards women's bodies, even though women prance around half naked all the time twerking as though all they had was their bodies. According to post-modern feminism/womanism, men's 'opinions' shouldn't matter, and if she wants to be the neighborhood whore, so be it. Modern feminism and our DEI Ebony bishops cheapen abortion, cheapen life, cheapen the actual power a woman has over the matrix of life, by suggesting that power is not worth or equivalent to the professional, academic, economic or political success such that men get? Modern Feminism and our DEI Ebony bishops cheapen Black life. Who told them we don't need as many Black babies as possible (as we can educate and feed in strong healthy stable nuclear and extended families because the European birthrate is collapsing)?

A female prostitute is free to ply her trade. She makes choices about what 'clothes' to wear or not wear. She is making sexual choices with her body about what 'Johns' to accept, and whether to get in the car with a strange man or not. She is exercising her freedom, but is she free? On the surface she's free as a bird, but she's that free sexually because she's a slave to drugs or her pimp/madam. When a woman's self-esteem is so low that she has sex with 3-5 men with no birth control whatsoever, within one month's time, and ends up on Paternity Court is she exercising her freedom? Is the culture that produces the phenomena a 'safe space' for women? Her children don't know their father! But she is indeed sexually free and that takes precedence over all according to the liberal socialist-atheist LGBTQIA+ social justice warrior class. Often this same Black woman is making those kinds of choices quite precisely because she didn't have a Daddy, guarding her chastity, before she had sense enough to guard it for herself. As for these so-called men she slept with, few of them will take responsibility for even liking her, let alone having sex with her if they don't have to (as in the famous, yes, I had unprotected sex with her, but I didn't ejaculate). They only admit that she was a 'friend with benefits' that ended up pregnant. Their excuse for not thinking it was theirs, was because she was 'friends' with a lotta dudes in the neighborhood, and apparently, she was handing out benefits to her male friends like DFACS. Is that court room, a trial by humiliation, a 'safe space' for women or children?

How can it be that feminists have won? American women marry for love and choice now, not finances and getting saddled with babies. Why are divorce rates skyrocketing. Women are free as they want to be, but not no one apparently, certainly not our children is any happier. If the world the feminists have created is so good why are so many Black women sad, unmarried and angry? Recent statistics suggest the divorce rates amongst lesbian women is even higher than the general divorce rate of 70%. They have all the abortion they can get, they are better educated than Black men, but not a soul is any happier, and even though the memes and myths of the 'super Black woman', #Blackgirlpower, #Blackgirlmagic are rife, Black women's success rates in raising children alone hardly inspires confidence in any of those memes and myths. The fact your child survived is not proof you were a good parent. The fact that you did the best you could by yourself, does not absolve of you of the negative impacts of the poor choices involved in choosing to do it all by yourself.

Many of these same independent Black women, come from busted families themselves with no fathers or problematic relationships with their fathers, and in that anger, resentment, and quite often rage, their response is to demand that they don't need men, men's values etc., at all for a baby, happiness, love or anything else. Beloved do you see where 50 years of that have gotten our families and cities. Crime rates are ridiculous. Schools are virtual prison camps with armed guards etc., because our children do not have stable home lives with stable mothers, fathers and extended families. Six Flags had to institute chaperone policy, the first in 55 years because early this summer our children were out there in roaming gangs fighting, looting, and shooting...at 6 Flags Amusement Park. Our present DEI Bishops would have you believe fathers are completely dispensable and disposable. But is this really the case, or socialist-atheist LGBTQIA social justice warrior propaganda? Is this really the case or are our DEI bishops doing a slight of hands magic trick on the Black community and the wider UMC church? That is to say, things magically appear and disappear with an 'abracadabra' hocus pocus incantation like gay flag placards and hocus pocus oft spoken incantations that revolve around completely unbiblical ideas like #Blackgirlmagic and #Blackgirlpower. All power is of God and related to Godliness. You do not get 'power' just from being Black or a woman. Any power you claim to get from such entities and means is all in your pathetic head.

Part II

At this juncture we go back to my bullying metaphor. The youngest kids are the runts. You are smaller than other kids in your class and the older kids, let alone adults. That is a biological fact. Equally factual is the harassment of peers and other kids due to your small size. Black people aren't the only ones who 'don't snitch'. Kids tend not to do it either, perhaps for similar idiotic reasons. However, telling an adult may not be an option, and it often backfires and makes things worse. At that point the only solution is to pick a bully, the most benevolent one you can find, and try to take refuge in his shadow from worse bullies. Perhaps even, he might be an encouraging bully that cares about you in some way. That was my survival mechanism through childhood. It worked and taught me a lot about life, families, schools, denominations, seminaries, jobs, and corporations. All have cliques, cultures, and 'centers' of power. Cruel and sadistic or benevolent, you will run into them all your life. How you navigate them is critical and we call these life skills. Many of our children don't have 'life' skills because our families are not transmitting them, and then we expect external authorities like teachers, administrators and police to transmit to them what they should have gotten at home in the rough and tumble of family, community, and school life. A child must learn how to wait their turn, follow instructions, perform the appropriate role in a hierarchy, these types of basic skills children should learn at home, thus are called home training. However, kids are quite capable of teaching one another, in the form of what might be termed 'bullying' or 'light hazing' that tends to occur.

And so now. How does that relate to feminism/womanism, DEI Bishops and the collapse of the Black family? The obvious effects the Black community is now living with, of raising generations of children that feel vulnerable, unloved, and unprepared to compete because they do not have live in fathers and strong families, for ideological reason our DEI Ebony Bishops must ignore in order to continue to promote the socialist-atheist LGBTQIA social justice propaganda that tells them women don't 'need men, and neither do their children need a father because they have #Blackgirlmagic and #Blackgirlpower. They don't have enough sense to connect the dots from the bizarro world they inhabit where they are going around preaching from the hills that they don't need a man for nothing...to the fact that have more than a reputation for being angry and pissed off at the world, quite precisely because they are vulnerable, and they have made themselves vulnerable. They are wondering why they feel so vulnerable and unprotected, but they consistently reinforce the fact that they don't need any help from no man, not father, not friend, not lover, not uncle. The only men she can tolerate are boys.

The success of the socialist-atheist LGBTQIA social justice propaganda amongst Black women has meant that Black children grow up with a terrible stigma. No, it is not a stigma the White man, racism, patriarchy, or the Bible and curse of Ham put on them. Not having a father or knowing who he is, or the fact that one's father is in jail or dead by violence is a stigma. It is a stigma on our children, that Black women are very cavalier about putting multiple generations of Black children in this stigmatic predicament. The fact that Black men and women have put generations of Black children in this predicament should qualify as child abuse. Children in a 'family' have older siblings and parents. Children know instinctively that they are little, and they need protection. This is biology 101 and the reason that crying children get picked up and carried. There is an innate fear of being 'left behind' kids virtually come wired with. This is an innate survival tactic. That process entails exposure to different older personalities in the familial setting. From older siblings, to aunts, cousins and of course parents, all fitting within a physical and emotional hierarchy of needs, beginning with a sense of protection and not being left behind when the clan goes places. Saints, these are not choices. These are not social constructs. We evolved to be in relatively close-knit families and communities of about 8-150 people radiating outward. This hierarchy of needs is well documented for stability, but the liberals don't want to admit that it is precisely the weakness of our families, our extended families, our communities, and our religion that is 'driving people crazy'! That's why there is an explosion in mental health issues all over the place. The traditional means of creating stability, order, and discipline in children is gone, and we leave it up to the tv, rappers, politicians, Hollywood, social media, and religious hustlers and agent provocateurs that are really socialist-atheist LGBTQIA social justice agents in sheep's (Christian) clothing. The family is necessary to mental health, everybody's mental health, the children, the parents, the grandparents, the aunts, the uncles and the cousins and the wider community. The family is the mechanism for the transmission of that stability and tradition, and that is civilization. And when we cede the authority of the philosophy of the family to outside parties, organizations, and interests, as opposed to God, then America gets what it is getting in terms of its rotten civilization and corruption of public and even world morality. A little leaven, leaveneth the whole loaf.

Yes, your mother is a bully to protect you, but imagine the consolation of knowing she has bigger bully, that protects her. Your father, who is significantly more physically imposing than your mother, is even more capable of defending you and her. Oh these benevolent bullies, called parents. These bullies have taken it upon themselves to name me and begin teaching me my ABCs and the ABCs of religion long before I knew how many existing options I had for a name or a religion. Most of us love and respect our benevolent bullies for protecting us until we were big enough to be bullies ourselves. These benevolent bullies had rules and regulations. They claim you should follow them for your own benefit and in exchange for their protection of you. They disciplined you and through being disciplined, you had discipline. Your bullies were so jealous over you, they wouldn't allow other bullies, even your siblings, to discipline you. They are the ultimate authority. Mom because she has dad, dad because he has mom. No one else can or should make bully like demands on you, that is to say, tell you what to do, or what you are, ugly, fat, smart, dumb, etc. The world's opinion and even its bullies are subordinate to your bullies.

Let us reflect on where all this 'princess' mythology comes from. Your head bully is King, and you are his female child. Not just his regular female child but a princess, his first-born girl, and he treats you like a princess and demands your mother, and siblings do to. Failure to protect you, or others even angering you, is a crime, even by his other children, and your father the king will discipline them for handling you wrong.

Your father barely lets your feet touch the ground. He demands your mother get your hair done and dress you like a princess. Here again I 'm talking about the psychology of why many little girls go through a princess phase and be in the grocery store with a Tiara and crinoline dress on.

Oh, how my father proudly shows me off to the other bullies on his level and tells me how beautiful I am and how proud he is of me. I was his little princess. How Father flashes with anger and rage when I cry out to him in pain at my oppressors. Now what is the opposite of that. What is a girl with no father...a slave or Cinderella. Beloved the princess myth is going nowhere and the fact that post-modern women are so unhappy is the proof that the socialist-atheist LGBTQIA has nothing to replace it with...unless we mean they replace traditional characters in princess/prince/hero roles with themselves as socialist-atheist LGBTQAI social justice warrior characters.

Chapter 15 - DEI Ebony Bishops and Mammy'

Chapter 15 - DEI Ebony Bishops and Post-Modern Mammy

One of my best ideas in seminary was to frame Oprah as Post-Modern Mammy. If Mammy somehow was reincarnated after slavery, Jim Crow, industrialization, the public education system, the digital revolution, and after the Civil Rights movement, what would mammy look and act because of course, Mammy has options now in 2024 that Mammy could never even have dreamed of. A Mammy could get rich in post-modern America. Doing what, the reader might be asking? The same thing she did in 1858, cater to White folks' emotional and physical needs. The folkish Black female self-help, the folk wisdom, the herbal remedies, salt baths, fragrances, and wellness products, that Mammy used in the 'big house' in 1858, Mammy is doing the same things in 2008 through her 'lifestyle' brands and 'book clubs'. Obviously there was a valid excuse for it in 1858. But in 2024 for Black women to be trapped in 'mammy mythology' is a curse. Mammy's book clubs are the symbol, if not the reason, Negro education and the Negro intellectual environment is in the sad state it's in today. Oprah Winfrey, Post-Modern Mammy is running the most successful book club in the country, all catering to White women's needs for wholeness, emotional healing, and self-care. Because of course, Mammy's entire audience has been traumatized and needs 'loads, and loads' of self-care, self-healing, etc. What else would a Black Mammy in 2024 be concerned about but White women's emotional healing and wellness? That is how she got paid (rewarded) in 1858, and it is how she gets paid in 2024.

'Super Soul Sunday' sounds just like something a 'Mammy' could have come up with in 1858. On Sundays Mammy takes over the 'big house' and runs her 'Super Soul Sun-day' where all kinds of traveling weirdos (White, Black, et al.) come by with spiritual opinions, insights, and beliefs, and concern themselves with White folk's health, wellness, and self-care. Because of course, Mammy is concerned about Masser's family and the big house. Sit right on down here 'missy' and let Mammy run you a hot bath with some of her 'special' lavender bath salts and give you a back rub. "Oh, Mammy, you've been more like a mother to me than my own mother, you're always there for me". Of course Mammy is Sugar, of course Mammy is.

Lawd Mammy is concerned about massa health and wellness. Every other day Mammy reviews a book on her book club that brings about spiritual transformation, self-acceptance and healing...every other day? How much renewing and pseudo-spirituality can they take Mammy! 50 years of Oprah's book clubs and the stench of African American and mainstream America's putrid rotting pop culture and its public-school systems has gotten worse. All this healing and renewing, reviving every day, and super soul Sundays and people are more anxious, and more crazy than they were before Oprah, excuse me, Post-Modern Mammy started her crazy products and designs. 50 years of her hyper moralizing, love, peace, self-forgiveness, self-acceptance, wholeness, and everything about Black and White mainstream American culture is worse than when she found it.

I had nearly forgotten about my ITC academic experience writing a paper that was a critique of Oprah as post-modern Mammy. Needless to say, as liberal and female dominated as ITC and Black theology is and was, that didn't go over well. Even today Oprah is a hero of Black feminism, a totem, taboo, and untouchable. To criticize Oprah is to criticize Black women writ large, and affront to all Black women. Occasionally, you find a hard core Christian Black female that is suspicious of all that hocus pocus self-affirmation styled spiritualism, but even those begrudgingly admit that what the America dream is, in the context of a Black woman's (Black body in 2024), she is living it. This is to such an extent that it would be difficult to imagine a Black woman getting further than Oprah in mainstream culture, economics, and politics. If Kamala wins, Oprah will have acted as a virtual 'kingmaker' (president maker) for Black people in America.

Enter our DEI ebony female bishops and killa Kam Harris, now anointed 'Mamala' by Drew Barrymore. All this talk about the country needing a mother figure and a giant hug. This is mammyish nonsense, as though the world doesn't need discipline and order, it needs a universal big Black mama archetype with ample breasts and thunder thighs to hug her, like Michelle Obama hugged the Queen. We've accepted the role of the world's mammy. It's one of the best hustles a Black woman can get. The world needs its own Big Black Mammy to hug it and say 'no you come on over here sugar and give mammy a hug, every little thing is going to be alright'! Let Mammy handle it and there will be no more racism, no more sexism, no more transphobia and no more homophobia. And there will be social and economic justice for everyone. That is how within a week of being the presidential nominee of the 2024 election, Killa Kam found it necessary to visit Ru Paul on his Drag Queen Drag race. I suppose that is how she prepares for summits with Putin and the Chinese Premier too.

This kind of mythology surrounding Black women is just as dangerous and entrapping as images of Black femineity generated by Cardi B, Sexy Red, Lizzo, etc. They are both demeaning and limiting, yet both well paid and paying. Usually what someone will pay you to do is what they 'want' to see you doing, preferring you do that over something else. That is not the same thing as freedom. Paying someone to dance in a cage is still keeping them in a cage, even though they are well paid. Perhaps in this way, you can fool a slave into staying in the cage. True freedom, that is to say behaving in ways not dependent on others paying you, can quite often be dangerous to the status quo...which is why elites would rather pay Black men to dribble balls, juggle balls, run balls, shoot balls, than run Fortune 500 Companies. Let them that have ears, hear.

We must understand boys and girls, that Mammy was an important figure on the plantation. The stereotype was that she was big, but at the very least she would have tended to eat better and be better housed than the field slaves. Also, Mammy functioned as a doctor, counselor, midwife, and in some cases, it was not uncommon that mammy could have wet-nursed old master and a couple generations of his brood from the time she got pregnant at 14, through her natural courses. Mammy was also the liaison between the Black community of the field slaves, and Master and the big house operations. A good Mammy needed to keep her finger on the pulse of the master classes and the slave classes. Both sides would have naturally relied on a good Mammy to walk the line. Both sides relied on Mammy to push their cause and the justness of their complaints. Master relied on mammy to smooth over the extra work during planting or reaping season. She had accessibility to master and his family at the most intimate (non-sexual for the purposes of this essay) levels. All these things made Mammy a powerful figure in the life of the Big House and plantation. Mammy's roles were crucial to the functioning of a well-run plantation. Her place in the order was secure all throughout slavery. There she is, almost like the family mascot or pet, master's favorite hunting dog in the family photos. Here's mammy on family vacation with master in the Mountains of North Carolina. Lawd they were dancing in the aisles to the old Negro songs of Zion Mammy sang. Oh, here's another photo '12 Years a slave' when master took the household, including Mammy to Europe for vacation.

Imagine the bunch being entertained by princes and royalty in England and the subject comes up, gee Mr. Foghorn Leghorn, you're a great planter. In the European press they say how bad you treat your darkies. My word, their saying it borders on the inhumane. And Mr. Foghorn leghorn plantation owner and master, gin and tonic in hands says ridiculous my good man. Look at this one over here, 'pointing to Mammy'. Does she look mistreated or undernourished? No my good man she weighs 300 pounds how can she be mistreated. Pointing at Mammy he continues, this woman has been with me all my life, she was my first and only wetnurse. I never even saw my mother's breast. She midwifed me and my kids, healed my family of their sicknesses and cured me of various ailments throughout the years with her folk wisdom, her #Blackgirlmagic and #Blackgirlpower. Mammy, tell the Prince and Princess some jokes. Tell em' the one about 'Precious' running down the street with a stolen bucket of chicken. Tell them the prophetic dream you had about a mulatto named Lizzo in the future. She is a singer, flautist, overweight exotic dancer, etc., and the White people of the time get upset because she finds occasion to play Founding Father of America James Madison's flute. Imagine her putting her mulatto lips on James Madison's flute. Tell em the one about Martin Lawrence, Eddie Murphy, and Tyler Perry all playing and parodying a version of you Mammy. Hilarious. Mammy is well fed and well paid. Does Mammy look unhappy? Your man servant butler looks unhappy. Our Negroes go prancing around the plantation all day, having a ball in the fields singing their little songs, and reproducing like animals, such that I have enough slaves to sell off. The 'darkies' wouldn't be reproducing like that if they were unhappy. Meanwhile Mammy has been continuing her skits and stories in the background and Foghorn Leghorn shushes her and says that'll be enough mammy, that'll be enough.

Oh no the Duke and Duchess interrupt. Before she goes, please let her sing one of those good old songs of Zion. Those spirituals and work songs, field hollars and field cries that so define the American Negro experience in the Antebellum and Jim Crow south. You heard the man Mammy, sing us one of those good old songs about Moses and Pharaoh that y'all sing on Sundays in the brush harbor after sitting in the balcony at the White church.

Oh how mammy is wined and dined in the salons and stately houses of Paris, Munich, Vienna and Milan. And yet back on the plantation the field slaves are getting restless. Generations of poverty, family instability, and ignorance took a toll on the quality of life for field slaves.

Many of the adolescent boys and young men were aimless and violent, unless they were being managed, supervised whip in hand and threatened with the stocks. As for the women, debauched to the point they are proud of it and enjoy it so much they call themselves 'boss female dogs'. We spoke earlier about the weak needing their own benevolent bullies in their lives. A Black man in such circumstances cannot protect her physicality, or her sexuality, or her daughters, or her mothers. Her man, benevolent bully or not, by default in the context of slavery cannot protect her from bigger bullies in the White mainstream southern plantation culture that will sell her, her children, her relatives and her man up and down the river. Add to that White men extracting sexual favors from them by any means necessary for the level of what they presume to want.

Bullies all around, but none to protect the Black woman. Her Father and her husband, certainly not her son, they cannot protect her even if they tried. They certainly couldn't protect her for long. The situation seems hopeless. How will the Black woman respond to being in such dire straits...socialist atheist LGBTQIA social justice rhetoric versions of equality with men seems as good an answer as any. So women define freedom as divesting from the traditional family and embracing the forces of nihilism, baby killing, chaos and anarchy. But is that the answer. Back in slavery days we were forced to have mass fatherless and even master's bastard children around as children and adults were sold up and down the river at the will of fate and the economic exigencies of their owners. Now we choose (fatherlessness) as necessary for individual sexual freedom. Talk about psychodrama, Afro-Europeans in Europe, and African Americans view the products of the rape of Black women, mulattos, as being standards of beauty for Black people.

Sister you do have a father. You do have a big bully father. And He is the bully of all bullies, the universal benevolent bully. That is your father. You are indeed a princess, destined to be a queen. And it doesn't befit a princess to be on paternity court trying to figure out who her baby daddy is. It doesn't befit a princess to be fighting other Black princesses with fake nails, fake hair, fake eyelashes, fake rear ends, fake breasts, but you want to be taken seriously, that is to say 'for real'.

But let us say a woman goes awry. What is her father's response. You're not going to act like that in my house. If you want to be like that, fine, you can do it somewhere else. General Hood from my church hipped me to a great saying. He had a commanding officer who would routinely walk up to soldiers on duty and ask them 'what are you doing'? Some would reply 'nothing'. At which point he'd say, 'well do nothing somewhere else'. Her father's response is 'you're not going to act like that in my house'. But when she hits rock bottom and wants to come home, she can. But when you are here, you will follow your Father's rules and submit to his discipline when you traverse them...but dad I read a book, but dad Sheilah and Michelle said...I'm off into a new religion and its teachers. And there your father is saying...my house...my rules.

But there is no escape to rock bottom. The UMC near committed suicide on Youtube Live at General Conference 2024. But you gotta go home baby, in order to get yourself together. It ain't out there in the streets running with your new partners. It ain't out there drinking and carousing with every Tom, dick and Harry, every two-bit philosopher or Yogi in a robe and sandals, or alternative this or that. Eventually you must go home and do it God's way. God's way with the disciplines, traditions, order, the Holy Ghost, and church institutions we've inherited. Something one inherits, one must loath changing. For the perpetual question is, is the problem me, or the discipline? To argue it's the discipline is to take the easy way out, and make a God of oneself and one's own opinions.

We will have to come home, or die trying to imitate the secular world living with one foot in it, and one foot in supposedly Holy Conferencing. We've said repeatedly that a little leaven, leavens the whole loaf. And do not think it is just Black women getting played. One thing I enjoyed about regional and national UMC conferences is the international representation. There would be Koreans, Africans, Polynesians, all in their cultural dress, all staged very craftily by the UMC Communications Office to suggest our darkies are happy. Sing for them 'onawapulea', on cue darkie. But if you are Conservative on sexuality, darkie you're old fashioned and you must update your thinking on sexuality to White western mainstream standards. Let us think for you darkie, just keep singing those old songs of Zion. This is the attitude of the liberals, who would ever have you believe they love their darkies and apologize to them for past crimes, and speak (beg) on their behalf. To the point they have forced their own conservative darkies out of the UMC as church after church in Africa, Asia, and North and South America have chosen a more conservative and traditional biblical interpretation of what a man and a woman are.

You might think present post General Conference 2024 intentions are good in forcing the global church to accept the pro socialist-atheist LGBTQIA social justice agenda or else. But how can one group of people, let us say early White Methodists in the colonial world be held accountable for forcing cultural and religious norms, imperialism, and a western Christ/Christology on the peoples of the world. But when our current crop of DEI Bishops and religious courts does the exact same cultural imperialism against the formerly colonial world, forcing 'new' Western socialist-atheist LGBTQIA+ sexual algebra notions of sexuality upon them it is ok...presumably I suppose because the liberals and DEI Bishops are 'forcing them to be on the right side of history'. That is the very same logic European colonials used to justify their appropriation of native lands and cultures, they were forcing these backward peoples into the modern world of the European mind, religion, and economic system...i.e. the right side of history.

Our current crop of DEI Bishops is asking them to sacrifice long held indigenous cultural assumptions about sex...so they can be on the right side of European socialist-atheist LGBTQIA social justice history? And then at the same time they are apologizing for the transgressions of early White Methodists in the colonial experience in the Americas, Hawaii and Africa. You are committing the very same sin using western post-modern sexual norms, as the standard for all sexuality, even biblical and mammalian sexuality. Our DEI Bishops want the historic White man to be accountable for his sins, but DEI Ebony Bishops don't commit sins because they have #Blackgirlmagic and #Blackgirlpower? This is the kind of liberal hypocrisy that passes for policy in the post-General Conference 2024 UMC.

Church let's repent and go back home to Dad's house. Let us follow God's rules and our inherited Discipline that was grounded and rooted in that fertile academic, theological, and even economic soil (the good ole Protestant work ethic). We don't have to give in to win, or save face. Our father is the big bully. And yes, He does allow suffering and no he's not going to apologize for it. A life, any life, is a beautiful precious thing, even with all the suffering that it brings bodily, emotionally, professionally, etc. There are countless stories of people who have experienced great tragedy, but still found a way to be thankful to God, not blaming him for their misfortunes.

This is a Joshua moment for Methodism. It has come to a head. On one side there the 'as for me and my house, we will serve the Lord' side. They will not serve a God of mistakes and incompetence, that we must correct and apologize for, on such mundane and basic matters as what a man and a woman are.

16

Chapter 16 - Is the current UMC a 'Safe Space'

Chapter 16 - Is it a safe space or are our DEI Ebony Bishops blowing smoke up our 'Old Testament donkeys'

Imagine with me Annual Conference in June here in North Georgia, dang near as I write. Imagine that the Conference wide staff of the North Georgia UMC Singles Ministry Committee is having a dinner/dance event; **all** invited and **all** welcome (even married people who love to swing). Imagine with me dear reader that there would be men dressed up like women, or in varying states and stages of surgical and chemical transition. And there would be women dressed up like men in varying states and/or stages of surgical and chemical transition. And at the Conference UMC singles event, there would be people there with AIDS, but its ok because they are medically undetectable, and can have unprotected sex without transmitting the AIDS virus as long as they take their meds. Oh yes, there would also be pansexuals there at the UMC North Georgia Singles Ministry dinner-dance and fundraiser. Imagine all that, and then ask yourself would you send your child or anybody else you love that happened to be single to that event.

You, a middle aged Black or White woman from a local church, knows a good-hearted woman that could use a good Christian hearted man in her, and perhaps her child's life. So you tell her what generations of women (Black and White) in America have told younger women; that they need to get involved in the church, travel with your pastor to other churches, and get involved in the Christian community. Perhaps she might find an honest sincere man. So you send her to the North Georgia Annual Conference singles dinner dance and even buy the ticket. She meets somebody alright, but that individual ends up being a woman dressed as man, or transitioning and fooled people including your young friend. How would you feel? Any sane person would be scared to send their beloved child to Church singles events with the church in its present socialist atheist LGBTQIA+ sexual algebra promoting alignment. No disrespect intended, but men and women who parade around with the intent of fooling people are not heroes, they are taking advantage of others. They are fooling others. They are running a scam on others. Someone is taking advantage of us when they have us believing that by dress and surgery, they weren't born the opposite sex. If you meet someone and fall in love, and in the midst of all that is required in a functional, respectful, reciprocal relationship, they forgot to tell you that they have AIDS, and use AIDS suppressing drugs, or that they were born a man/woman, there is nothing sanctified about that relationship. Altogether worse, if LGBTQIA+ sexual algebra practitioners are cruising singles events at the North Georgia Annual Conference 2024, looking for hookups, encouraged by DEI bishops, and General Conference 2024, you are a fraud. The church is committing fraud, practicing fraud, and supporting fraud, and this is the state of our UMC today. Let us never forget that the best way not to get AIDS, unwanted pregnancies, or any other sexually transmitted diseases is to get married; one man, one woman, and hold committed to it (as best as humanly possible). At no point in the Bible does it suggest young men and women should go off exploring their sexuality, just doing whatever they want to do or whatever their loins and inclinations seem to be pointing them towards. But the new post-General Conference UMC desires that world for us. Everything goes.

All this dating, and pressure to look a certain, way, that ain't bible. People are anxiety and angst ridden, and as 'ole dirty bastard' the rapper said, 'taking all types of medicines', trying to fix something that when they got it from God, it wasn't broken. No one in the bible is complaining of 'irritable bowel syndrome', and Paul's remedy is hardly a matter of genius...drink a little wine with meals. In biblical days, if you got a disease, it wasn't a 'made up disease'. Folk didn't get 'restless leg syndrome', they got 'no leg' syndrome like Mephibosheth.

2Samuel 4:4 And Jonathan, Saul's son, had a son that was lame of his feet. He was five years old when the tidings came of Saul and Jonathan out of Jezreel, and his nurse took him up, and fled: and it came to pass, as she made haste to flee, that he fell, and became lame. And his name was **Mephibosheth.**

If all Mephibosheth had was restless leg syndrome, he would have been happy and not complained at all. For that matter, how tall was Mephibosheth's nurse? What possible height could she have dropped him from and in what way, caused both his feet to be damaged? When she fell in 'haste to flee', did she fall with her full body weight on the boy's feet! He was crippled, lost his family, and lost his grandfather's, father's and his own kingdom. But the Bible doesn't give the impression he blamed God or thought God owed him and apology. It appears as if Mephibosheth was not resentful and angry towards David either. It is not unusual to see a person so angry at another for perceived past wrongs, that they would never sit at the same dinner table (in peace) with them no matter how sumptuous the meal. Those days are a long way from our angry and resentful DEI bishops determined to apologize on behalf of God for the way God does Divine Providence. Our DEI Bishops would have told Mephibosheth he needed to protest David and go on social media discussing all the crimes David did to him and his family historically, and how he deserved more than a meal at David's table. You deserve reparations Mephibosheth, even though David had restored to Mephibosheth his father's land and they were fertile productive lands. No, according to our DEI Bishops God gave a Mephibosheth a terrible hand and everybody owes him an apology. As a matter of fact, when the adolescents and young adult men have foot races and spar in battle or sport, they should let him win. When Israel goes to battle, they should put Mephibosheth out there so that the 'crippled' community in Israel should be represented and Israel can prove it is on the right side of social justice history by having a crippled military leader leading the battle. I'm trying use humor but it seems to me that is DEI Bishops actual thought process.

Anyway, Church what happened to Jesus and Jesus alone. I'm not 'joaning', my legal and marital history is no secret. But the ideal must be Jesus and Jesus alone, not Jesus and 28 other medications, big pharma, 2 therapists (and you're unsatisfied with them and looking for another), and what the government told you to do, to keep your job or keep from dying. This is supposed to be better than Jesus and Jesus alone. Sanity is living the 10 commandments. A sane society is one that lives the 10 commandments. Any other society is not only insane, insolvent and unstable, but bound for the scrap heap of history and the hell fire, whichever comes first. This is why everybody in America is crazy and needs all this therapy, self-help, self-care, self-healing, self-pampering...etc. They are trying all sorts of means to make excuses for the fact that they feel like failures. They feel like failures quite precisely because they constantly (via social media), compare themselves to their perceptions of other people. These are all the signs and symbols of a narcissistic, self-indulgent, arrogant prideful society that loves the gods of affirmation, way more than they love a God of correction and discipline. They serve a soft god that apologizes to them for things like making people men and women, and Black, White, and brown, rich or poor. Instead of complaining, take what you got and make it do! But you sit around complaining about what other people owe you, and change religion into serving a mistake prone, apologetic god.

Part II

Brothers and sisters, let us close on this wise. Earlier I mentioned my integrated/integrating White flight elementary and middle schools. I was in the integrating phase, and one of the remnants of when country White folks ran things, was the square-dancing program(s). On the surface, the whole concept of dancing around country western style annoyed the Black students (even in elementary school). This was probably due to the influence of older siblings who had more control over their PE Choices. But Square Dancing had one redeeming quality that trumped even political and ethnic considerations and loyalties. Boys and girls would pair off, and periodically switch partners and 'doe see doe'. There is a twisting phase where the girl turns around as you hold your hand above her and the like. We'd rehearse in class with the 'PE' teacher and at the end of the semester there would be a performance style competition to see which grade level class was the best.

I loved it because it was the first time I got a prolonged opportunity to hold hands with girls, to look in their eyes, and sense their physicality and form as they sweep by me in rhythmic motion. Having a legitimate reason to touch a girl, got a shy bookish athlete interested in the subject of girls proper. Note that it is the forces of post-modernism that find debutant balls, tom thumb weddings, proms, and events that pair and presuppose traditional sexual roles as oppressive. How so? Why? Making us square dance and pair off in traditional sex roles was oppressive, subversive? The people who are making these kinds of arguments are DEI Bishops in the post-General Conference UMC. Dances and proms were big deals because they were presuppositions of what was to come, marriage. It is a foretaste. Dancing with a girl, presupposes one day I will dance with a woman in marriage. There is a reason our ancestors built these kinds of 'normative' traditions into children's activities. They were geniuses, that is the reason, not oppressive tools of the dictatorial patriarchy. These traditions are grounded in biblical and mammalian history and tradition, as well as widely different cultures from the most primitive to the formerly most advanced. Now the most advanced capitalist civilizations go around pretending like they don't know what a man and a woman are. The DEI Bishops responsible for teaching that doctrine, serve a god that doesn't know what man and woman are or has been lying about it to western civilization for 4000 years. That is why our DEI bishops needed the socialist atheist LGBTQIA social justice community to define what a man and woman are for god, and to educate god to what terms to use, and made god apologize for ever having presumed to know what a man and a woman are in a biblical sense.

Oh yes, there is a reason fairy tale princes and princesses exist that lies deep in human and mammalian psychology. When we abandon them in favor of the vanity of our own imagination, we are doing so at our own peril. You know dang well our parents knew how rough marriage and family are, but every time we turned around there were rituals that reinforced the need to do so, even if it was a fantasy that completely hid the difficulties of marriage. What parent doesn't tell his children that one day he or she wants to be a grandparent and see the fruit of his or her loins prosper and thrive....socialist-atheist LGBTQIA+ social justice warrior parents with a suicidal conception do, and now it has infected the church. In the old days, every man had a princess, every woman a prince, even if it was a fantasy. Every man had a princess to save, every woman a prince to save. Let them that have ears, hear. Every boy had a partner, every girl had a partner in elementary school square dancing. You could not know the girl/boy you had as a partner. That was the way the system was designed. They paired us off by numbers. Leftovers pretended like they had a partner until they switched, and he did have a partner, until the required amount was drafted. All we were frogs, paired off by the vagaries of natural mammalian physical endowment. Ah, but the kiss of the beloved princess, transforms frogs into princes, and the heroic sacrifices of princes turns bar maids into princesses. Clearly that is a fantasy, and yet it has survived for so many generations, and I believe will survive much longer than socialist-atheist LGBTQIA+ sexual algebra/sexual alphabet soup mumbo jumbo. I'll admit princes and princesses may be patriarchal fairytales, but so is the idea that just from cutting your penis off and taking enough hormones and steroids to make an elephant forget, that a boy can be a woman. What is more, a person can be disabused of thinking relationships are fairytales, but once you believe in the fairy tale that you can cut you penis off and take hormones to be an 'actual' woman, like Pinocchio wanting to be a 'real' boy, you cannot walk that back and re-suture your penis back on, and undo having taking powerful hormones for 10 years of your adolescent and young adult life.

Why has the love story between a man and a woman survived? Even if it was pure fiction and set up false premises about marriage, it has survived. Even though the 'happy ever after' presumed by such fairy tales, usually ends up involving marital discrepancies instead of bliss, the fairy tale survives. The Hallmark channel and others like it are basically 24/7 love stories. And yet, it's almost like a cruel joke our ancestors played on us, to teach us the fantasy that every woman has a prince, and every man has a princess, even if they are frogs to begin with. It was a kiss, affection, belief in, encouragement, trust in, that transitioned that frog into a prince and princess. To use a proverbial story from recent African American history, it was a kiss that turned a gangly, awkward pot-smokin, occasionally cocaine tooting grad student into Barrack Obama, the first Black White president of the United States, presuming Bill Clinton was the first Black president of the United States.

Oh these myths, handed down. They are fantasies and patriarchal dreams the liberals tell us. The only thing is the liberals and their DEI bishops have nothing to replace those dreams with but the North GA Conference 2024 singles dinner/dance fundraiser, where you better be prepared for anything, whether you go to the men's restroom or the women's. And this situation the current DEI Bishops and liberals would tell you is not only fair, but that there is someway to do that in a way that is 'decent and in order'. Imagine being at a church singles event, 'Holy Conferencing' no less, and you see a cute young lady on the dance floor. Y'all dance together in the dim flashing light and then after the song you take a bathroom break after talking to some friends. When you get there, there is your dancing partner you thought was so cute, peeing in the men's standup urinal, because the women's was too crowded (as women's bathrooms are won't to be). This your current crop of DEI bishops calls 'decent and in order' and making sure the UMC is on the right side of history. Local churches are supposed to send their children, adolescents and young adults to that?

I dare anyone to tell me I'm lying or that the conclusions I'm drawing are beyond the pale of what is now possible in UMC assemblies, Holy Conferencing or not. Even if you thought it was right, you wouldn't send your children there. And if you would send other people's kids there but not your own, you are a hypocrite and a phony; surely more likely to be a child of hell than a child of God. It is the post-modern equivalent of the biblical 'passing your children through the fires of Molech', sacrificing them. Except we are sacrificing them to the post-modern socialist-atheist LGBTQIA social justice agenda which is a philosophy of mutilation and death. Biological children is the aim. If the lifestyle doesn't/can't produce biological children, it cannot continue the grandparents, parents, DNA, the same way a biological female and male can.

Chapter 17 - How to do Theology with a Hammer!

Chapter 17 – How to Practice Theology with a Hammer

Nietzsche famously claimed (amongst other things) that he 'philosophizes with a hammer'. According to him, the purpose of this philosophic hammer is to destroy idols. Of course, 'his hammer was too short to box with God' and that fact drove Nietzsche crazy, but that is another discussion. The purpose of this book is to do public theology with a hammer. I have no doubt about the good intentions of the former liberal wing, now dominant wing of the UMC. I don't doubt the liberal's intelligence, and/or their love for, and commitment to the UMC. It will seem like it however, when I get to throwing hammers like ninjas throw stars and flip nun chucks. I might accidentally knock a few people upside the head who were just at the wrong place at the wrong time in my ardor. Thus please do not take it personally. But our church, the UMC as it was, got stolen, taken for the 'okey doke'. Our church ran away from home in spite and anger at our Father, seeking freedom, but it has come at a terrible cost, and it turns out we ran into some thugs and gangsters that ended up taking advantage of us and sex trafficking us. That is to say, using us for sex. And the confluence between sex and money, like the UMC is in the business of endorsing transexuals because Budweiser accepts it as normative, and all sorts of corporations view it as normative too, trying to appeal to as wide an audience as possible. Corporations have valid reasons to reach 'all' audiences and segments 'by any means necessary', the church does not. The UMC got fooled, hoodwinked, and bamboozled by our 'new friends', the socialist-atheist LGBTQIA social justice warriors, who promised us freedom, money, and being on their right side of history. In exchange for 'freedom' (as they define it), our new friends have gotten us nothing but a busted-up church, and an irrelevant public witness in an America that needs spiritual 'clouds of witnesses' now more than ever. Your witness, and the power of your witness, doesn't come from being on the right side of human temporal history. It comes from God, the eternal word of God. Our new friends prostituted us as we celebrated the triumph of their flim-flam at General Conference 2024. Imagine their smiles as we celebrated by dancing in the aisles wrapped in gay flags (idols), and celebrating with kisses, hugs, and banging tambourines like it was some kind of pagan ritual.

Church it's time to get off the streets, prostituting ourselves at the behest of our pimp, the socialist atheist LGBTQIA social justice warriors. They criticize us all the time, slap us around, and we can never do enough apologizing and paying reparations for them even taking the time to 'help' us. Even when we turn tricks for them, they take all the money. Let's go home saints. Even the prodigal son eventually realized it was not only best, but easiest to just go back home. We need to run away from our new socialist-atheist LGBTQIA masters and go home to our Father and faith. Yes, we've been out here prostituting ourselves for our new pimps and we've defiled ourselves, but Father will take us back. Our DEI Bishops however, are telling us this is the new normal and our father's house is old fashioned too stringent. There our DEI bishops are telling us that it's the new thing, the happening thing, the hip thing, and we the church have got to keep up and be on the right side of the whims of human temporal history. But wait, our faith invented the division of history! We use the terms BC and AD. How can people who don't even know my Father tell me what the right side of history is?

These folk, these socialist-atheist LGBTQIA bullies told us, like Hitler told the Jews on the sign atop the deathcamps that "Arbeite

Macht Frei". They told us if we went their way, we would be free, like a God to use an Edenic phrase. But it did not lead to freedom, only an intensification of suffering, sold to us as the price of seeking our freedom. What is freedom compared to tens of thousands, perhaps even hundreds of thousands of American citizens and even children, cutting their penises and breasts off in the name of sexual freedom. This behavior the post-General Conference 2024 and our DEI bishops calls heroic and applauds.

The UMC and our DEI Bishops fell for the worldly hokey doke, and killed itself trying be like the world. It hacked itself into its most sensitive areas trying to be sexually free and welcoming. The UMC as we knew it fell for the old bait and switch. The God we inherited was an omnipotent God who never makes mistakes, and is not a man that he should lie, nor the son of man that he should repent. To our current UMC that god is dead, replaced by an idol god that not only makes mistakes in allowing people to suffer, but a god who can't even apologize for himself and our DEI Bishops must go around wheeling him out on platforms and dais and pedestals, through hocus pocus prayer incantations, and 14 pages of apology. We were taught the necessity of owing the God we inherited from our UMC fathers and mothers. We were to apologize to him, not he has to apologize to us for making us a male, female, Black, White, skinny, plump, whatever. He did not make a mistake in his word or you by making you in particular categories. He doesn't owe you an apology for his mistake, and you can't legitimize going around hacking your penis or breasts off because 'God' made a mistake. This is as though you shouldn't be expected to live with god's mistake, when you'd feel better about yourself with $125,000 worth of plastic surgery and taking enough hormones to kill a small horse. And our current DEI Bishops call this behavior heroic! The God we inherited from our UMC fathers and mothers was omnipotent. Our DEI Bishops have replaced him with an idol god who is not omnipotent, because he doesn't know what a man and woman 'really are' and needs our DEI Bishops and their socialist-atheist LGBTQIA sexual algebra social justice warrior pimps and thugs to tell him.

Some 23 years ago in a jail cell under the supervision of the GA department of corrections fearing for my life, I prayed. Up to that moment I'd considered myself a bright worldly fellow. I hung out with Muslims, Rastas, 5 Percenters, Buddhists, etc., and enjoyed the lingo, and the religious and social events as well as the general religious feeling and imperative. But on that bunk in jail, so fearful I couldn't sleep, all I had was prayer. With so many religious experiences, I tried every approach I could wrap my mind around, meditation, tai chi. But I learned the hard way, sitting in your bunk at 3AM sweating with fear is not the time to be confused about, or even entertain doubts about how you can approach the throne of grace in time of need.

By then I had many diverse religious experiences and Knowledge. By then I had read the Quran once or twice. I had read most of the bible but learned the language and tone of how Rastafarians practice hermeneutics and do exegesis, even though I didn't have the language to describe it that way yet, as I had not gone to seminary. Obviously, my own Christian experience in the UMC, in the choirs, confirmation, and youth programs had impacted me. But for whatever blessing these activities were in my life, I had to deal with the very real fact that I had all that, and God still let me und up in jail, with $100,000 bond like I had killed somebody or had sold as much opioids as the folk behind oxycontin. I am told the reason my bond was so high was because the computers were down and they didn't know whether I had an extensive criminal record or not, and while 4 pounds of reefers is hardly Nino Brown, to a rural town with budget problems, I looked like I was going to post a 10th of the entire town budget just getting out of jail, let alone the fines and fees I will pay on supervision.

But on that bunk that night, the god that I had vainly imagined I could worship on a whim in whatever way interested me, at the time and made me happy and self-satisfied with myself spiritually and intellectually, when I felt like it and why I felt like it; that seemed idol like.

As good as my intentions were and however much I enjoyed these experiences, they were not rooted.

So what did I do. My grandparents George and Annie had a profound impact on me. The consistent weekly outings to their AME church, where my grandmother was on this board or that, this or that committee and aid society, her church hats and gloves, her uniform of choice, had a profound impact on me. Making me say my bedtime prayers. Bible stories as bedtime stories. It was a simple faith and simply prayer they taught me (Now I lay me down to sleep, I pray the Lord my soul to keep, if I should die before I wake, I pray the Lord my soul to take). There is a version some moderners do that is not quite so morbidly depressing in tone, but I prefer the original wording because it is the truth. It is certainly much truer that you can die in your sleep, than it is true that you can cut off your penis and breasts, and go prancing around as the opposite sex. It is certainly much 'truer' than that you can hold people accountable for calling you your new sexual identity, even though you still look like your old one for the most part. And you expect that everybody, nay even God, owes you a 'full' life as a person of the opposite sex. As a matter of fact, even God owes you an apology for making you the 'wrong' sex in the first place (wrong as defined by you and the socialist-atheist LGBTQIA sexual algebra social justice warrior community).

As I said it was a simple piety. My grandmother didn't take to exotic theologies, and the few televangelists that she would have been exposed to on television and the radio were tame compared to the vultures on Christian television today. The local church was her nexus. Her sisters Rebecca and Sadie (my great aunts) went to the same church with their families. Radical Christian or other theologies that drew her away from that nexus, she just wasn't particularly curious about. Her faith was a kind of everyday faith and praxis, that had little to do with esoteric knowledge or (as it were) gnostic knowledge only available to select 'initiates' or that type of hocus pocus theology. What the Holy Ghost didn't give her and hip her to, she didn't need. That kind of faith. She certainly would have rejected the idea of a church driven by the agenda of the socialist-atheist LGBTQIA social justice warrior community, or the churches quid pro quo capitulation to those same forces. It would have been very alien to her.

I wasn't thinking about any of the post-modern culture wars however, sitting in bunk in jail that night with tears streaming down my face because I thought either someone will try to kill or violate me, and/or I will end up possibly fighting, maiming or killing someone to defend myself. Desperate, not knowing what to do I prayed to my Grandma's God (true story), like on some Jewish, Christian, and Islamic appropriation of 'the God of Abraham'. Abraham, I didn't know, but my Grandma said she served the God of Abraham, Isaac, and Jacob and I was supposed to. That is how she handled me every single time I was around her. Desperate not knowing what else to do, there in the Washington County jailhouse, facing imminent threat, I prayed to my grandma's God, as she knew Him. I asked that God and Grandaddy George's God to save me. I didn't think I had earned enough merit, not enough esoteric knowledge, not enough yoga, and Tai Chi, Meditation, Salat, and foreign religion, to stay out of jail, so I called on the God of my grandma and grandad in their merit to save me and please help me.

...Finally I went to sleep, for a few hours. That morning, I got up, read some bible, and meditated and prayed like usual. I got in line to get a work detail post, or go to an outside church led bible study, because in my mind, it was better than sitting around doing nothing and being bored. At least it got you out of the dorm. Two dudes were in the dorm with me that had committed major crimes. One had shot his girlfriend in the face and led police on a wild high-speed chase filled with rolling gun battles and even hostages; until he ran out of ammo and crashed. The other was there for an attempted murder, of which the details didn't come out until later. Unfortunately, because post-modern American society is producing so many criminals, there was not enough space in the State Prison system at the time, for them to go immediately to State Prison as opposed to remaining in the county jail, where they were in the same population with dudes in there for DUI, bad checks, simple assault, slapping his baby mama, etc. The GA Department of Corrections was waiting for people to die in State Prison, or be released before they allow 'new' inmates in.

While they were waiting to go state prison for the above noted crimes, they were in a dorm with me, white dudes, Black dudes, and Mexicans on public intoxication, DUI, and simple fighting or domestic violence charges. The problem was that they had nothing to lose. The others and I basically just wanted to do our time and get out, while they knew they weren't getting out anytime soon. The guy that was in for attempted murder had home training, and while he was 'bout it-bout it'; he wasn't insufferable. Tony on the other hand, especially after having shot his girlfriend in the face, had nothing at all to lose, not even what home training he may have once had. He'd intimidate people, show the contents of his bunk and his latest shanks, and imply that he liked to have sex with men. He avoided me for a while, but I could feel him feeling me out and taking greater and greater liberties around me and to me. Thus, my feeling that eventually he was going to say something crazy or handle me wrong grew. I also understood instinctively that if he handled me this way publicly, I'd need to give him the business end of whatever natural martial skills and endowments I could bring. I certainly had no shank. I certainly had no posse. I am the quite sensitive guy always reading a book, meditating, getting a work detail, and that had never been a fight in his life except one, and it was more a tussle, in front of people I knew would break it up immediately. Unlike Michael Jackson, I'm a reader not a fighter. That night when I went to sleep, I decided in my mind that if Tony said something to me privately, I would let it ride and fob or laugh it off. But I had seen him operate, and how he liked to publicly humiliate people, and I said if he did that to me, I was just going to jump on him and wail and pummel, until somebody or the guards pulled me off (if I was lucky enough to need to get pulled off). I also knew that if his little clique jumped in it, I could possibly be done, so with that in mind, I determined to have no brakes; to pummel, hit and wail intentionally and repeatedly, like an animal and not stop. I knew dang well, big as I was, I could possibly kill somebody. But I knew once I was disrespected and let somebody treat me like a chump, EVERYBODY would think that's what I was and take advantage of me too (Note to current DEI Bishops and post-General Conference 2024 UMC). But God, apparently the God of Annie and George, in addition to being the God of Abraham, Isaac, and Jacob did an interesting thing when I woke up the next morning with that 'human, all too human' declaration and willingness in my mind to run the risk of possibly killing somebody.

I got up, did my usual mediation, bible reading, and got in line for a work detail, and there behind me in line was 'the other craziest' dude in the dorm; the other guy waiting to go to state prison, albeit his crimes were not as dramatic as Tony's. Don't get me wrong, they were as numerous, but not as dramatic. I later found out he was waiting to go to state prison for whooping his girlfriend and the dude she was cheating with, to the point that he was charged with attempted murder on one or both. I never asked him for details, and we never had a conversation about exactly what he was going to State Prison for. But the story I had heard from others was that he caught his 'old lady' cheating, and dang near killed her (like the anti-Hosea). I never asked and he certainly never told. What he did say that I will never forget, is when he came behind me in the work detail line that morning. It was as follows:

"Hey, I been checking you out (fear in the author's heart). Yeah, how you read the bible every morning, mediate and pray, and how you get a work detail instead of laying around in the bunk pretending to be asleep, so you can be lazy and stay in the dorm sleeping and lazing around all day talking crap (they didn't read or go to sponsored bible studies)."

Somewhat startled, I told him thanks and kind of fobbed it off, like chuckle, chuckle, nothing else to do around here. Then this came out of his mouth, within 6 hours of me praying to my grandma and grandad's God, that he save me from myself and the situation I've gotten myself into. The dude reputed to have beaten the brakes (if not the hell) out of his girlfriend/wife said to me:

"I think we should start a bible study twice a day."

Needless to say, I was flabbergasted and stupefied. The idea of that was as hardly pleasing as it was out of left field. Picture these men looking at me, long familiar with the vagaries and miseries of life. There they would be, looking at me like I was supposed to say something good, meaningful, or important. That was scarier to me than having to fight somebody. Thus, I was wondering what I could possibly tell this man to back out gracefully. But there was no way to back out gracefully. How do you tell a man in the County Jail only because there wasn't enough space in the State Prison, convicted of something that resembled attempted murder on a 'loved one', that you'd prefer not to do a bible study. The nightmare is that he interprets it as either you think his idea for a bible study is dumb, or you think there is something wrong with him. I had one enemy in the dorm, I was not going to create another simply because he felt 'inspired' to think I could lead a bible study.

I told him that I'd co-lead with him, but that twice a day was too much. I suggested we start out with once a day (and trust me, that proved relatively sufficient even though there is a place for a two-a-day in a correctional facility setting). As a matter of fact, I like the concept inherent in AA and NA which is that in a big enough city there are multiple meetings each day, at varying times, with the theory that whenever you feel vulnerable, there is a meeting going on somewhere.

Ladies and gentlemen, that is my call story. As you might imagine, when varying committees on ordained ministry in the UMC heard that, they weren't as impressed as I hope the reader is. Starting a bible study with about 6-8 guys in jail was my first 'ministry' (other than participating in Sunday school and youth choir). At varying points in this work, I refer to bullying and/or light hazing. When we started our bible study Tony, the guy with the shanks waiting to go to State Prison stopped intimidating and terrorizing guys associated with us. Not because of me, though at 250 and athletic I knew how to make it 'do what it do' in a pinch. It was because the guy that started the Bible study with me was not only waiting to go to State Prison too, and had nothing to lose himself, but was acknowledged to be just as crazy as Tony. That was just enough shelter for the quiet dudes, younger dudes, even White or foreign dudes (the Mexicans had their own hustle) and others that just wanted to do their time and leave without being terrorized or traumatized.

This is not to say my 'co-laborer' in the vineyard was perfect, even with his aspirations to two-a-day bible studies. One day he was playing cards with a few other guys at one of the communal tables in the dorm. In a flash, I didn't have time to notice what led up to it, my co-laborer jumped up and slapped the bejeezus out of one the younger big mouth brats, who are really adolescents, but they are in jail, convinced of their silly childhood and neighborhood ideas of what bloods, crips and other gangs are. So 'them young boys' act a fool in jail. Many of them come from broken homes, with no fathers, and mothers who are in problematic circumstances. Whatever happened that day I am sure it revolved around my co-laborer feeling disrespected by the boy, so he jumped up, slapped him and they started tussling. Both were put in solitary confinement as punishment for a few days, and I had to labor on with the Bible study by myself for a few days. I was not worried however, and nothing changed because, as scary as it was to see my co-laborer jump up and slap the brakes off somebody, no one dared say anything crazy to me, especially after that because it just solidified in their minds how crazy my 'co-laborer' was. Everybody knew that if somebody handled me wrong, and I told my co-laborer when he got out 'the hole' and came back to the dorm, my co-laborer would have a serious, serious problem with you. That being said, he never handled me wrong, always respectful, but I was scared as crap of him.

Part II

Please be patient with my call story. I want you to know who you are reading. After about 3-6 weeks of relative order and calm with my co-laborer and bible study in the county jail, I got transferred to a probation detention facility under the GA Department of Corrections called, I W Davis. It is now closed. It was approximated or intended to be something like a 'boot camp'. This was supposedly better than the state prison I was entitled to go to for possessing 4 pounds of marijuana with the intent to distribute. The canteen was better. There were more and varied work details. And the prized thing about I W Davis was that they sold Newport cigarettes in the Canteen, and one could 'smoke their back out' if they wanted to. I got sick off the first 3 and sold the rest. I never had time to get addicted to cigarettes, I was too addicted to weed at the time. There were church services and bible studies 3 or 4 times a week and I enjoyed them all, every denomination. When you get saved (literally), and God does something miraculous for you, you're really gung ho.

It is interesting to note the denominations that had a presence at I W Davis. I went to everything. The services would be in the cafeteria or 'education room'. The Catholics came to the jail, but only for the Catholics and they were certainly not proselytizing unless it was by magic. I even enquired about going to something Catholic, and desired to meet the Priests, who would be in full garb, but I was told it was just for Catholics. Cool. Unfortunate, but cool. Worse, no UMCs, AMEs, or CME's, Episcopalians, Anglicans etc., just lots of White and Black variations of Baptists and non-denominational types. One of my favorites was an old country White man. He was so hillbilly and so country, his English was worse than anything Blacks are rumored to have done to the Kings English since we got it. Deep country. Here again, that real simple humble piety. One of the proudest moments of my 'saved' life at the time, and my beginning to have signs of commitment to glance towards Jerusalem (if not set my face towards it) occurred in one of his Services.

Many young men went to the church services simply to get out of the heat, noise, cacophony, and din of the dorm. One time the old guy was there to hold service as usual, but the air conditioning was out in the rec room/visitation room/education room. The old man must have been at least in his late 70's then. He was ready to preach, sweltering heat, like nothing was wrong. He started up his usual 'thing' and many of the guys left when they found out the air conditioning wasn't working. Some left after a half hour or so in the sweltering room, that was hotter than being outside. I stayed to the very humid end. I was embarrassed for the old man. He was taking the heat and sweating with an old ragged dingy white handkerchief teaching the word, and here we big Negroes and White boys were complaining about the heat and walking out on the word. My fellow inmates shouldn't have done that old man like that.

But mainly I liked the old man's theology and schtick. It was old-fashioned. Ruggedly old-fashioned. He didn't do a whole lotta exegeting. He didn't tell you what stuff meant in the Greek or the Masoretic text. Just the word, the King James, the best he could exegete and all his exegesis was through the hermeneutic lens of holiness and personal piety. That is to say, cultivating holiness, rectifying one's life, purifying one's life, sanctifying one's life. For me, that was the forerunner of wrestling with Wesleyan notions of Sanctification. The old man was deeply rooted in traditional southern Christianity. It wasn't a lot of frills, but it was real stable. It is also memorable, because it was the first time in my post-Jail House Conversion and Call Experience when I had a chance to go hard for what I now believed. Going hard for the old man's word, in the sweltering heat, as others bailed, I had a chance to go hard for what I now believed. To be willing to preach to others, not for competition, but for the sake of God, that I was willing to go hard, go faster, go longer, in the name of Jesus. It was a small triumph, but it presaged others, far more painful than the heat we had to suffer to prove obedience to God.

A Black non-denominational church visited weekly or bi-weekly as well. The inmates called them 'Batman and Robin' because one was tall, and the other was short. Their schtick (if you will) was a tag team approach like Burt and Ernie, Laurel and Hardie, Abott and Costello, Amos and Andy, etc., except riffing on different scriptures and subjects from the Bible. It was very entertaining and spirit lifting in such a dark, dour place. Also stopping by periodically was a White husband and wife team that would hold service. He played guitar and they both sang. I think both had long hair. They were 'hippy' type Christians, and I wouldn't even be surprised if they had on tie-dye. Their theology was traditional, even if the package wasn't. Believe it or not, Black and Hispanic inmates like them. The main thing I remember was that they seemed very earnest. As a matter of fact, that was the central characteristic they all had, because you have to be earnest and believe to do prison ministry without being paid, with your spouse. It is not for everybody, certainly not our DEI and Ebony Bishops.

That isn't a criticism, however. When I got back in the UMC Church after getting out of I W Davis, I went to my Father in the Ministry (though I had not claimed him as such then) and told Rev. Dr. Thrower that we should have a prison ministry in Douglas County Jail. We regularly visited nursing homes, hospitals and the like and I figured it wouldn't be too much of a shift to do ministry in jails and prisons sometimes. I learned a lot going around with him. I certainly thought he had the type of personality that would work in a prison context. But when I told him, he looked away distracted, and simply said that wasn't his gift. As I've grown in ministry, I've learned the importance of to some extent knowing your 'gift', working within your 'gift', and stretching extremely selectively. Like spending more time consolidating than seeking. In ministry, it's best if you're not afraid to tell folk the limits of your gifts and graces. Everybody can't do homeless ministry, either because they were traumatized or perhaps their physical and emotional constitution is such that just the thought of the smells, human and otherwise that run across such settings is more than they can take and even cause physical revulsion and throwing up.

On the other hand, there are others that are so wired with gifts and graces that they can wade through the sickest, the poorest, most distressed, leprosy, open putrefying wounds like Lazarus, almost like Jesus in ease and grace. Either way, as a rule, you should do what you're best suited for. But some kind of way our DEI Bishops think that doesn't apply to your biological sex. God was confused when he made me a male or you a female? And then I go find me some DEI Bishops willing to say God regularly makes mistakes of this kind and nature? When the habitable parts of planet earth maintain a temperature within a range of -10 or -20 Fahrenheit to 120 Fahrenheit, and anything thing consistently colder or warmer would kill us among many other species of flora and fauna...and that system is suspended in a solar system, galaxy, and universe this size is amazing. Praise the Lord for His works. A God that can do that, how is it possible that he doesn't know what a man and woman are? There are gazillions of galaxies in the universe. The God that can keep them all, and keep the temperature on earth in habitable zones within 100 degrees or so of what can quite clearly kill us, makes mistakes like birthing people the wrong biological sex? Really? Really? This is the idol god DEI Bishops serve that needs help knowing what a man and woman are from socialist-atheist LGBTQIA sexual algebra/alphabet soup social justice propaganda.

The official representative of God, the official chaplain of I W Davis Probation Detention Facility under the supervision of the GA Department of Corrections would visit us in our dorms once a week or so. As he made the rounds, he didn't say anything in particular, but would ask if people need prayer. Occasionally someone would ask him if he could contact loved ones or help them in some other way, but of course he couldn't, as none of the visiting ministers could. That being said, he was no help to the inmates and nearly everybody ignored him when he made his rounds. Even religious people such as I, didn't put any stock in him. He'd walk around each dorm shaking hands and saying God bless to those interested. Then he'd immediately put hand sanitizer on his hands when he came out of each dorm, within full sight of the inmates. But of course, he had to do that to protect the inmates (wink, wink, nod, nod).

That being said, for the most part I enjoyed my rebirth in Christianity and the immediate aftermath of my jailhouse conversion and call. The Bible study started in the county jail, but it continued in different ways in I W Davis. At I W Davis, my spiritual habits (morning prayer and meditation, hot for my work detail, reading a lot) were the same. Oh yes, brief interjection, in jail I read a lot of westerns and crime novels, books people had donated over the years. This experience greatly helped me as a writer. To be frank, it was almost like I read 40 westerns and Nero Wolf, Sherlock Holmes style crime novels in the 60-90 days I was in. No doubt this improved my writing because it improved my sensitivity to narrative and the basics of a strong narrative theme and pulse. All of this brought some kind of more or less positive attention to me from the authorities and the other inmates. I wouldn't make the argument I was Joseph...more like Joseph light, or Joseph redux, Joseph abridged.

It was interesting how I was assigned a work detail (here again being eager for one). The jail went through a great pretense of interviewing you so they can assess your education level, and skill level, and presumably be doing something suitable. Baloney. In my interview, with me being a college graduate, I thought they'd find me something commensurate with my skills. The officer looked my background over and said, "oh wow, a college graduate, we don't get many of you in here. You look like a big strapping fellow; I'm going to put you on the bush ax crew". The bush ax crew was the most physically demanding of all the crews. It was the crew they used to discipline inmates who didn't know how to talk to guards, had too much mouth, and kept up too much. 5 days a week, 8:30-9:00 to about 2:30 or 3:00 I was on bush ax crew beating back weeds, overgrowth, in rural Washington County, Banks County, Commerce, and that area of Georgia.

And yet every cloud does indeed have a silver lining to the patient and wise, or those willing to learn to be patient and wise. When it rained, we went out, posted in the van and waited for it to stop...talking, laughing, and listening to the radio. White guys wanted to listen to one radio station, Blacks another. Our guard regulated by making the time between the two until everybody forgot, and it was left wherever it was. When it didn't rain, it was bush axe time. Oh, my memory of the rolling hills and over abundant plums, figs, blackberries, etc. White and Black rural farmers would see us keeping the overgrowth back, in key places and some would invite us on their land to eat the fruit. I grew up in urban/sub-urban SW Atlanta. There in rural Georgia, every day I saw snakes, buzzards, turtles, possum, racoon, deer, wild turkeys and hogs. The country boys of both races would play with the kosher ones. The country boys also knew the best fruit and how to eat it, as well as home remedy type stuff.

The landscapes we would see were amazing. This immersion in the natural world, 35 or so hours a week, gave this city boy an appreciation for nature I had only experienced visiting my grandparents in SC. It is not an understatement to say that quite often we on the bush ax crew were walking around picking berries and fruit like we were in Eden. But I was in jail on a work detail working on a sentence of 60 to 90 days, the least amount one could be sentenced according to the sentence structure. Gung ho for the Lord though, which nearly automatically means filled with the Holy Ghost (or some variation).

As you work your work detail you get to know one another, and learn each other's histories, backgrounds, and communications styles. You build a unit of sorts. Many of those deep country boys were damn near illiterate. They could tell if it was going to rain and how long, or catch a rattlesnake with their bare hands, but the simplest ideas would be virtually unfamiliar to them. Many of them were good solid hard-working dudes that would eventually 'catch up', but you could see a profound level of early and consistent ignorance. Even the hardcore city dudes, within a week or two on the Bush ax crew calmed down because they were too tired. You couldn't swing your bush ax and walk 3 miles without being tired. Plus I think nature and all those organic fruits and berries does something to the soul of a man.

Our guard who loaded us up in the van, took us to our duties, and supervised us was a married older country no-nonsense White dude. He was probably in his early 60's and chain-smoked. He was no-nonsense and didn't take a lot of crap, but he was one of the fairest guards. Rain or shine we were out there and in the middle of the summer it would be

90 degrees or more. The correctional facility gave us coolers of water like the one's football teams use, and li'l hugs juicy juice cool aid cool 6-8 oz drinks to have with our sandwiches for lunch. In 90-degree weather the water would run out and the juicy juices were meant as an adornment to the sandwiches, not reliable hydration. When that would happen, the guard would take his own money and buy a couple jugs of water and get us some more paper cups. Another reason the Blacks, Hispanics and White guys liked him was because he smoked these cigarettes that were brown like cigars but filtered like a cigarette. Once he got to know you, and you were relatively easy to get along with he'd give you one during a break. I was gung-ho for the Lord (at least at that point) so I was not indulging even if it was free, and you could get a cheap dizzy nicotine rush/high. The bush ax crew cleaned up crazy White dudes too.

I give White dudes in jail credit for being married and attempting to stay married in jail. They spend way more time on such matters than Black men. There is nothing like a guy running himself crazy worrying what's going on at his home when he is in jail. During my 60-90 days under the supervision of the Georgia Department of Corrections, it seemed every week at least one man (most often White), got served divorce papers. Many of them would be dang near inconsolable. It was amazing to me that in the White community, even the poorest men, illiterate and doped up get married, at least once and often multiple times. The poor and less well educated a Black man is, the least likely he is to get married. This proves that our Black marriage rate has more to do with culture than economics, with all due respect to economic issues and factors impact on marriage and family life.

As I intimated earlier it was observable by staff and other inmates that I went to all the church services, meditated, stayed in the bible or other religious materials available in the I W Davis Detention Facility Library. The library looked (and felt) like somebody got the bright idea to put up bookshelves in a 6x6ft closet. Like the county jail there were lots of westerns and detective novels. Many of my fellow dorm mates, Black and White would come to me with life questions or problems, which to be honest, call or not, I wasn't interested in or prepared to deal with. Many of these men were people that if I knew them on the outside, I would not choose to be around them. Some of them I would be afraid to be around on the outside. I had few answers, but all the time in the world at that point to listen. Learning how to listen is a difficult skill that deserves its own book.

It should be noted that jailhouse evangelism is quite different from the evangelism of our DEI Bishops and our post-General Conference 2024 UMC. Amazing how they don't have the same energy for prison ministry, they do for encouraging the cutting off penises and breasts. Jailhouse evangelism is easier in one great regard. Repent for past sin, try life God's way, based on God's word and fellowship in his church, the Body of Christ. Jailhouse evangelism is not rocket science. That message did not require seminary and missiology classes. That message doesn't require fancy robes and Bishops trained in 'safe sanctuaries' even though I am tempted to ask once again, is a sanctuary that encourages your children to cut their penises and breasts off if they want to, a 'safe' sanctuary? That message doesn't require a PHD or an M.Div. There is no better place for the repent message either. Doing it your way got you to this point of sitting in jail, your baby mama shacking up, with some dude giving your daughter baths at night and tucking your daughter and your baby mama in, while you in jail. This cell is where doing it your way got you. I wish I could convince our DEI bishops that doing it 'their' way is what got us to a split up, busted up, weak and witnessless post-modern UMC church. We need to repent, just like I did and just like I encouraged others around me in jail to do.

My Rasta days did yield one great benefit that manifested itself at this time. Many people look at Rastafarianism as though it were another religion. It really should be looked at like a version of Christianity; perhaps even Afro-Caribbean folk Christianity, complete with its own exegesis, its own heroes put on par with biblical heroes like Marcus Garvey and Bob Marley. The fact that it was based in a particular kind of music, with particular kinds of religious lyrics made it a transportable faith.

The Reggae band Steel Pulse had a song with the title 'Chant a Psalm a day'. There are quite a few reggae songs and Nyabinghi chants that derive straight from the Psalms, quite often word for word. On that basis, during my Rasta days I did precisely that, and read at least one Psalm a day.

So by the time I was in jail, I was somewhat familiar with them and of course many of the themes resonate with people in jail. If I had to give credit to one scripture for getting me cleaned up, scrubbed up, wrapped up, and tied up in jail, and wrapped up and tied up in Jesus, in jail is Psalm 119. I'd read and meditate on it every day. The part that I doubled down on, and that I told my pastoral care inmates were the lines:

Psalms 119:9 ¶ BETH. Wherewithal shall a young man cleanse his way? by taking heed thereto according to thy word.

And the line:

Psalms 119:67 ¶ Before I was afflicted I went astray: but now have I kept thy word.

And the line:

Psalms 119:71 ¶ It is good for me that I have been afflicted; that I might learn thy statutes.

When a man gets that in his spirit and believes it, and believes that God indeed has afflicted him to correct him not kill him, and out of love, not anger, then he is ready for a 'born again experience'. Absent that 'feeling', I'm not sure one can really be born again. Did you come to God because you're so smart and you make good choices in the natural, or God's words lined up with your beliefs, or did you come to God because you were doing it your way, it didn't work, and you decided to try it his way?

That is to say, even though you may be in jail, get served divorce papers, etc., God doesn't owe me an apology. God was not unfair to me when I look back over the entirety of my life and add it all together. Guess what else, the criminal justice system doesn't owe me an apology and my cheatin, lyin wife doesn't either. As a matter of fact, even in such a case as this I still owe God an apology, because even where we were in the wrong place at the wrong time, in most cases there is still a lot of clear indications of bad decision making on our parts. The selling point is, somehow, someway, if we quit trying to do it our way and do it God's way, biblically speaking, your life will get better. Your community will get better, and America will get better. Until now and a UMC influenced by socialist-atheist LGBTQIA social justice philosophy, repentance has always been the core of evangelism. And since the days of Jesus 2000 years ago until General Conference 2024, it has not only worked, but been the guiding theology of the church (universal). Do it His way, according to His word as best you can and slowly but surely, one way, and then another, line by line, precept upon precept, your life will get better. Trust the process, trust your brothers and sisters in Christ in your local church because they are going through the exact same process, but in different stages.

After I finished my 60-90 days under the direct supervision of the GA Department of Corrections, I was as gung-ho out of jail as I was in jail. I got married and joined Golden UMC in Douglasville GA under the leadership of the man I call my 'Father in the Ministry'. Of course, like all Black fathers, sons and daughters, that relationship can oftentimes be problematic. But there are just some things, if one is successful in any regard, one must give his or her 'father' credit for. I got involved, went to men's bible study, the male chorus, the United Methodist Men, and another remnant from my former Rasta life made itself useful (in context). Nyabinghi drumming, chanting, singing, involves playing the drums, specifically, varying forms of hand drums, shakerees, bass drum. Because Nyabinghi sessions would go on at least 3 or 4 hours, drummers would take breaks, and if you got to know one, when they took a smoke break, or a chat up a sistren break, you could play until they got back. If you had your own drum, you didn't even have to ask to sit in. But trust and believe, if you played something that didn't go with the basic Nyabinghi beat or you stepped on toes at the spirit drumming session, you would quickly be checked. Imagine my surprise when I get to Golden UMC, and they have a beautiful pair of congas. One higher register tone, one lower. I probably should have tuned or tightened them, but other than that they were in good shape. Altogether better, no one was playing them, they were just sitting there. I told Thrower I played around in the old days, asked could I play, and it worked out. You might say things worked out so well I decided I wanted to go to seminary. That story deserves to be told as well.

Part III

Theologically sound or not, I had been in the business of striking deals with God since I was in the 6th grade. Well, I have credentials before the 6th grade but the deal making started then. My mom had a MLK Jr Commemoration Bible with fake gold trim around the page edges. On the back or front blank page I traced my hand on the blank page, and promised to God that I would read it every day. It was a promise soon forgotten, but later taken up more or less in earnest. Also consequential to my youthful understanding of God was an incident I had after I learned about prayer from grandma, my mother, Sunday school and the like. Grandma et al, said you can ask God for anything you want. He might not give it to you, but you never know. That made sense to me, so one Sunday at church (Trinity AME on Lynhurst Drive in Southwest Atlanta) I prayed to God to go to Six Flags Amusement Park. The very next day out of the clear blue one of my mother's close friends from her alma mater and mine, South Carolina State University, invited me to go to Six Flags with her children. Wow, prayer really does work. Not only is God real but he can hear and might grant you your prayer. Some kind of way I associated it with praying at church and trust me, I couldn't wait to get back to church to pray for something again the next Sunday. I worked up a list, but I figured it'd be best not to be greedy, and to just ask for one thing a Sunday. I prayed hard for something, what it was I can't remember because it either didn't come, or didn't come soon enough for me to notice! Thank God He worked it that way, because in my disappointment, it resonated deeply with me that God might give it to you, or he might not, but He can! That experience was probably the root of my sense of a relationship with God based on 'remembering' (as in Jesus counsel to the church that part of the role of the Holy Spirit is to 'bring things to rememberance', remembrance as in understanding the significance of). i.e. the famous mantra of the Black church 'when I look back over my life, and I think things over, I can truly say, that I been blessed, I got a testimony'!

My next home on the Methodist map, having left Trinity AME, was Ben Hill UMC under future Bishop C L Henderson. I joined around the age of 12. More scholarship needs to be done on him and that period in Atlanta Black Christian history, but off the top of my head, his experience at Ben Hill was important for 3 very important reasons. #1 he, a staid and stolid United Methodist in a mainstream White denomination had the first mega church in new integrating and transitioning Southwest Atlanta, and South Fulton County. He set the pattern for aspiring UMC pastors and nondenominational pastors and preachers. #2 in that growth he showed what could be done with a coalition of newly middle class and affluent Black people, who tithe and are on one page. #3 this kind of blending of 'disciplined', staid, and stolid structures and theologies of White mainstream 'UMC' Methodism, were blended with High Negro spirituals sung by Sharon Willis and Oliver Suing, and a full-fledged gospel choir of a quality and size any Baptist and Pentecostal, church would admire (The Gospel Choir). Willis and Suing were highly trained and gravitated to the Sanctuary Choir, which tended towards a more 'refined' style. This recipe was magic to the nascent SW Atlanta Black Middle Class that now had Bourgeois religion to go along with their college and graduate degrees, their business success, and their professional success in the government and White mainstream corporate world.

But back to my little soul at Ben Hill UMC where I had my 3rd religious experience. My mom put me in everything for youth at Ben Hill. This was not just to keep me off the streets, but as a teacher she knew the importance of music, travel, and exercises on the intellect. So she was big into camps and children's stuff. Usually I resisted, preferring the neighborhood and my friends, but I went because in those days, parents weren't trying to figure out what their children's learning styles were, they'd put them in enough activities, forcibly or not, for the child to figure it out on their own and hope something sticks. I think from the ages of 12 to 18, I participated in every youth and children's event Ben Hill could come up with. I was in Boys RISE (Ready in strengthening Ebony-how ironic), Sunday School, Vacation Bible School, Youth Choir, Confirmation class. I went to everything and whether I wanted to go or not, I loved it. I sang in the children's choir at Trinity. The Youth Choir at Ben Hill was near professionally done, and sang the gospel standards of the time, and between the two I developed a love of not only choral singing, but particularly religious singing. Even as a kid, you can feel the energy of the audience. It is the supreme contradiction for children in terms of their relationship to Church as an institution and theologically. Something at once so pointless, meaningless, irrelevant to a child, can generate the most intense emotions in adults. And the more choirs you sing in you learn to blend your voice, you learn to sing parts, you learn to follow improvised direction, you learn to rock from side to side and clap on time, and you know what it sounds like and feels like when things are clicking and when they are not (rhythmically, harmonically, and spiritually). This is even without a stitch of musical training. It is no coincidence that many of the early Black finalists in the American Idol and other similar shows, had their start in the Black church. I'll never forget the first song I learned on my first day at Ben Hill youth choir rehearsal. If I'm not mistaken Keith was the choir director. The song we were to sing the next Sunday was the Soul song 'Love Train, with the refrain 'People all over the world join hands, get on the Love Train'.

I thank God for my youth choir experience. Oh, halcyon days indeed. I had a Volkswagen Rabbit, but every once in a while, I'd trade my Rabbit for one of my neighborhood friends motorcycle, and ride it to youth choir rehearsal some Wednesdays. No helmet, trying to look cool! I'd take a young lady on a ride before or after choir rehearsal. Thank God I didn't kill anybody's baby girl or myself! One choir rehearsal, the

Sunday before a Sunday we didn't sing, a girl I was sweet on, who shall remain all but nameless, because her dad was an on-air personality at the local PBS affiliate, me, my best friend Joe, 'old girl' and another young lady cut choir rehearsal and went to the mall. The company was fine, and it was worth the convivial companionship, but we all felt bad about not being there for rehearsal and then having to lie about aspects of our evening when we were supposed to be at a church related event. When we returned in the immediate aftermath of choir rehearsal dismissal, the girls were able to sneak back in anonymously. Joe and I got noticed, someone told Mr. Denson (then the Youth Choir Director) that we cut choir rehearsal, and his punishment was that we had to miss singing the next Sunday. But we went anyway and just blended in. At that time the Youth Choir at Ben Hill had about 125 youth.

In a stroke of genius, Rev. Henderson had a famous way of recruiting for the youth choir. We eventually got good enough to sing at the 8:00 and 10:45 services from the choir loft and had our own concert repertoire. Whenever Rev. Henderson noticed youth in the congregation he'd jump up after we sang and extoll our greatness. He'd say to the assembled, that the youth choir is recruiting, and rehearsals were every Wednesday at 6 PM. Then he would ask all the youth in the audience between 12-18 to stand. When a certain number of them stood, or perhaps any of them stood, he'd invite them...no request that they come up in the choir loft right now and sit with us. Preachers don't have the 'balls' to do that kind of evangelism amongst our angry angst ridden, anxiety riddled, phone addicted youth for fear of offending them or making them uncomfortable. Humorously enough, Rev. Henderson fundraised much the same way. But he was ahead of his time in many ways, and I am disappointed Black North Georgia Methodism didn't produce more Black male and female elders with his unique appreciation for the possibilities in ministry, and taking advantage of socio-economic trends.

There were some very notable people in the Youth Choir at Ben Hill during the early to mid-80's when I participated. Sleepy Brown from the Dungeon Family (Outcast, Goodie Mob, etc), Keisha Lance Bottoms, Kaseem Reed, kids from Mays, Douglass, Westwood/Westlake. 130 strong, it was a special time, and we were very well rehearsed and trained.

One of my fondest memories is doing a concert at Ebenezer. Yes, that Ebenezer. The old one, not the new edifice that is the seat of Warnock's liberal socialist-atheist LGBTQIA social justice machinations. But I digress. Rev. Roberts was pastor of Ebenezer then. Rev. Roberts son Carlyle went to Douglass with me, and we had a few classes together and were friends. He lived in Heritage Valley, damn near within walking distance of my home. Apparently, Rev. Roberts and Rev. Henderson were friends as well as professional colleagues such that they would preach revivals for one another. The Ben Hill Youth Choir, here again about 130 strong, sent 2 or 3 Coach buses full of youth in our matching outfits. The theme was pink and gray. The boys had grey suits with pink cummerbunds and bow ties and the girls had pink dresses that to my mind looked like prom dresses. After the concert at Ebenezer (the old building), they had a reception for us. It was heady stuff for teenagers. I stared at Angela the whole time. We get to seminary and get PHD's in theology and ministry and put fancy spins and 'unpackings' on words like 'spiritual formation' and 'Christian education' but Saints it is in praxis, your own personal praxis and piety and that which you expose your children to.

Contrast this with the state of Ben Hill Vacation Bible School (VBS) program when I brought my adolescent son there a few years ago, because I was dumb enough to think that he could possibly experience the same or similar experiences as I did during my teen years at Ben Hill. Beloved, the only people there were old people and little kids. There were so few teens, that the 'youth' pastor at the time said there was not a teen VBS, and that the 5 or so teens that were there, were just going to follow her around helping with the little kids. That same young lady is an Elder in Full Connection now with a cross racial appointment at a

White church somewhere. She graduated from Candler School of Theology I think.

130 strong youth choir to 5 teens at VBS in 2018-2019. The pastor at Ben Hill under such a phenomenally dismal youth program and youth presence is now a District Superintendent. And not coincidentally, when I got rejected twice before the district committee on ordained ministry he was on there. Berneice Kirkland was the other. And I think I mentioned earlier a man from the Ben Hill of my youth was the lay representative. I don't say these things to condemn them. I'm just telling a story. I have no doubt between my credit history, my criminal history, and my failed marriages, anyone that wants to list all sorts of reasons I was unacceptable to varying committees on ordained ministry, is merited in so doing. No doubt it was why many of my phone calls were ignored. But without a doubt, the UMC certainly hasn't done any better without me. Notwithstanding my credit, my criminal history and my failed marriages, I know what a man and a woman are, and will stand on it, instead of socialist-atheist LGBTQIA sexual algebra social justice propaganda.

I was an acolyte as well (No Star Wars Pun intended); a process of about 3 or 4 Saturday's training, maybe from 10-1. Then we hit the floor that next Sunday, each child on a rotation thereafter. Ruth Tucker did that ministry, who happens...well...I don't want to start naming DEI Superintendents and Elders in this context in a way that is unfair. I don't mind being unfair to people, and I will critique them for the mess they heaped upon the Black UMC and the wider UMC denomination, but not for their personal choices. Anyway. Ruth Tucker had a picnic at her house, the last Saturday of acolyte training. The hot dogs, the girls, the games, everything I needed was there. Confirmation class was much the same way. A few Saturdays and an introduction/induction program at church the next Sunday where we took pictures with Rev. Henderson. I still have that picture and if I have the nerve, I will place it in this current volume. Hot dogs, hamburgers, girls, sports, and games...and all I must do is acolyte, go to Sunday school, choir rehearsal, confirmation class, join the youth usher team etc! Sold, no theology necessary. I was a youth usher and sometimes when the preacher was preaching a few of us with cars would go to Mrs. Winners and get sausage biscuits and cinnamon swirls. If I wasn't singing, ushering or participating in some other way, I would oftentimes cut church, show up around communion time walking in taking care to make sure my mom saw me, by waving at her as I walked through the communion line to show her I was there for communion. I'd take communion and walk right out the back door. I had perfected this deception. Back then, quite often the youth sat in the balcony, where of course we'd be youth, eating candy, laughing and talking and the like, but at least we wouldn't be disturbing most people.

Which leads us to my next significant religious experience which occurred at Ben Hill. I got the Holy Ghost for the first time. One Sunday the spirit was high and service was running longer. I came in a little too early. Time I hit the narthex while the ushers were still actively seating people, I got caught up in the press and got seated. The song 'Soon as I get Home' was huge them, and I remember the Majestic Choir singing it. The sanctuary was packed. Folk were getting happy and falling out in the choir loft, in the pews, and the ushers couldn't keep up. I was in the back left rear of the main sanctuary. As the song began to crescendo and fade, then crescendo and fade again, the lady right next to me began shaking and rocking. Oh Lord, here we go I thought, this woman is bout to get the Holy Ghost. As she got more and more amped and physical I looked around for an usher, but they were busy with others. Finally after a few frantic looks, the adults near me started fanning the lady and telling her everything was going to be alright. And I started feeling the same energy and pulse in the music, the people around this lady fanning her and telling her everything is going to be alright. For some bizarre reason I started feeling like everything was going to be alright too, even though I didn't know anything was wrong. And somewhere between the song and people fanning the lady right next to me and chanting a mantra of 'its going to be alright', something started sweeping over me. I knew exactly how I felt, a kind of emotional swelling and catharsis. I felt in sympathy with the woman, I felt in sympathy with the people fanning her and telling her it's going to be alright. There was not an ounce of my being that doubted God at that moment. Orthodoxy and 'means and ways of approach' I had debates about, but from then on, pretty much I knew God was real. I'm about 14 as these feelings swell up inside me that Sunday, and suddenly I had this tremendous urge to cry. I knew dang well I had no reason to cry. I'm sitting there not knowing why I feel like crying, but in truth, probably in the natural, sensing the woman's grief, and the people's concern, and my proximity, I was overwhelmed. But I wasn't a naïve teen. I cut church too much and did what I wanted to do too much to get overwhelmed by a single event. I had seen people get happy before. My other teen friends and I would sit in the balcony and laugh when the same old ladies got happy every Sunday. I thought these thoughts rationally as I sat there, tears swelling in my eyes with nothing to cry about. The wonderful out of control-ness sensation (not coincidentally common to the feelings associated with drugs and alcohol), kept coming upon me. I could feel it very palpable. I was afraid that if I let it get much further, I would not be able to stop it and perhaps I'd burst out in tears and rhapsodic spiritual ecstasy like the lady next to me. The only way I could stop the ride I was on was to detach myself from my feelings. Detach from the music and wonderfully morbid lyrics of the song, detach from what was going on around me, and detach from my own feelings. Dunno how wise it was but I can certainly tell you it was quite an exercise in spirituality for a 14-year-old.

And yet the experience had a profound impact on me. I kept thinking, how could they tell her everything was going to be alright? Of more concern to me was why I wanted to cry and dance to it, and I knew of a certainty that if I had let myself go, that is precisely what would have happened. From then on, I might not be able to dance the Holy Ghost, but I made a habit of doing my best to detect it, and know when it authentically broke out. That is because when the Holy Spirit breaks out, it is a sign that the presence of the Lord is there, way more than in a ceremonial 'holy conferencing' way. Plus when it authentically breaks out, I am a firm believer that whoever is present (and even some that aren't), can get a little bit of it. The bigger your cup and the more you sit under the Holy Ghost waterfall, the more you get. And it helps all manner of things, physical, spiritual, mental, emotional, etc., but I digress again.

After being Treasurer of the UM Men under Thrower, I started taking more public roles for this or that. In the spirit of that 'deal making' as a kid, I attempted a 'deal' with the Lord back when I was selling weed, drinking and smoking blunts like 75/85 runs North/South, my friends and I getting shot at, carrying guns. During the midst of those days, I told the Lord that if anything traumatic ever happened to me, I would go to grad school and if it was traumatic enough, I'd go to seminary. 2 years before the county jail and the probation violation sentence of 60-90 days in I W Davis Probation Detention boot camp, I was trappin' at a local hotspot, and living there as well because my girlfriend at the time had left me and moved back to her hometown in Camden, South Carolina. My partner ran the spot, I took trips to Atlanta to get the weed, generally from 4-10 pounds a week. Late one night, a 'robber boi' kicked the door in and started shooting. I jumped out a second-floor window and ran into the woods in my thermal underwear, in the middle of a winter's night. My friend was dead. They shot him with one of his own guns, which they found in the closet, along with most of the weed. Even that was not traumatic enough because thinking of all the money that could possibly be made, I was going to start the trap back up, reunite the click version 2.2, only to get locked up myself leading to my sentence to 10 years' probation (1st offense) for four pounds of weed. I did about a month in Washington County Jail and about 75 days at I W Davis Detention/Bootcamp facility after I violated the terms of my probation after getting caught the 2nd time with marijuana in my system. I was only supposed to be on intensive drug test probation, 1 year, but due to a back log in processing the paperwork for people who had satisfied the terms, you were still under intensive until the government completed your paperwork and said you weren't on intensive probation anymore. Thus some year and a half later I was still on intensive when I violated by flunking a second drug test.

I had about 500 hours of Community service, over seen by Fulton County department of corrections probation and parole services. Some community service 'details' were better than others and I actually enjoyed working at Rice St in the warehouse area, and cleaning up the Sherriff's locker rooms and stuff. Sometimes we put soap, draws and socks or something in a little bundle for inmates when it got out of the washers and dryers. With as many hours as I had and my personality, I met many sheriffs and of course there was a constant stream of offenders and violators of 'all' stripes coming through.

I also enjoyed my hours at the Fulton County Health Department when it was by Grady. My fellow offenders and I liked it because you'd be in the health department facility quite often, where attractive women employees and clients were plentiful. They also had an area down there by the loading dock with a pool table and radio, so when we weren't technically working, we would be listening to the radio and playing pool. I was never good enough at pool to last long at the table, but technically it's better than the bush ax crew back at I W Davis. Also, the warehouse county employees would take us along when they made deliveries to all the different health offices in south Fulton County. Here again the eye candy was a great justification for the entire travail. There was a Hispanic guy that used to work there. The drivers could pick who they wanted depending upon how many community service people they needed to do a job. One day the Hispanic guy took a few of us out, and just in making conversation, I told him that I like mariachi music.

It was true of course, because of the Hispanic presence during my time in rural South Carolina. In rural South Carolina, going to local and regional flea markets is like a religion, probably because it's not that much else to do for entertainment and socializing. There would always be some Mexicans at a table or booth dressed like cowboys, selling mariachi cds and tapes (then), and blasting Mariachi music. After a while I heard a few things I liked and went to the table or booth and asked what they were just playing, and I'd buy it. Also I was a huge fan of the British Alt rock band 'The Smiths' in high school and Morrissey, the lead singer and 'The Smiths' repertoire is huge in Mexico. After watching documentaries on 'The Smiths' I knew this, so the Mexicans always had a soft spot in my heart. Good thing I did, because after I told the Mexican County employee that I liked Mariachi, every time after that, if he only needed one guy, he'd get me.

Of course I did the classic community service project as well which is walking the streets and byways of South and North Fulton County picking up trash and other things along the high way. In hindsight it would have been immediately better had I not had all that community service (500 hours) and used that time getting a real job, getting stable in that job, and integrating myself in the law-abiding wider community. As it stands, I had 500 hours, and extra hours added for varying infringements such as missing appointments or not doing the requisite number of community service hours per week. I was in jail for about 90 days, and then I came right out and spent 500 hours, hanging out with offenders, violators and criminals far worse than anything I had done or how I grew up in Black bourgeois middle class Southwest Atlanta. And yet, I learned a lot about people, places and things during that time, that I had not known before. I matured emotionally and spiritually in ways I didn't previously think necessary or possible. My economic prospects suffered however as my background prevented me from some jobs, including a negative checkmark from our beloved UMC, as well as my poor credit, and poor decision-making skills with regard to women and 2 divorces. Temp jobs, part-time jobs, pieces of jobs, hustle jobs, even selling knives and cutlery.

Part IV

When my friend got shot, I tried to restart the trap version 2.2 and the 'White man put them papers on me' with 10 years probations, and locked me up for 60-90 days, and that was enough trauma for me. My original deal with God was to go to some graduate school in political science and/or history. But between my friend dying and me getting locked up, terrified and terrorized, that was enough trauma for me that combined with my natural gravitation towards spiritual subjects, I should go to seminary. Keep it in mind. I didn't want to preach. I wanted to be an academic theologian; a Black professional academic (an even rarer breed). Like a dummy, young and dumb in my late mid to late 30's, I thought I could teach somewhere or another with an M.Div and/or get a doctorate. I told Rev. Thrower all of that and he said it would be best to take the practical ministry route, which included the possibility of ordination or becoming a local pastor. Of course he was right. The problem was that I wasn't right for the UMC even of that more conservative time. The UMC was/is highly administered and computerized, where psyche tests, credit scores, criminal history, in context or outside it, or your job in the fortune 500 world or medical field, determine more about an ordinand than personal piety, temperament or gifts and graces.

I knew my background. I knew the staid stolid folks (at least then) heavy off into the Discipline, probably would never ordain me. Of course I was correct (presently construed), as you can very well see from what you've been reading. But the Lord ministered a strange thing to me one afternoon, when I was thinking about how I would be wasting my time going to seminary and seeking ordination. I was content simply to go to seminary and serve a specifically United Methodist Church in a lay capacity, but I felt I'd never be ordained. And yet there was a part of me that still wanted to do it. Yes of course, part of it was a sense of 'loyalty' going back to my grandparents and Williams Chapel AME, Trinity AME, Ben Hill, Cascade, Laster Chapel, Gammon, and all that. Part of it was taking the advice my father in the ministry gave, that I should take the practical ministry ordination track. All that was wonderful, but it did not make me continue. What made me continue even with the realization that I would never be ordained, was that the Lord ministered to me that 'it wasn't my test, it was their (the UMC) test'. The Lord ministered to me that it was not 'I' that was being tested, but they themselves, meaning the administrative bodies of the UMC that were being tested. Little did I know how much they were being tested far and above my situation! From that perspective I had to persevere as long as possible, relative to my mental health (to use a phrase). It wasn't literally worrying me, because however far I got in the candidacy and ordination process was infinitely further than I thought I would get. At the time and even now, I didn't interpret it as the UMC wasn't being 'fair' to me. I knew exactly what was coming and walked into it...fresh out the jail-house with a credit score that would shame Evander Holyfield. To the extent I feel like they put me through something intellectually, spiritually, emotionally, and professionally, that didn't bother me, I like taking tests. My critique is that the 'powers that be' make it easier for some people than they do others.

I can very well forgive the UMC if I were angry at it or resentful. But as I have mentioned elsewhere in this book, thank God the Methodists did reject me, or I'd be somewhere pretending like I don't know what a man and woman are for the sake of the socialist-atheist LGBTQIA social justice warrior agenda. If they would have accepted me, I'd be a part of that foolishness they had going on at General Conference 2024 as the socialist-atheist LGBTQIA social justice community danced in triumph with their flags, kissing and hugging in the aisles, like some kind of pagan ritual that evidently was a prophetic vision of what we would later see at the Summer Olympics opening ceremonies in Paris. What is altogether worse, being I am such a great writer and polemic, what if they had paid me to promote that foolishness...as good at it as I would naturally be. For $80,000 a year would I marry two homosexuals, or two dogs, or bless two unions of purebred Siamese cats. The truth of the matter is I'm tired of being broke and I owe the Student Loan corporation $120,000 and by the time I pay it off, it will be $150,000, all for my sense of loyalty to the UMC for some ancient halcyon days of what it meant to me back when I was becoming me as a teen...and I like me.

The best thing that ever happened to me (in some order I guess), intellectually, theologically, spiritually, etc., was after my rejection, and instead of spending years focused on what it took to be an ordained UMC preacher, I concentrated on what it took to be a child of God in piety, faithfulness and personal spiritual discipline (as best I could). Furthermore, as one sees in the present volume (which is selling well), and my preaching engagements at Methodist, non-denominational, and other denominational churches, my preaching career (such that it is) is healthy, like Isaiah being fed and watered at the brook by the ravens. UMC rejection was the best thing to happen to me. Being 'the stone that the builders refused' was the best thing that ever happened to me...and United Methodism in post-modernity. When I lie...tell me I'm lying and why.

I am free to make critiques many Black UMC pastors and churches can't make because they can't afford to. Many would prefer a more traditional and conservative line on Church discipline. Between books, speaking engagements, I make out decent, so don't think my critiques of the current class of DEI Bishops and Elders, and the White liberals that promoted them is based simply on anger, resentment or jealousy, though indeed I have felt all those things in the past.

How can I be jealous of Christians and pastors who because of political considerations and 'correctness' must pretend with a straight face and all seriousness, that they have no idea what a man and woman are, and must resort to throwing letters around and practicing hocus-pocus sexual algebra. This LGBTQIA+ sexual algebra, our DEI Bishops and Academics got from the nihilistic socialist-atheist LGBTQIA+ social justice warrior community. That is what they now base their theology on, instead of the Bible. How can I be jealous of that? What makes it worth it...$60,000 a year with benefits, $125,000 to be a DS and/or $250,000 to be a bishop running around pretending like I know God, who I can't see and have not seen...but that which I can see, the physical difference between a man and a woman I ignore? How do we define 'gaining the world, and losing your soul' in the post-modern church? They pretend like they know this God so well they can apologize for him with their hocus-pocus 14-page apologies to anybody who's ever been hurt by 'the Church' or God made a 'mistake' and made them a biological woman or man but that's not what they want to be. So, God needs to apologize for giving you life, but the wrong sex organ? They pretend like they know God, whom they have not seen, but they have seen men and women all their lives but will not act like they don't know what a man and woman are. What can you possibly be paid to justify acting that stupid with a straight face! What level of self-delusion can possibly make you pretend like you don't know what a man and woman are, male mammal and a female mammal, and then try to convince people that you are on the right side of history. Whose history, certainly not mammalian, reptile, and flora and fauna history! Yep, that's right. I'm jealous of UMC foolishness and pastoring churches with 16 people, 12 of them are over 70. Yes, I'm jealous of not pastoring a church in a denomination that is hemorrhaging members like a gunshot victim hemorrhages blood, with multiple gunshots to vital organs.

How can I get paid enough to endorse a God, who I spend all my time apologizing for what God has said and done in the past that hurt people's feelings. Would they rather be dead, than a man, woman, Black, White, poor, rich, etc., if one day they wake up and say that how they were born was a mistake? Whose mistake, theirs or God's?